RECLAIMING
ENGLISH KINSHIP

At the source of the longest river
The voice of the hidden waterfall
And the children in the apple-tree
Not known, because not looked for
But heard, half-heard, in the stillness
Between two waves of the sea.

from 'Little Gidding', in T. S. Eliot,
Four Quartets, London: Faber & Faber, 1944

RECLAIMING ENGLISH KINSHIP

Portuguese refractions
of British kinship theory

Mary Bouquet

Manchester University Press
Manchester and New York

Distributed exclusively in the USA and Canada by St. Martin's Press

Published by Manchester University Press
Oxford Road, Manchester M13 9PL, UK
and Room 400, 175 Fifth Avenue, New York, NY 10010, USA

Distributed exclusively in the USA and Canada by
St. Martin's Press, Inc., 175 Fifth Avenue, New York,
NY 10010, USA

British Library Cataloguing-in-Publication Data
A catalogue record for this book is available from the British Library

Library of Congress Cataloging-in-Publication Data applied for

ISBN 0 7190 3026 9 *hardback*

Printed in Great Britain
by Bookcraft (Bath) Limited

CONTENTS

FIGURES

ACKNOWLEDGEMENTS

This book developed in various places and times, as these Acknowledgements indicate. It would almost certainly have remained in several pieces without Marilyn Strathern's initial and sustaining encouragement and constructive criticism. Janet Carsten's suggestions have also been indispensable. I would also like to thank Brian Juan O'Neill, Martin Southwold and Ana Verde Oliveira for reading parts of the manuscript. Martine Segalen generously helped to sharpen my understanding of the differences between French and British approaches to the study of kinship.

Former colleagues and students at I.S.C.T.E. in Lisbon provided an intellectual atmosphere that was challenging and rewarding in countless ways. Naming the names of those to whom I am indebted in Portugal would scarcely be a straightforward matter. I refer throughout this book to 'Portuguese students', and I would like to apologise for lumping together in such a clumsy manner persons who left an indelible impression upon me. Brian Juan O'Neill and Jorge Freitas Branco must, however, be named for their friendship, comradeship and substantial help both during and after my time as I.S.C.T.E. I would also like to acknowledge the *simpatia* and many *conversas* with João Leal, Cristiana Bastos, Manuela Reis and Teresa Matos.

Frenk Driessen is thanked for drawing Figures 4.1, 4.2, 4.3 and 4.4, and Michael Fitch for carefully reading the manuscript. Any remaining inaccuracies are my responsibility. No reference is made to Marilyn Strathern's *After Nature* (C.U.P. 1992), or to *Anthropology and Autobiography* edited by Judith Okely and Helen Callaway (Routledge 1992), both of which were published after this manuscript went to press.

Without Henk de Haan's *ondersteuning*, on many different scores, this book could, quite literally, never have been written.

The very existence of Hendrik J. M. R. de Haan has been closely tied up with its writing – as has his collusion in rereading some classic children's literature. Tabitha, Duchess and Ribby stalk the pages.

Reclaiming English Kinship is dedicated to the memory of my father, Michael Rome Bouquet (1915-88), whose personality was reflected in the books I found waiting on my childhood book-shelves; and it is no less for my mother Joyce Bouquet, who read and reread them to me.

Mary Bouquet, Bennekom, 2 March 1992

INTRODUCTION

The British 'classics' are export artefacts on the late-twentieth-century international anthropology scene. The use of these texts for pedagogical purposes among non-native English-speaking students raises practical, political and theoretical issues.

The questioning of certain notions in British set texts in mid–1980s Portugal brought to light an area of implicitly *English* assumptions. The Portuguese reading of those texts effectively problematised an early-twentieth-century English middle-class intellectual 'background' as the hidden standard against which the comparison of other people's kinship took (takes) place. The specificity of that understanding of kinship became steadily clearer through the attempted exploration of Portuguese kinship using the genealogical method. That exploration showed the need to consider a range of sources and materials alongside those conventionally defined as kinship-related.

The intensity of British anthropological interest in other people's kinship is puzzling given the relatively few (compared, for example, with French ethnology) studies by British social anthropologists of kinship at home. The plot is thickened by the belief that English middle-class kinship is of limited scope, with personal rather than a structural significance. The issue of how early-twentieth-century British anthropological 'obsession' with kinship be elucidated was inspired by Portuguese questions. The 'voice' which speaks through British kinship theory obviously belonged to 'persons' who developed it. But what sort of persons were they?

The decision to incorporate the *Peter Rabbit* stories into this account reflects upon the English notion of 'background': this usually refers to 'where a person comes from', connoting birth and

1

growing up. 'Background' includes a repository of cultural materials. I have ransacked the stockpile and pulled out one example. While certainly neither definitive nor exhaustive, this was not a random choice. The *Peter Rabbit* stories provide a kind of native exegesis on the composition of the (English) person. Fished out of English middle-class background, and set alongside the notion of *pedigree* – which underlies the genealogical method – the *Tales* of Beatrix Potter may constitute a way of tackling the discrepancy between an efflux of discourse on others' kinship, and taciturnity about our own. These two disparate sources address an English middle-class notion of the person: his or her origins and composition, and the nature of 'relationships' between like and unalike persons.

What sort of anthropology is this?

The title of this book refers to several orders of things. *Refraction* is a term borrowed from physics, but used here in a layman's sense: the deflection or deviation of a wave, such as a beam of light, from one straight path to another when passing from one medium (such as air) to another (such as glass), in which the speed of the transmission is different. The term can also refer to change in the apparent position of a celestial body due to the bending of light rays coming from it as they pass through the atmosphere. The notion may, as a consequence, also refer to the correction to be applied to the apparent position of a body.

The bodies in question here are hardly celestial: they are, in fact, selected anthropological texts dating from about 1910 to 1960. The genealogical method is conceived as irradiating through the British approach to kinship during the first half of the twentieth century. The method and, 'behind' it, the indigenous input to that method, are conceptualised as artefacts of pedigree; or, in more colloquial English, chips off the old block. Genealogical waves are still pulsing in the late twentieth century, several anthropological generations later, not least for students of social anthropology in countries where the metropolitan strains of the discipline are a recent import. Such students must become conversant with (amongst others) the classical British founding fathers.

A central problem of this book is what happens when classical British works are placed in the hands of late-twentieth-century readers who are not native English-speakers. What are the effects

of putting a British anthropological artefact, such as the genealogical method, at their disposal? The plurality of the refractions
is not misplaced. The 'British' notion of kinship begins to splinter
at the moment its tacit assumptions are questioned by those for
whom the implicit theory is anything but taken for granted. The
refractions of the title refer, then, to splintering. The smithereens
produced by passing British artefacts through the eye of another
language open up unexpected vistas onto a quite specifically
early-twentieth-century English world. This is not to deny the
nineteenth-century and earlier roots of British social anthropology, nor is it an attempt to transpose the burden of one authority figure onto another. My aim is different. Much is certainly
excluded or neglected by narrowing the focus to a single artefact,
the genealogical method. It does, however, allow for picking up
the pieces in another way: exploring the dark side of a dismantled
image – the genealogical method – which I shall refer to as
'pedigree'.

The direction of attention away from English bourgeois life, to
which the majority of British anthropologists conformed in (written) voice if not in actual affiliation, towards 'other worlds', bred
an incapacity to deal with matters too close to home (middle-class
kinship being a prime example) which may be peculiar to British
social anthropology. Within the imaginary world of English
children's literature there is, however, a miniature ethnography of
early-twentieth-century bourgeois views on difference and com-
mensurability. The hypothesis is that much the same parameters
that informed the personalisation of the natural world in these
children's narratives, were also implicit in the 'British' way of
familiarising the exotic.

It would be difficult to find a single label for the eclectic story
outlined here. It criss-crosses the twentieth century at various
speeds and gaits, and it refuses to be pinned down to a single
ethnographic locality. It is about the practical, empirical effects of
theory, but not the theory which usually occupies centre stage.
The adjectival form of 'refraction' is 'refractory'. 'Refractory' is
synonymous with 'unruly': resisting control or authority; stubborn, unmanageable; resistant to treatment or cure. If some kind
of label must be attached to this 'sort' of anthropology, then this
one would do as well as any. The next section tries to be more
precise.

Artefacts

Each facet of the roughly triangular argument sketched so far needs plotting into contemporary debates within anthropology. Firstly, the debate over the place and interpretation of artefacts within anthropology. The genealogical method is an artefact insofar as it results from the imposition of prior conceptual form upon material substance (Ingold 1986, pp. 344–7, cit. in Ingold 1988, p. 85). The value of such a general definition of artefact is that it allows us to get away from the polarisation of 'material' culture and (immaterial?) culture which accompanied the fieldwork revolution, particularly in Anglo-American anthropology (Strathern 1990). Artefacts may 'be' objects, texts, images. The point is that the production of artefacts depends on a capacity for symbolic thought that is based on language. This capacity, according to Ingold, allows for innovation by deliberate invention, for the transmission of design by teaching and for the active acquisition of culture, which is in turn responsible for the cumulative and progressive growth of knowledge (Ingold *loc. cit.*).

Clifford's point about collections relies on a similar notion of artefact:

A history of collections (not limited to museums) is central to an understanding of how those social groups that invented anthropology and modern art have appropriated exotic things, facts and meanings (...). It is important to analyze how powerful discriminations made at particular moments constitute the general system of objects within which valued artifacts circulate and make sense (Clifford 1988, pp. 220–1).

Ethnography can be seen as a form of culture collecting, in Clifford's view. This highlights the selection, gathering and detachment of diverse experiences and facts from their original temporal locations. These selections are given an enduring value in a new arrangement. Anthropological culture collectors select what gives form, structure and continuity to the world, from complex historical reality. The genealogical method is remarkable for being itself an artefact while at the same time allowing (directly and indirectly) for the production of other artefacts by anthropologists. It is telling that Clifford uses 'genealogy' as a metaphor for tracing the chain of events by which a plethora of non-Western artefacts and customs were comprehended and incorporated, albeit temporarily, by the mid twentieth century, using two strategies. Objects were reclassified as primitive art. The discourse and institutions of modern anthropology constructed comparative and synthetic images of Man drawing even-handedly from among the world's authentic ways of life, however strange in appearance or obscure in origin (*ibid*, pp. 235–6). Genealogy as metaphor continues to evoke a powerful notion of 'primordial' (cf. Fabian 1983, p. 75) connection even for post-modernist writers!

Clifford writes that anthropological collections and taxonomies are constantly menaced by temporal contingencies, and especially by 'an emergent present' (1988, p. 245). The anthropologist is confronted by more and more to know: a heady mix-and-match of possible human combinations. By emphasising the artefactual nature of the genealogical method, it can be reinvented 'to tell other stories, local histories of culture survival and emergence' (*ibid*, p. 246). His example of the encounter between a Fox Indian painted animal skin in a Paris museum, and the grandson of the Indian circus performer who sold it to pay his passage home, contains some parallels with the genealogical method as a British artefact 'recollected' in a southern European pedagogical context some 70-odd years after Rivers's formulation of it. Clifford observes that the objects of both art and culture collecting are susceptible to other appropriations. I would add that this applies not just to the objects, but also to the means of collection. My concern will be with the deferred or hidden meaning of Rivers's text in its wider resonances as British kinship theory. The aim is to locate the point of production, the template which fixed Rivers's 'design' for collecting materials. 'Pedigree' is the term used to designate this underlying conceptual cluster.

Translation

The second facet of the argument may be shorthanded as the problem of two-way translation. Portuguese refractions of British structural–functionalist texts have the effect of problematising the world (or worlds) of English concepts. This world of concepts is obviously not limited to the explicitly anthropological 'objects' of the discourse. It refers to a corpus of shared understandings and mutual intelligibilities internal to the texts, beyond the 'external' reality to which they make explicit reference. This second framework seems to have been taken for granted and carried forward beyond the original context where it could perhaps be assumed. As such, it resembles Lévi-Strauss's 'imperceptible clue': the many conventionalised figures and images that pervade ethnographic and popular reports on encounters with Others. As Fabian remarks: 'All statements about Others are paired with the observer's experience' (Fabian 1983, p. 91).

The 'observer's experience' is profoundly structured and coloured by the language into which they relay their observations. If, however, like the early Christian missionaries, contemporary anthropology's pedagogical activity can involve translating the Word into foreign tongues, then the conventional sense of anthropological translation may be profoundly altered. By engaging in conversation and discussion of anthropological concepts originally phrased in English, in another language, then the English metaphors, figures of speech and colloquialisms with which anthropological (like any other) texts are filled, suddenly acquire what might be termed 'analytical relief'. They lose their seeming innocence and self-evidence: 'something' is disclosed. Questioning and contestation can range over the meanings acquired by seemingly descriptive analytical concepts in the historical–political context of reading, to specific turns of phrase containing assumptions about the order of things not necessarily shared even between the 'oldest allies' of western Europe!

This process complicates Tyler's idea of ethnographic evocation: 'No object of any kind precedes and constrains the ethnography. It creates its own objects in its unfolding and the reader supplies the rest' (Tyler 1986, p. 138). The assumption is that the reader only needs reminding. Reading ethnography remains firmly in English-(or some other major language)-speaking hands (cf. Gerholm and Hannerz 1983). This is very clearly not so in late-twentieth-century anthropology, and makes Tyler's notion of post-modern ethnography a limited one. Evocation depends on the shared assumptions of Fabian's 'second subject' (*op. cit.*) being professionally and temporally removed from the main subject.

Asad refers to this configuration as the inequality of languages, suggesting a need for anthropologists to explore the asymmetrical tendencies and pressures in the languages of 'dominated and dominant' societies, in order to determine how far they go in defining the possibilities and limits of effective translation (Asad 1986, p. 164). I would go further. The possibilities and limits of effective translation help to illuminate 'the sense of a British, middle-class, academic game' (*ibid*, p. 159). This case study provides substance for turning the one-way street of ethnography (Clifford 1986, p. 22) into a two-way thoroughfare.

Apart from the implications of inequality between languages within academic anthropology for the issue of translation, there is the problem of incommensurability or difference in metaphysical ideas (Overing 1989, p. 71) about relatedness between two Western anthropologies. Overing defines the problem of translation as one of relevant emphasis, knowledge, experience and creativity. She has some interesting remarks on the genealogical meaning of kinship terms to which componential analysis returned:

> The method and assumptions about the world in formal semantic analysis of kinship domains can be an impediment to knowledge and to the outsider's comprehension of the use of kinship terms in most 'traditional' cultures. While formal analysis can impose an order with only minimal knowledge of the domain, it can preclude the possibility of learning the metaphysics of others (*ibid*, p. 80).

The present case study does not, at first sight, appear to concern a 'traditional' culture; nor is the formality of the genealogical method equivalent to that of componential analysis. Nonetheless, the methodological disposition (rather than simply the method in and of itself) proved a stumbling-block to exploring another western European 'kinship system'. Instead of translating that alternative world into the British labelling system, I leave this part of the account open-ended. The focus shifts instead to the need to make explicit much implicit English ethnography through the attempt to relay British anthropological concepts in another language. But where is the ethnography of kinship among English middle-class intellectuals during the first half of the twentieth century?

Possible worlds

The third line of approach, developed in Chapter 5, tries to explore a possible world of English persons and their interrelatedness. The starting-point is the undercover concept of 'pedigree', which surfaces at several points in the book, and apparently supports the 'original' genealogical meaning of kinship terms. The final chapter is an attempt at opening out the English notion of pedigree, and using it as an instrument for identifying some of the unwritten theories embedded in the technical vocabulary of kinship. The hybrid 'persons' of the imaginary 'world' to be considered can be read as a complementary source to Rivers's method. The characters resemble, in some respects, the monstrous (Plinian) races identified by Mason as translators between the known and unknown worlds of Europe and America (Mason 1990). They too can be made to translate ambivalent ideas about animal and human worlds, and irreconcilable differences between species of persons. Mason argues that European representations of the hybrid concern, in most cases individuals, not races, and therefore fall outside the scope of ethno-ethnology proper (*ibid*, p. 113). The characters discussed in Chapter 5 may, however, indicate a device for locating the imaginary English world which informed a particular British view of others' kinship.

Organisation of the text

The first two chapters deal with the 'artefacts of kinship', discussing the British anthropological texts from several angles. The first part of Chapter 1 focuses on the issue of *reading* anthropology, while the second part considers understatement, particularly in introductory texts. It then moves on to discuss understatement with respect to the genealogical method, drawing a brief contrast with French ethnological approaches to kinship. Chapter 2 looks at the way kinship was portrayed in a series of studies from Malinowski to Leach, and at the difficulties of attempting to extend this approach to English middle-class kinship.

The next chapter relocates the historical texts in the context of 1980s Portugal. The first part describes the processes of assembling a second-year undergraduate course based on the authors discussed; the second deals with the attempt at mediating Portuguese and English understandings of certain British set texts. Chapter 4 switches perspective by considering the students' problems with exploring Portuguese kinship by means of the genealogical method. The pedagogical aim was to clarify some basic presuppositions underlying later developments in British kinship theory in a practical way. What in fact emerged was a series of discrepant understandings concerning the basic terms in which the genealogical method is cast – starting out from names. The second part of the chapter pursues Portuguese constructs such as *nome, pessoa, saudade, simpatia* and *conversa* to the point where the idea of genealogy becomes unrecognisable. The final chapter (Chapter 5) begins by exploring the connotations of pedigree, arguing that these were not so easily discarded by transforming pedigree into 'genealogical method' – hence the problems with lack of 'background knowledge' on the part of non-English readers. Then it tries to find an imaginary ethnography which can provide a commentary on the implicit theory which has been identified. The conclusion briefly recapitulates the case for an ethnography of the rather specific view of human relations which informed the British kinship classics.

CHAPTER ONE

HOW BRITISH SOCIAL ANTHROPOLOGISTS LEARNED TO 'LOOK TO KINSHIP'

This is not to say that the scientist himself may not have his own personal predilections, based upon his upbringing and social environment, his temperamental disposition, his aesthetic values. He may regard the culture of a primitive, half-naked set of people in an island of the Solomons as a pleasant way of life, giving expression to the individuality of its members in ways alien to western civilization; he may regard it as something he would like to see endure, and he may strive to preserve it in the face of ignorance and prejudice, pointing out the probable results of interference with ancient customs. This he does as a man; his attitude is part of his personal equation to life, but it is not implicit in his scientific study. The greatest need of the social sciences to-day is for a more refined methodology, as objective and dispassionate as possible, in which, while assumptions due to the conditioning and personal interest of the investigator must influence his findings, that bias shall be consciously faced, the possibility of other initial assumptions be realized and allowance be made for the implications of each in the course of the analysis (Firth [1936] 1983, p. 488).

The simple distinction between biological and social kinship is thus insufficient. Biological kinship is always and everywhere a set of cultural conceptions. But these are of two kinds and their import is different. The first is that set of cultural conceptions called 'science' in European culture. The second are the folk science or ethnoscientific conceptions of all cultures, including European. Even in European culture there may well be a difference between the beliefs of science and the generally held beliefs about the reality of reproduction. It is with respect to the latter that kinship is studied (Schneider 1984, p. 111).

I. Reading British social anthropology

The first part of this chapter tries to problematise the relationship between English kinship and British social anthropological studies of kinship in other societies. This approximates a distinction made by Schneider between Western social scientific ideas, and the folk notions with which he believes them to be saturated (1984, p. 1). The main difference with Schneider is that while he leaves his distinction at the level of European/American/Western, I am concerned with breaking down certainly the first and the last of these gross categories. The second part of the chapter will attempt to deepen this insight by considering the problem of understatement, and by briefly contrasting the place of the genealogical method in the British and French traditions.

British kinship studies and the lack of studies of English kinship
In the quotation with which this chapter begins Firth stresses the need to separate personal disposition from dispassionate science. It is necessary to become conscious of the conditioning, personal interests and assumptions which are involved in and may bias the analysis. If it is only towards the end of the twentieth century that we have become aware of the extent to which folk notions may permeate scientific concepts, the process is of course much older. We are, in fact, heirs to the obscurity of that interaction.

English kinship is not just an example. British social anthropologists, particularly during the first half of the twentieth century, made kinship the classic focus of their empirical research and theoretical ambitions. This interest is usually traced back to nineteenth-century legal thought, and the significance of kinship in evolutionary theory. W.H.R. Rivers was responsible for the revival of British kinship studies in the early twentieth century. Rivers's formulation of the genealogical method became one of the enduring methods of both fieldwork and the presentation of data. Twentieth-century functionalist anthropology regarded kinship as the very foundation of social organisation in primitive societies. Attention given by British anthropologists to kinship at home was, by comparison, rather limited. Studies were carried out, many in the community studies genre, but they often had a geographical list towards the 'tassels from the Celtic fringe' (Frankenberg 1966, p. 45; Arensberg and Kimball 1940), or were 'historical' (Lancaster, 1958). Notable exceptions included Firth and his colleagues' research in London (Firth 1956; Young and Willmott 1957; Firth, Hubert and Forge 1970). There were attempts to examine conceptual problems in the study of family and kin ties in the British Isles (Lancaster 1961), but these remained rather isolated contributions which failed to inspire concerted research on the home front. Compared with historical systems, or with contemporary primitive systems, English kinship seemed of secondary 'social' importance (Strathern 1992). The tone was set by Rivers in 1914 when he remarked on the great 'paucity of definite social functions associated with relationship, and ... the almost complete limitation of such functions to those relationships which apply to individual persons and not to classes of persons' in 'our own system of relationships', when compared with classificatory systems (Rivers 1914, p. 13 1968, p. 46) cit. by Lancaster 1961, p. 323).

In the first place, England seems not to have been considered the proper place for real anthropological study. This attitude persisted well into the 1980s (Cohen 1990a, p. 293; 1990b, p. 218). It may have been that the rest of the world, meaning the British Empire, seemed just too exciting for the first generations of anthropology students. There may also have been a sense of trepidation at trespassing on the territory of sociologists and historians. Cohen speculates on the perceived marginality of such studies to the discipline. Britain was a research option to which resort should only be made if fieldwork elsewhere was impossible. Lancaster raises the problems of comparison due to regional differences within the British Isles (1961, pp. 320–1). Apart from that, non-unilineal (or 'bilateral', or 'cognatic') kinship is a residual category,'a sort of grab-bag of shapeless bits of institutionalised behaviour' (*ibid*, p. 322).

Community studies were criticised by sociologists for being 'discrete and idiosyncratic: ... of no use to grand sociological theory' (Jackson 1987, p. 11). It is true that Frankenberg tried to show how such studies might be used in his combined functional and morphologically evolutionary approach, which ranged studies already made along a rural–urban continuum (1966). But the classification of such studies as 'rural sociology' or indeed 'community studies', reinforced a sense that they were not really anthropology either. Frankenberg evokes a vivid image of this feeling, when describing his arrival in Glynceiriog in 1953:

When I went to Glynceiriog I was always conscious of my anthropological colleagues' anecdotes of how they sat in the centre of African villages while life went on around them and encompassed them. They could not avoid becoming part of the social processes they wished to observe. In my early days in the village I would often climb a hill and look sadly down upon the rows of houses of the housing estate and wonder what went on inside them (1966, p. 16).

The vanishing effect

English kinship was not really a priority on the British anthropological research agenda, seeming to pale in significance beside kinship 'elsewhere'. It was problematic without being a problematic. Strathern has written of the 'vanishing effect' as kinship 'disappears' into class or some other social phenomenon (Strathern 1984). One of the questions posed by this book is whether the vanishing effect is a linguistic one. What happens if we rephrase such a piece of 'information' in another language, for a different audience? This book will consider the effects of recasting certain British anthropological concerns in Portuguese.

Anthropology has made a good living out of translating ideas from foreign languages into English. Some of these texts became 'classics', and hence stock items on the reading lists which later generations of anthropology students must read. As the classics are translated into other languages, anthropology enters a new phase. We need to consider the significance of putting ideas originally expressed in English into other languages. The procedure creates new relationships and tensions between anthropologists, and affords new perspectives on the knowledge which is their concern. One effect of these new relationships is that they bring certain English assumptions into fresh perspective. This may not be the single most significant outcome of the complication of anthropological knowledge several generations on. It is, however, a peculiarly appropriate topic for a British social anthropologist in the 1990s: not as an act of 'expiation' (Gellner 1990), but as a means of reclaiming English kinship for anthropology.

The set of circumstances which precipitated this account was four years teaching British kinship theory to Portuguese anthropology students in Lisbon (1983–87). The students' questions about their 'set texts' brought with them novel perspectives on the contents. They drew attention to fundamental differences in

14

approach and style between their English and French bibliographies. They asked, for example, where the British equivalent of *l'ethnologie de la France* could be found? There is, of course, no equivalent. 'Anthropology at home' only took off in Britain in the 1970s and 1980s, and in rather a different manner to French ethnology.

It is as though British anthropological studies of other peoples' kinship, during the first half of the twentieth century, pre-empted or anyway curtailed discussion of the matter on the home front. Kinship was certainly 'found' in the countryside of upland Britain and in old urban enclaves such as Bethnal Green. But it was mostly seen as a local, empirical phenomenon rather than a central British (let alone English) assumption about social organisation. Perry Anderson has suggested that the vision required to conduct holistic research at home would have run counter to (bourgeois) intellectuals' interests there, and that the approach was exported wholesale instead (Anderson 1969, cit. by Gerholm and Hannerz 1983, p. 17).

Yet this assessment is still not radical enough, for it leaves unanswered the question of how English kinship might be studied. This book will suggest that one way of going about it might be by examining how 'British' knowledge of this area was produced and is 'inherited', translated and circulated. This involves overhauling the conventional notion of fieldwork. Extending Schneider's (1984) train of thought, British anthropological kinship notions are likely to be suffused by English folk ideas. The British/English distinction is made advisedly.[1] It refers, firstly, to the English language as the dominant means of communication among Britons, and of course the hegemony of the English language within academic anthropology. Secondly, it addresses the political dominance of England and the English over the remaining three territorial components of the United Kingdom. Analogously, it is customary to refer to social anthropology as it is practised in United Kingdom universities and similar institutions as 'British' rather than English. My hypothesis is that 'British' social anthropology as it developed during the first half of the twentieth century, drew on some quite specifically English, middle-class concerns. Although many leading British anthropologists of this period were 'recruited' from 'outside', in terms of class or nationality (cf. Leach 1984), they nonetheless brought their discourse

15

into line with the dominant concerns of the 'intellectual field' surrounding them (Bourdieu 1969).

Genealogy

I shall argue that the development of kinship theory depended upon the genealogical method, as formulated by Rivers, and that this is a constant although not always explicit feature of the classic studies which were published during the first half of the present century. The English notion which I think informs genealogy is pedigree. Anthropologists have indeed used the two terms interchangeably since W.H.R. Rivers's time. There seems to be a contradiction between the common-sense notion of pedigree, and the image of cognatic/bilateral/non-unilineal English kinship introduced at the beginning of this chapter. I shall argue that the contradiction makes sense when we consider how theories of lineal and non-unilineal kinship developed in tandem (cf. Strathern 1992). Both tendencies, which are present in the indigenous system 'at source', were drawn upon in various ways by anthropologists, who of course themselves occupied specific positions within this configuration. That 'internal' manoeuvring is in my view an integral part of the story that was told about other peoples' kinship.

An analysis of the prescriptions made in the genealogical method of anthropological inquiry, as formalised by Rivers, first suggested a means of localising some underlying folk ideas (Bouquet 1989). 'Pedigree' will be used as a catalyst to explore a series of related ideas: about human beings, but also animals; about reproduction, or breeding; about distinction, and the way that is achieved. Points of contact and inter-filtration between a particular set of folk ideas and a particular set of scientific ideas can be established by exploring notions associated with pedigree, such as those just mentioned. This procedure leads, as might be expected, to the identification of similar sets of concerns in a totally disparate form of literature, which (like the genealogical method) has demonstrated remarkable staying power long after and far beyond its point of production. The intellectual concerns of the English kinship with which this book will be concerned do not vanish. They have been (and still are) transposed, transplanted and translated – even mass produced. Yet the effects are far from predictable. Schneider's claims about European kinship require not only specification and verification, but also elaboration. Fifth-and-sixth generation anthropologists, often studying texts written in languages which are not their own, and in times and places far removed from the original writers and their audiences, complicate the stories of contemporary European anthropologies. If anthropology is to be more than a one-way flow, then these complexities have to be dealt with seriously (cf. Vale de Almeida 1991a).

It should scarcely be necessary to say that I am not making claims about the practical importance of kinship in the twilight of the Welfare State. This task has been very ably undertaken by others (e.g. Finch 1989). I do, however, tackle one of the issues which Schneider and Finch raise concerning the notion that 'blood is thicker than water'. In searching for motivations for the mutual assistance given by kin under certain circumstances, Finch comes back to this common axiom. Schneider considers it to be one of the fundamental premises for the Doctrine of the Genealogical Unity of Mankind from which all comparative studies of kinship start out. This, he says, is rooted in our own beliefs about biology and the enormous value which is attributed to human sexual reproduction in (what he calls variously) Western/European/American cultures. The projection of this implicit value in the pseudo-scientific guise of kinship theories is at the heart of Schneider's critique. What he fails to spell out, however, is the specificity of the genealogical method which may, I think, account for certain differences in style and content between the anthropologies he lumps together variously as 'Western', 'European' and 'American'. This is a serious omission since anthropology itself has become an 'export' discipline, nurturing hierarchical relationships between what Gerholm and Hannerz refer to as 'mainland' and 'island' traditions.

Diversity

The materials brought to bear in the present exploration are undeniably diverse. In a sense they could not be otherwise given the circumstances under which anthropology is taught and produced in the late-twentieth-century. The studies of kinship made by British social anthropologists in the first part of this century seem remote enough from contemporary British concerns, let alone those of non-native English-speaking readers. The processes of teaching and studying these texts therefore involve elaborating historical and cultural contexts – not only for the peoples portrayed, but for the people writing about them and, as this study recognises, those reading the texts. My emphasis on the genealogical method within British social anthropological theory should be understood in these exegetical terms. It provides a theoretical connection between a series of texts. These texts are almost routinely grouped together for teaching purposes. They are set texts; they have to be covered in one way or another. Doing so involves reactions, problems and feedback which mostly remain in the shadows. Here they will be used as a means of getting a hold on the texts.

Apart from the way in which the genealogical method underlies British kinship studies, it contains an empirical injunction: it is an invitation to collect comparable materials. While this invitation was eagerly taken up by the students, it soon became apparent that there was a mismatch between certain Portuguese ideas, and the notions which inspire the genealogical method. The built-in limitations to exploring Portuguese kinship with this instrument nonetheless suggested a further set of materials, contemporary with but rarely considered alongside the genealogical method: Beatrix Potter's Peter Rabbit stories. The Portuguese perspective enabled the two sources to be considered quite sensibly alongside one another.

The inventive potential to late-twentieth-century ethnography, is a reflection of the new order of international relations – inside as much as outside anthropology. The early-twentieth-century order of things has been transformed, and yet the legacy of middle-class English intellectuals (and others who conformed with the strictures of their discourse) continues to haunt certain areas of the discipline of anthropology. There are two good reasons (at least) for examining what has happened. Firstly, to try to elucidate both the sense and the nonsense of British texts with which non-English-speakers have to grapple as part of their anthropological training. Secondly, to explore the ethnographic possibilities of playing off cultural incommensurabilities, to illuminate (in this instance) some obscure areas of the indigenous (English middle-class) system of thought which might otherwise remain unnoticed. There is no promise of resolution in this restless toing and froing between sources, traditions and ways of thinking.

If one result of the swing towards 'reflexive anthropology' has been the discovery that much of what passes for 'theory' in the social sciences is nothing but elaborated common sense (Smith

1988, p. 581), then it is of interest to try to document both the contents and the mechanisms by which it infuses the social sciences. The complex pathways by which this occurs may themselves inspire new structures of ethnography. The categories Sybil Wolfram believes to be defined, expressed and preserved in the systematic relationships of kinship, need looking into, but also away from. Relatedness, which is what kinship is all about, involves two-way traffic.

From ethnographic writing to reading anthropology
Much critical attention has recently been devoted to the problems of 'writing culture'. The process of writing has emerged from the penumbra of the written form. Whole areas of textual silence are being brought into audibility. The ethnographer's authority has been called into question perhaps for the first time since participant observation became the trademark of the social anthropology;[2] the 'many voices' of post-modern ethnography clamour for the reader's attention. In a parallel movement, considerable emphasis is now placed on understanding precisely how previous generations of anthropologists managed to convince their readers *qua* authors (Geertz 1988).

The focus on ethnographic writing has to some extent pushed issues concerning the propagation of anthropological knowledge into the background (cf. Sutton 1991). The accumulated writings or texts of preceding generations of anthropologists are, by now, an integral part of 'reading anthropology'. Reading the classic works of Morgan, Rivers, Malinowski, Evans-Pritchard and the rest precedes fieldwork for a considerable number of students. The categories by which these texts elucidate native life in a thousand times and places around the globe are absorbed, with varying degrees of critical appreciation, by each successive generation.

Reading anthropology deserves a place in the limelight presently and rightly accorded to writing ethnography. Reading, using indexes and bibliographies, feeds into ways of conceptualising and translating, writing and rewriting ethnography. The language(s) read in a given country influence what can appear on university reading lists. Expectations about linguistic versatility condition decisions about which texts shall be published in which language(s). They also effect the extent to which students are prepared to read ethnographies in their original language, or only in translation. Pedagogical policy about which texts shall be studied also reflect Asad's 'inequality of languages' within anthropology. All these factors make nonsense of the simple sliding between 'American', 'European' and 'Western', as done by Schneider. In what measure do the languages in which anthropological texts are read contribute to the making of social anthropologists?

In the case examined in this book, translations of some texts were available in Portuguese, or French – a language seen by many senior Portuguese intellectuals as 'closer' and more 'comprehensible' than English. Quite a number of texts were, however, as yet untranslated so that students were forced to try to make sense of the English phrases and concepts supposed to convey anthropological meanings. The difficulties encountered in this process, together with the questioning and discussion of certain Portuguese or French renderings of these ideas proved extremely provocative. The problematic nature of the English language for Portuguese-speakers was unambiguous. The style of writing, the examples chosen, the figures of speech, and the very rules of grammar, sometimes transformed what is self-evident to the native English-speaker into a convoluted source of confusion. The historical nature of the ethnographic 'present' in which many of the texts are written cannot simply be brushed aside with anti-imperialist rhetoric. Those writing in the early twentieth century did so in specific contexts, drawing selectively upon a stock of customary usages acquired as gradually as consciousness itself.

A major hypothesis might be formulated as follows. Anthropological discourse, in seeking to render intelligible unknown worlds and their inhabitants to a readership assumed to be 'like us', drew upon that which was already familiar. Peter Mason has demonstrated how the language of monstrosity 'translated' unknown 'America' into terms which allowed Europeans to assimilate that continent (Mason 1990). The British anthropological language of kinship performed an analogous operation, if on a less grandiose scale. Just as the Plinian races of Antiquity provided a body-language through which the inhabitants of America could be imagined before the continent was even discovered, so 'pedigree' was forerunner and later travelling companion to the genealogical method. If pedigrees were the prerogative of the landed and the aristocratic, all the more reason for their incorporation into the bourgeois scientific methodology of genealogy. Middle-class kinship defined itself negatively, lacking both the distinction of (upper-class) pedigree and the ramifications of working-class cognatic kinship. Middle-class anthropologists seem to have gone one better. They drew upon the kinship dialect of their internal 'betters' (aristocrats and 'great' families) to formulate a scientific methodology, from which they themselves were exempted, in order to assimilate as knowledge the connections they felt must exist among the external (or internal as, for example, 'working class' or 'farmers') others they studied.

Texts, pretexts and contexts

The perceptions with which this book is concerned have slowly acquired substance since leaving Portugal in 1987. In a way they are a retrospective interpretation of the four and a half years I spent there. The constant need to recast English thoughts and expressions in Portuguese offered a vantage point from which to scrutinise the language, and also the Englishness of the language in which British kinship theory is written. It should, however, be stressed that I did not conceive of what I was doing between 1983 and 1987 as 'fieldwork'. Fieldwork is a term which has mostly been reserved for activities among people who do not share the professional presuppositions of the anthropologist.[3] It would, of course, be possible to redefine those years as new-style ethnographic fieldwork; to claim that 'dialogues' with students pressed me into a new understanding of the activity. Professional parameters encourage this kind of juggling with dates and experiences.[4]

The problem is not the length of fieldwork. It is knowing where to draw the boundaries of relevant experience. Since writing is so closely tied up with learning to read, and since rereading brings new meanings, isolating a single period of physical dislocation can seem arbitrary and senseless. Arbitrary, in that the processes of thinking through and writing stretch out before and after time spent physically 'elsewhere'. Senseless, in that much of what it is possible to think and write about a place and its inhabitants is only discovered through writing itself, when the writer is at the mercy of the language in which she writes. There seems, in fact, to be no limit to further vantage points.[5] The Portuguese students could be presented as the 'native population'. But apart from insulting those who are now colleague-anthropologists, this plays down the other, quite diverse influences at work. It would also miss the point of the texts themselves, which often worked as pretexts for discussing Portuguese matters, and the specificity of anthropology in Portugal. The vexation of some students at having to study authors and ideas so remote from their notions of what anthropology is or ought to be, must also be taken into account. There was, of course, an imbalance of power involved in these discussions which is inescapable in any pedagogical system. The fact that many were mature students, studying in the evening (from 18.00 to 23.30 hours) after a full day's work, tempered the imbalance to some degree, but did not transform it.

Nothing could have been further from studying anthropology in mid-1970s Cambridge. One of the main differences is between studying a subject where almost everything you are expected to read is written in or translated into your own language (English), and a situation where the very act of studying implies familiarity with a number of languages other than your own. These central differences between European traditions of anthropology involve hierarchies of various kinds among their practitioners (cf. Gerholm and Hannerz 1983). Such imbalances must profoundly affect the directions taken by the discipline.

Distinctions between European contexts

The simple contrast between two 'European', 'Western' contexts in which anthropology is studied (1970s Cambridge and 1980s Lisbon) heightens the absurdity of collapsing these categories into one another. British kinship theory discussed in English, in Cambridge, had a totally different meaning from British kinship theory discussed in Portuguese, in Lisbon. Portuguese provided a kind of scaffolding by which to separate the formal 'British' identity of the texts from the 'Englishness' of the language in which they were written, and a set of assumptions which they contain. The same construction also afforded a different perspective on the riddle of British social anthropology's emphasis on kinship elsewhere as opposed to England. Such emphasis is only apparent, of course, when the British tradition is set beside other European traditions. The contrast with the depth and variety of kinship, marriage and inheritance studies carried out by French ethnologists in different parts of France is one example of this remarkable specificity.

Schneider writes, 'Kinship has been defined by European social scientists, and European social scientists make use of their own folk culture as source of many, if not all, of their ways of formulating and understanding the world about them' (1984, p. 193). The problem is *which* European folk culture, and *which* social scientific tradition? Is it sensible to assume that what Schneider calls the Doctrine of the Genealogical Unity of Mankind belongs to pan-European/American folk culture, elevated to social scientific wisdom? As he says, the doctrine assumes that mothers (for example) can be compared by holding constant the single fact that they bear children, and then examining all the variations. He writes:

As an American observer, I certainly believe that women have children, and that to do so they certainly must have had sexual intercourse, regardless of what other conditions may be required such as God's will or being physically capable of conceiving and so on. I certainly believe that Americans, and those sharing European culture generally, as Americans do, believe that relationship is, if not sacred, at least of immense value. But I am equally convinced that most anthropologists project that particular set of meanings onto all peoples everywhere, and since they rarely if ever raise the question, there is no reason to believe that it is universally true as assumed (*ibid*, p. 198).

Many Europeans would contest the idea that they 'share European culture', with each other or with Americans. Although this may not be an American perception, that in itself may underline the point. Portuguese anthropology students' difficulties with reading *Argonauts We, The Tikopia* or *The Nuer*, or struggling with notions of pedigree, descent and breeding, are not simply the other side of the coin. The radical asymmetry of what they were doing also provides a means of assessing the specificity of what British anthropologists call(ed) kinship. The Portuguese device does not, of course, substitute a Portuguese norm for a British one. Instead it allows one to explore the analytical potential of playing off the component ideas of these 'European' versions of kinship against one another.

A personal 'background' note

In a perceptive, and in many ways predictive, discussion of the fourth phase of British social anthropology, Raymond Firth speaks of its inward-turning disposition, and the rolling-back of the spirit of inquiry upon itself (Firth 1975, pp. 8–9). Anthropologists in the first three phases were primarily concerned with charting the world of social phenomena they observed. They recognised that the nature and position of the observer were significant to this. One of Firth's 1930s colleagues even suggested that every field report should append the anthropologist's c.v., including IQ! Firth explains that the magnitude and urgency of the anthropological task as they saw it, led them to regard the 'observer-effect' problem as peripheral to their job of recording and interpreting. They opted for a 'common-sense' approach, for which they had to pay the penalty in a period when common sense was out of fashion. Interest turned to the meaning of what was being said, not just by 'informants', but also by the anthropologist. Firth poses a central problem: 'What is the significance of the language he is using as his own means of expression, his own frame of ideas, not just as a medium of communication with people in his own field?' Since, he writes, the anthropologist's perception of a situation is coloured by his own previous experience and commitment, should the notion of an 'objective' account be abandoned? 'Is there then no 'reality' in the descriptions given by social anthropologists, but only a series of personal versions or 'refractions'?' (*ibid*)

If, as Evans-Pritchard (1962) thought, the basic structure of a society is a set of abstractions derived from analysis of observed behaviour, but fundamentally an imaginative construct of the anthropologist himself, this does not mean that 'the anthropologist' is a singular individual. Part of that person is an anthropologist, meaning 'with anthropological connections', but there are of course connections with all kinds of significant others. Imaginative constructs are not private day-dreams: Mason's view, that reality is constructed through the work of the imagination, can be extended to anthropological discourse, although that refers to an external reality. The selectiveness of the imagination is what confers on objects their striking attributes (Mason 1990, pp. 14–15). There is a connection between the imaginary worlds (ensembles of names) such as those of childhood, and the world as we come to 'know it'. For the English, literary 'middle class' that connection is, above all, found in intellectual activities: from listening to bedtime stories as children, through reading and studying, to writing.

There is a certain ethnographic imperative, in a text which dwells so much upon 'background' knowledge, to include some specification of my own. My origins are provincial:[6] I was born and grew up in rural Devon, and went on to study for seven years in Cambridge. Family identity, as conferred by father's surname, is French Huguenot. My father's family was middle-class with Anglican connections. My grandfather studied Theology at All Souls', Oxford. His cousin, A.C. Bouquet, became lecturer in the History and Comparative Study of Religions at Cambridge (1932–55). Grandfather became an Anglican clergyman, and married my grandmother, who was the daughter of a provincial bank manager. My father grew up in St Giles (Dorset) before being sent away to school, his lip trembling as my grandmother's diary records, while still a little boy. The family later moved to Eastbourne. After my grandmother's death in 1941, grandfather remarried: the devout and wealthy daughter of a northern industrialist. My father studied History at Queens', Cambridge.

My mother's family forms a striking contrast to the middle-class, Oxbridge, Eastbourne, Anglican connections on my father's side. Her father and stepmother lived, when I knew them, in a semi-detached in a suburb of Exeter. During my mother's childhood, they had lived in a back-to-back terraced house, more familiar from the industrial towns of the North. My mother's strong identification with the city of Exeter, which she remembers fondly as it was before the wartime 'blitz', stems from the implantation of her paternal and maternal families there: disinherited rural migrants who sought refuge from poverty in rural–urban migration in the county town during the later part of the nineteenth century. My maternal grandmother died young, before my mother was three years old, and Grandpa remarried rather hastily before being posted to India. My mother's only solace, left in the charge of an unaffectionate stepmother, was Auntie – her mother's sister – whom we visited with probably greater frequency during my childhood than 'Grandpa and Nanny'.

The disparity in my parents' social backgrounds provided living insight, from earliest childhood, on the differentiated connections we call English kinship. How this 'background' is worked out in the narrative of the present book is for the reader to decide.

II. The genealogical method in the British and French traditions

In his comparative study of human societies a social anthropologist has learned to look to kinship as a major element in the operations of a society. Among the ties of kinship those of the elementary family (...) are primary. But in most societies historically studied by anthropologists the extra-familial kin ... are at least of comparable significance. So much is this the case that the structure of the society may seem to depend upon such groups as lineages recruited on an extra-familial kin basis, and the elementary family may even be denied recognition as a structural unit.The comparative studies of social anthropologists have revealed the structural and organisational significance of kinship in a great range of societies. Kinship is a core of social relations, a basis of education, a medium of transmission of economic rights, a framework for social obligations and often for political alignment, even ... a focus for moral ideas and ritual procedures (Firth *et al.* 1969, pp. 4–5.)

Understatement

In what was surely not an accidental move, Raymond Firth, Jane Hubert and Anthony Forge chose to introduce *Families and their Relatives*, the study of kinship among middle-class north Londoners published in 1969, by looking back over the twentieth century. The second part of this chapter will trace the way British social anthropologists during the first half of that century 'learned to look to kinship', to a specific source. Firth and his colleagues' mixture of tenses obscures both the specificity of the perspective, and the way in which it was constructed over time. Their 'social anthropologist' is an understated figure. The indefinite article suggests that it could be any social anthropologist at any time; equally open-ended is the society ('a society'): it could be any since all could be compared. The identity of the figure is in fact unmistakable; it is an amalgam of British social anthropologists, who studied societies particularly in Oceania and Africa during the first fifty years of this century.

Understatement presupposes tacit understanding in the reader, making it unnecessary to spell it all out as I have just done. Yet the implicit 'Britishness' of the vision can prove baffling to students, especially non-native English-speakers. While it is relatively simple to gain a general impression of British 'obsession' with kinship, neither the motivations nor the means by which the authors went about their chosen task are clear to all readers.

The 'social anthropologist' invoked by Firth, Hubert and Forge is, in fact, a series of texts which express a vision put together by what are loosely termed 'British' social anthropologists, writing in English. These include selected writings of W.H.R. Rivers, A.R. Radcliffe-Brown, R. Firth, E.E. Evans-Pritchard, E.R. Leach, M. Fortes and J.R.Goody. As Firth has commented, 'By comparison with today, the relevant literature was very limited and the scholars involved very few' (Firth 1975, pp. 2–3). Fortes has gone even further, describing anthropology in the British Commonwealth at the outbreak of the Second World War as 'still only a minority intellectual movement, almost, from some points of view, a lunatic fringe' (Fortes 1978, p. 4). The language they developed to discuss the nature of social organisation in primitive societies was very specific, and this imbues the writings with a kind of identity.

Stocking has been tempted to explain the 'infection' of so many intelligent anthropologists by what he sees as a sterile viewpoint, in terms of 'British intellectual character' (Stocking 1985, pp. 181–2). But in what does national intellectual character consist? What was the source of the 'infection'? While many have traced the intellectual and theoretical roots of British structural–functionalism, few have ventured into the more recondite cultural and linguistic corners of the intellectual field.

The separation of the 'personal' (individual, private, out-of-bounds) from the person-as-author of the texts, has led to considerable obscurity. The error has been to equate 'home frame of reference' with 'private lives', both of which remained largely unmentionable – for reasons of good taste as much as a certain vision of science. Anthropological translation needs to become a two-way process, however, rather than a one-way street (cf. Clifford 1986; Asad 1986; Bouquet 1991). Not only did British social anthropologists 'learn to look to kinship' in a certain way. Later generations of students are also put through the motions. This is less because kinship is nowadays regarded in the same way: the texts and authors concerned now belong to the anthropological 'classics' (cf. Firth 1975, p. 5). Kinship is, furthermore, still regarded as a field of distinctively anthropological competence (Barnes 1980). If anything, greater imaginative exertion is required to read and understand structural–functionalist texts now that we take a critical distance on them. If this is the case for many British students of anthropology, well-versed in the vagaries of twentieth-century English, the effort required of non-native English-speakers should give pause for thought.

The problem of understatement will be pursued in the following section by means of a well-known introductory text.

Introductory texts

Much of what latter-day generations of anthropology students initially 'learn' about the subject is culled from introductory texts. One reads about the fieldwork of others long before undertaking it oneself. The same goes for subject matter – anthropology's 'famous four': kinship and marriage, politics, economics and religion (cf. Barnes 1980, p. 293). It may therefore be useful to examine how one such text synthesises and propagates anthropological knowledge concerning kinship.

The reading list sent to students preparing to read the Archaeology and Anthropology Tripos at Cambridge in the early 1970s included Lucy Mair's *An Introduction to Social Anthropology*.[7] The choice is justifiable in terms of the esteem in which this work is held by professional anthropologists. An obituary of Lucy Mair written by Elizabeth Colson makes this clear. Colson cites John Davis, who refers to Mair's lapidary style, predicting that the major syntheses she produced between 1960 and 1970 will be recognised as the *summa anthropologica* they are. The six works include *An Introduction to Social Anthropology* (1965, but frequently revised). Colson adds, 'At an age where most of us regard our major work as over, she found new vigour in pulling together what social anthropologists had learned from all that field investigation' (Colson 1986, p. 24).

Mair's chapter on 'Kinship and Descent', in *An Introduction*, indeed 'pulls together' the legacy of British social anthropological thinking on these topics as follows:

In societies of simple technology most statuses are ascribed. This is another way of saying that a person's place in society, his rights and duties, his claim to property, largely depend on his genealogical relationships to other members. The primary social groups – the ones to be found in all such societies whatever other principles of organisation there may be – are all linked by kinship, and in many cases their membership is fixed by descent. The terms kinship and descent are not identical, and they are not always distinguished clearly enough. People

28

are in one sense kin if they have what is popularly called 'common blood' – that is to say, if they have an ancestor in common. In this sense, of course, nobody knows all his kin; in a highly mobile society such as ours, it may not even be possible to discover the 'next of kin' of somebody who has no close relatives. The phrase 'next of kin' has interesting implications for the social anthropologist. It is not the biological calculation of 'common blood' – actually genes – that measures nearness of kin; it is the law of any given society. As Rivers put it, 'kinship is the social recognition of biological ties' (Mair 1965, p. 69).

The exposition is, until we encounter Rivers's name, a synthetic one: a distillation of several positions published after his death in 1922, but concerted enough to permit this formulation. The vocabulary is unmistakable: statuses, rights, duties, property, and genealogical relationships; groups, principles of organisation, kinship and descent. Rounding the synthesis off is the ancestral figure of Rivers. It is to him that 'we owe a number of concepts still fundamental in the analysis of kinship' (*ibid*, p. 29).[8]

There are various salient points in the passage quoted. Firstly, the equation of genealogical relationships with biological ones; a distinction follows between these basic relationships and the social recognition given to them. Kinship is about the social recognition of certain genealogical (= biological) relationships. There is a further important equation between the calculation of social kinship and the law of any given society. These socially constructed relationships expressed, as Mair suggests, in a 'biological idiom', serve all kinds of juridical purposes in technologically simple societies: claims to land for cultivation, to other kinds of property, to mutual assistance in the pursuit of common interests, to authority over others. The recognition of kinship also requires the fulfilment of obligations which complement these claims: those in authority should look after the welfare of subordinates, who in turn must obey them; and everyone must cooperate on occasions where this is appropriate (*ibid*, pp. 69–70).

The social recognition of biological ties – kinship – is distinguished from descent. Descent refers only to membership of a particular kind of kinship group, according to Rivers, whom she cites as the authority on the matter. Descent was limited to membership of what he called unilateral groups, and it was evinced by tracing ancestry through the male (patrilineal) or the female line (matrilineal).

The resonation of one of Rivers's famous definitions in an introductory passage on kinship, typical of those to which students were referred as recently as the 1970s, captures the impetus he gave to British kinship studies. Firth and his colleagues' reference to ideas developed from the beginning of the twentieth century, as they turned their attention to middle-class English kinship, reiterates this point. Rivers breathed new life into some of L.H. Morgan's ideas, published in 1871 under the title *Systems of Consanguinity and Affinity of the Human Family*. Morgan's 'discovery' of classificatory and descriptive systems of kinship terminology, interpreted as 'survivals' from previous forms of social organisation, facilitated the reconstruction of human history within an evolutionary framework. The debate on kinship faded during the closing decades of the nineteenth century in Britain, after McLennan's dismissal of these ideas. The 1874 edition of *Notes and Queries* reflects, in the number and scope of questions, which were the topics of the moment. While there are 245 questions on religion, the section on 'social relations' is restricted to a single descriptive sentence (Urry 1972, p. 47). Rivers transformed this situation and helped to make kinship central to the ethnographic study of social organisation by British anthropologists.

Why should (the American) Morgan's ideas have proved so fertile for the development of British social anthropology? If some of the specificities of British interest in kinship can be observed 'at source' in Rivers's genealogical method, this also provides an opportunity to examine the interpenetration of folk and scientific conceptions identified by Schneider. Biographical details of anthropologists are frequently presented as the 'background' against which publications and career are set, but the two are seldom related in other than 'individual' terms. Kuper, quoting Slobodin, writes that Rivers was born in 1864 into an old Kent family, solidly middle-class, with Cambridge, Church of England and Royal Navy connections (Kuper 1988, p. 153). It is presumably considered superfluous (for what is assumed to be an Anglophone readership) to do more than signpost: south-east England, Cambridge, C. of E. and R.N. effortlessly evoke the 'background' from which 'our Rivers' (the anthropologist) steps forward.[9] Writers such as Langham and Slobodin have tried to bring Rivers's background into the anthropological foreground, carefully relating his theoretical ideas to his personal trajectory.

30

Yet when Leach assures us that Rivers (like Haddon) did not belong to the right social class which would have made the success of ethnology at Cambridge a foregone conclusion (Leach 1984, pp. 4–5), this suggests another direction in which personal biographies might be taken. Leach proposes 'Englishness' as one of the component variables in the interesting spectrum of personal characteristics displayed by British social anthropologists, which are reflected in their respective contributions to anthropology (*ibid*, p. 16). If this is so, then 'Kent, Anglican, Cambridge and the Royal Navy' are indeed signposts which lead into specific zones of English life and culture, exerting an influence on Rivers's thinking and writing. They cannot be treated as if they were assumptions. Leach remarks that British academics were still far too sensitive about matters of social class and nationality even in the 1980s (*ibid*, p. 3). Yet such historical, linguistic and class specificities cannot be bracketed aside from an author's 'work', for nicety's sake, when they are not part of the reader's background or general knowledge. Such information forms a submerged area of knowledge which, like an iceberg, may be crucial to comprehending the 'tip' which is exposed as text. How far might this work for Rivers?

W.H.R. Rivers and the genealogical method of anthropological inquiry

Rivers was born in Kent in 1864, the eldest son of a vicar who was also trained as a speech therapist. He studied medicine at the University of London (St Bartholomew's teaching hospital), graduating in 1886. He became interested in the physiology of the nervous system and in sensory phenomena and mental states while still in London. He travelled widely, as ship's surgeon, as well as studying for some time in Jena. While based in London, Rivers came into contact with a wide variety of people. He moved to Cambridge in 1893 where he held a University appointment to teach the physiology of the senses. It was here that he was invited by A.C. Haddon to join the 1898–99 Torres Straits Expedition. Rivers had just completed a critical account of the main theories of colour vision and space perception, and he was to be the expedition physician–psychologist.

Haddon, who was a zoologist by training, had first visited Melanesia to carry out research on marine biology (1888–89). While in the field he became interested in the oral literature and art of the Papua and Torres Straits peoples – an interest that was fostered by J.G. Frazer. Frazer urged him to record the rapidly changing societies and customs of Melanesia before it was too late. With this encouragement, Haddon set about organising the Cambridge Anthropological Expedition to the Torres Straits. Haddon's interest in primitive mentality was distinguished from 'that of every early anthropologist and almost every philosopher since the Enlightenment' by his determination to 'undertake precise and systematic measurement of psychological characteristics in the field' (Slobodin 1978, p. 19).

Rivers's work on the cultural conditioning of perception (spatial relations and colour discrimination) coincided with his 'conversion' to ethnology. His main contributions to the ethnological report were on genealogies, kinship, personal names and totemism (Kuper 1988, p. 157). The genealogical method, regarded as a major contribution to scientific methodology in ethnography, was also developed on this expedition. Rivers's natural-sciences training almost certainly influenced his approach to ethnological methodology. He argued that 'facts' by themselves were not enough: it was the manner in which they were collected that was important. Genealogies or pedigrees provided, in Kuper's words, a powerful tool with a variety of uses, but above all they allowed the scientist to record with a new precision the crucial data – terms for kinsmen – which permitted the reconstruction of the social structure (*ibid*).

There were two distinct stages: first, a pedigree comprising the proper names of relatives was collected; next the terms of relationship for addressing and referring to each of these persons were assembled. This procedure allowed the ethnographer to 'mimic the thought processes through which indigenes apprehend abstract ideas via concrete facts' (Langham 1981, p. 75). Rivers published his method in 1910, and a succinct description of it already appeared in the fourth edition of *Notes and Queries on Anthropology*, which came out in 1912. The sixth and most recent edition of this methodological manual (1951) still contains instructions which although unaccredited are largely as Rivers wrote them. Let us consider the method in more detail.

The genealogical method

Pedigrees had been collected by, for example, Morgan and Co-

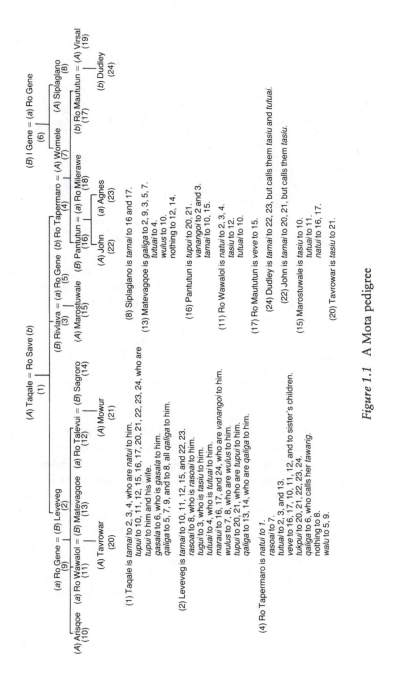

The relationships in the pedigree:

(A) Taqale = Ro Save (b) (1)

(B) I Gene = (a) Ro Gene (6)

(B) Rivlava = (a) Ro Gene (3)   Ro Tapermaro = (A) Womele (4) (7)   (A) Siplaglano (8)   (A) Virsal (19)

(a) Ro Gene = (B) Leveveg (9) (2)   (B) Matevaqoe (13)   (a) Ro Talevui = (B) Sagroro (12) (14)   (A) Marostuwale (15)   (B) Pantutun = (a) Ro Milerawe (16) (18)   (b) Ro Maututun = (A) Virsal (17)   (b) Dudley (24)

(A) Arisqoe (10)   (a) Ro Wawalol (11)   (A) Tavrowar (20)   (A) Mowur (21)   (A) John (22)   (a) Agnes (23)

(1) Taqale is tamai to 2, 3, 4, who are natui to him.
tupui to 10, 11, 12, 15, 16, 17, 20, 21, 22, 23, 24, who are tupui to him and his wife.
gasala to 6, who is gasala to him.
qaliga to 5, 7, 9, and to 8, all qaliga to him.

(2) Leveveg is tamai to 10, 11, 12, 15, and 22, 23.
rasoai to 8, who is rasoai to him.
tugu to 3, who is tasiu to him.
tutuai to 4, who is tutuai to him.
marawi to 16, 17, and 24, who are vanangoi to him.
wulus to 7, 8, who are wulus to him.
tupui to 20, 21, who are tupui to him.
qaliga to 13, 14, who are qaliga to him.

(4) Ro Tapermaro is natui to 1.
rasoai to 7.
tutuai to 2, 3, and 13.
veve to 16, 17, 10, 11, 12, and to sister's children.
tukpui to 20, 21, 22, 23, 24.
qaliga to 6, who calls her tawarig.
nothing to 8.
walu to 5, 9.

(8) Siplaglano is tamai to 16 and 17.

(13) Matevaqoe is galiga to 2, 9, 3, 5, 7.
tutuai to 4.
wulus to 10.
nothing to 12, 14.

(16) Pantutun is tupui to 20, 21.
vanangoi to 2 and 3.
tamai to 10, 15.

(11) Ro Wawalol is natui to 2, 3, 4.
tasiu to 12.
tutuai to 10.

(17) Ro Maututun is veve to 15.

(24) Dudley is tamai to 22, 23, but calls them tasiu and tutuai.

(22) John is tamai to 20, 21, but calls them tasiu.

(15) Marostuwale is tasiu to 10.
tutuai to 11.
natui to 16, 17.

(20) Tavrowar is tasiu to 21.

Figure 1.1 A Mota pedigree

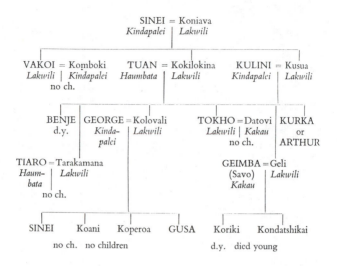

Figure 1.2 The pedigree of Kurka or Arthur of Guadalcanal

drington before Rivers went to Melanesia. It is interesting to compare Codrington's pedigree of a Mota family (Figure 1.1) with the small pedigree of Kurka, or Arthur, of Guadalcanal in the eastern Solomon Islands (Figure 1.2). Codrington's chart is presented as almost self-evident. Rivers, by contrast, takes his reader through the steps by which he collected the material as a concrete illustration of the methodological potential of the device.

The informant, Kurka or Arthur, was first asked to name his 'real' (as opposed to classificatory) father and mother, check for previous or other marriages, then list their children, in order of age, their marriages and offspring: 'Thus was obtained the small group consisting of the descendants of Arthur's parents' (Rivers [1910] 1968, p. 97). Next, he obtained Arthur's mother's pedigree – since descent on Guadalcanal was matrilineal: her parents, other possible spouses, the names of children, their marriages and descendants. The most extensive pedigrees could be collected, according to Rivers, using only five terms of relationship: 'father', 'mother', 'child', 'husband' and 'wife', thus avoiding what he

34

considered the more problematic terms: 'brother', 'sister', 'cousin', 'uncle' and 'aunt'. The fifth edition of *Notes and Queries* advises: 'terms such as brother and sister, and still more cousin, uncle and aunt, must be altogether avoided' (*Notes and Queries* 1929, p. 45). Barnard and Good question why *Notes and Queries* treats some genealogical positions as less problematic than others. They suggest that there is an implicit lineal bias pervading the entire method. Lineal relationships are consequently seen as less ambiguous than collateral and affinal ones (Barnard and Good 1984, p. 28). We shall return to this point.

Information concerning the social condition, locality(ies), totemic or other group affiliation, together with any other relevant facts, should then be recorded for each person named on the pedigree insofar as this was possible. Information collected in this way permitted the study of an extraordinarily wide range of topics. Its main use was for studying social organisation; this meant, in the first place, working out the 'systems of relationship': that is, the terms of reference and address used reciprocally between the informant and all those named in his pedigree. Differences of sex, age and birth order were all to be noted. Rivers estimated that at least three separate pedigrees would be required to obtain the relationship terms. A second way in which the material could be used was for the study of laws regulating marriage: an analysis of the statistical frequency of marriages allowed, enjoined or prohibited. Rivers thought there was a gradual transition in progress from a situation in which marriage was regulated chiefly or entirely by clans or other groupings, to 'one in which the regulation of marriage depends on actual consanguinity' (Rivers [1910] 1968, p. 103). Thirdly, the laws regulating descent and the inheritance of property could be obtained. Each person in Arthur's pedigree, for example, belongs to his mother's clan. Chiefly succession could be examined in exactly the same way. Furthermore, the divisions and subdivisions of property, such as that involved in the inheritance of a piece of land, could be followed with some facility using the method. The migration of Melanesian bush populations to the sea-coast from about 1860 onwards could also be studied from the information concerning the successive localities in which persons had lived.

Beyond the study of 'social organisation', Rivers saw further uses for the method in the study of magic and religion: 'very definite functions in ceremonial are assigned to people who stand in certain relationships either to the performer of the ceremony or to the person on whose behalf it is being carried out' (*ibid*, p. 105). He went on to suggest that:

exact inquiry rendered possible by the genealogical method would show that these functions connected with relationships are far more general than current anthropological literature would lead us to suppose, and further that the duties or privileges of kin discovered in this manner can be much more closely defined (*ibid*).

Rivers describes working with his book of pedigrees by his side, looking up the names of participants and seeing how they were related to the performer or subject of the ceremony, so that they 'become real personages to me although I have never seen them'. This is a crucial observation. Later generations of anthropologists extended this genealogical 'plotting' beyond the study of magic and religion, into economics and especially politics. Genealogical plotting became more than simply a way of gathering materials; it became closely identified with the presentation, or even the translation of other ways of life, to such an extent that Barnes could describe genealogical charts as part of the ethnographer's 'minimum obligation' for making his fieldwork 'intelligible' to others (Barnes 1967, p. 121). He did warn against the hazards of confusing terminological and prescriptive (marriage) diagrams which use the skeleton of genealogical charts: 'Analytically these two features are quite distinct, and it is important not to confound them, as well as to avoid the even more serious error of thinking that the diagram is a genealogy' (1967, p. 125). Yet he would scarcely have warned against these errors had they not been possibilities – as, for example, Southwold has shown to have been the case with Mrs Fallers's analysis of Baganda kinship terminology (Southwold 1971, p. 37). The moulds and constraints imposed upon Ego's genealogical knowledge by the ethically inspired techniques of questioning identified by Barnard and Good, had perhaps equally resonant effects among anthropologists. This, at least, has been one of the hypotheses making the genealogical method so decisive to the present account.

Protopathic and epicritic

Langham suggests that the protopathic–epicritic distinction, usually associated with the experiments performed on Head's arm in Cambridge, dates in fact from Rivers's face-to-face encounter with 'savages':

Rivers's concept of the protopathic embraced the emotions, subjectivity and 'concrete' modes of thought. His concept of the epicritic embraced emotionless objectivity and abstractly rational forms of cognition. With 'protopathic' and 'epicritic' interpreted in this broad fashion, Rivers's fascination with aboriginal man may be described as arising from his desire to uncover the protopathic elements in humanity – to see beneath the epicritic veneer to 'the dog beneath the skin' (1981, p.75).

Genealogies reveal, in Langham's view, how mental operations which men like Rivers perform epicritically, are accomplished by those in whom the protopathic predominates. Langham thus connects Rivers's scientific interests with his psychological constitution. Fascination with the protopathic mental abilities of the aboriginal was transformed by Rivers into an efficient, objective tool for rendering ethnography more scientific. He regarded the genealogical information obtained in this way as 'bodies of dry fact the accuracy of which, especially when collected by the genealogical method, is about as incapable as being influenced by bias, conscious or otherwise, as any subject that can be imagined' (Rivers 1914).

The enduring significance of the genealogical method within British social anthropology deserves attention. What attractions did the method hold for anthropologists? Ethnology's institutional insecurity at the beginning of the twentieth century makes the legitimating idiom of scientific method fairly predictable. It is perhaps more remarkable that the notion of pedigree should have been identified as suitable for transformation into a scientific procedure.

Pedigree

It is tempting to apply the protopathic/epicritic dichotomy to Rivers's personal biography, and to interpret the incorporation of pedigree as a kind of commentary on his own feelings about kinship. Rivers never married, and never assumed the responsibilities of domestic life. During the London years he lived in lodgings, and later he resided in St John's College, Cambridge, where he 'might have been a man without a family' (Slobodin

1978, p. 45). His family of reference remained the one into which he was born, with whom he was in fact 'on affectionate terms' (*ibid*). He visited the family in Kent during most vacations, before and after going abroad. He accompanied his two (unmarried) sisters on several trips abroad; and he used to check his brother's farm accounts. He also took the opportunity to visit relatives in India and in Australia when he was carrying out research there. Slobodin observes that Rivers's study of social organisation was 'supported by his view of it, and especially kinship patterning, as the most fundamental part of a culture, the most covert and hence the slowest to change' (*ibid*, p. 147).

Was this hidden factor of stability in Rivers's rather varied life translated into intellectual terms? Was he seeking in the pedigrees of others, translated into scientific terms by means of the genealogical method, refuge from his own (protopathic) longings in this direction? This kind of reasoning might also help to account for the lineal bias which (as we have seen) later commentators argue pervades the entire method. Rivers never married: of course affinal relations seemed more problematic than those of descent ...

For all its attractions such an explanation is restrictive. By limiting the effect to Rivers's psychological condition, the argument is effectively contained at the level of a rather singular individual. But are there more satisfactory ways of relating the properties of the genealogical method with the unmistakably (upper) middle-class indices (S.E. England, C. of E., Cambridge, R.N.), which are usually relegated to the status of 'background' (i.e. understood or assumed) knowledge? The success of the genealogical method in British social anthropology may have depended as much on assumptions implicitly shared among those drawn into what was a very limited intellectual field at the outset.

Rivers was certainly 'author' of the genealogical method but, like any other author, he depended on attracting an 'audience'. There is a clue about why he conceived of kinship as the most fundamental, covert and enduring aspect of culture, and saw the genealogy as the key to documenting it, at the beginning of his 1910 paper:

It is a familiar fact that many peoples preserve long pedigrees of their ancestors, going back for many generations and shading off into the mythical. It is perhaps not so well-known that most people of low culture preserve orally their pedigrees for several generations in all the collateral lines so that they can give in genealogical form all the descendants of the great-grandfather and the great-great-grandfather and therefore know fully all those whom we should call second and third cousins and sometimes their memories go even further back (Rivers [1910] 1968, p. 97).

The point was that Rivers could assume that his readers were familiar with pedigrees. When Rivers was a medical student at St Bartholomew's Hospital, staff were expected to pay attention to patients' life histories (Slobodin 1978, p. 10). A number of immigrant patients were interested in and knowledgeable about their own genealogies. The example chosen by Slobodin from Sir Norman Moore's history of the hospital is that of an Irishman who 'came into the Casualty department, and when asked his name replied, 'Michael O'Clery'. 'An illustrious name', said the physician ... The scavenger explained accurately to which part of the family of hereditary [Irish] historians he belonged' (*ibid*).

In 1914 Rivers published some 'Notes on the Heron pedigree collected by the Reverend George Hall'. Here he is even more explicit about the overlap between pedigree and genealogy among 'ourselves':

The practical importance of the subject of genealogy is well recognized. Our own pedigrees are collected and preserved as the means whereby to show rights to property or rank, and those of animals have long been an indispensable instrument to guide the breeder and the fancier. It is only, however, in quite recent times that the value of pedigrees as instruments of scientific research has been recognized; and just as they have been found to be of practical utility in law and breeding, so is it in the sciences of sociology and biology that their value is making itself felt (Rivers 1914b, in Slobodin 1978, p. 219).

We shall return to some of the points about 'breeding' and 'recording' made in this passage in Chapter 5. The aim so far has been to introduce the genealogical method, and postulate its centrality for subsequent developments in British anthropological theory. Barnes, indeed, has described the collection of genealogies as part of the ethnographer's stock-in-trade (Barnes 1967, p. 104). We shall try to document this claim in the following chapter. The next section will emphasise the *Englishness* of British social anthropological interest in kinship by means of a brief contrast.

A brief contrast with French ethnological approaches to kinship
There are some striking contrasts between the way the British learned to look to kinship, and French ethnological studies in this field. French ethnologists showed a remarkable lack of interest in kinship studies during the inter-war years (Segalen 1991, p. 377), at the very time of their proliferation in Britain. On the other hand, studies of kinship in Britain were rather half-hearted by comparison with overseas research. There seems also to have been more interchange between French scholars working at home and abroad.

There are clearly important differences of an institutional and intellectual order, which partly explain the respective emphases of the two traditions.[10] Folklore and museology laid the groundwork for the ethnology of France.[11] There was also a significant input of ideas from the École Sociologique, particularly through Mauss's lectures at the École des Hautes Etudes from 1926 onwards, and published posthumously as the *Manuel d'Ethnographie*. Van Gennep systematised the enormous accumulations of folkloric traditions using the framework of *les rites de passage* in his *Manuel de folklore français contemporain*. Although Durkheim lectured on the 'Origins of the family' in Bourdeaux in 1888 (Segalen 1991), this interest did not carry forward to the inter-war years. Mauss's lectures were mostly concerned with the collective origin of primitive beliefs, the empirical study of 'total social facts', and the development of the classificatory method.

The advent of the ethnology of France coincides, for some authors, with the founding of the Musée National des Arts et Traditions Populaires, in 1937 (Chiva 1987a; Segalen 1990). One of the effects of having the museum rather than the university as the institutional framework for the discipline was that it ensured the place of objects in the world charted by French ethnologists. The material world was not partitioned off from ethnographic research in quite the way it had been in Anglo-American anthropology (Strathern 1990a). The Musée not only housed the contents of the former Salle de France, which was transported from the Trocadero but was also a place where research could be carried out alongside the conservation and display of objects. G.H. Rivière had been instrumental in establishing this *musée-laboratoire*: (cf. Chiva 1987b).

Ethnological research based at the Musée National during the

Vichy period was concerned with a 'rather specific vision of the rural world', and particularly 'peasant values' (Segalen 1990). During the post-war era (1945–50) the ethnology of France began to discover its identity, mainly through the pioneering work of Maget and Dumont. The first monographs published in the 1950s, Dumont's *La Tarrasque* (1951), Wylie's *Village in the Vaucluse* (1957), and Bernot and Blancard on Nouville (1953), reflect the incorporation of methods and concepts from social anthropology (Cuisenier and Segalen 1986, p. 42). Cuisenier and Segalen have argued that the impact of structuralist analysis on the ethnology of France was indirect. It consisted in a way of perceiving reality which stressed similarities rather than inventorising differences (cf. Le Bras and Todd 1981, p. 18; Zonabend 1986), rather than a structuralist analysis of phenomena.

An imported artefact?
When Cresswell and Godelier published a collection of essays on practical aspects of fieldwork in the mid-1970s, they observed that 'the descriptive monograph is dead' (Cresswell and Godelier 1976, p. 17). Theirs, they said, was not a manual of the English type (they were almost certainly referring to *Notes and Queries*), nor did it resemble Mauss's *Manuel d'Ethnographie* in providing the researcher with a list of questions that must be answered in the field in order to cover all aspects of the society's functioning.

This tacit reference to an intersection between 'old-fashioned' French and British methodological treatises deserves closer scrutiny. Firth reports that Mauss was wellknown, although not present at Malinowski's seminar (Firth 1975, p. 2). Mauss was personally acquainted with Rivers, referring to him as 'mon pauvre ami' (Mauss 1924, p. 289). It seems reasonable to assume that one of the ways in which the genealogical method made its way into French ethnology was via Mauss. Mauss equated British social anthropology with French moral and juridical sociology (Mauss 1947, p. 110). One section of his *Manuel d'Ethnographie* is devoted to this field. It deals with political and social organisation at the level of the State, and domestic organisation which is divided between politico-domestic and familial–domestic. The methods available for studying this area included the case study, the biographical method and direct observation (*ibid*, p. 114). The genealogical method is presented as a more specific means for studying domestic organisation. Mauss seems to have envisaged 'applying' the genealogical method to family biographies and auto-biographies, in order to obtain the exact kinship nomenclature of the society being studied.

The genealogical method, as Mauss understood it, consisted in collecting all the kin terms employed by an individual as they were used with respect to the different members of his family, where the exact kin tie with the informant was known. These terms, recorded on the genealogical tree of the family being studied, revealed different classes of kin: the 'father' class, comprising all the father's brothers; the 'brother' class, including all maternal and paternal cousins, and so forth. There is a reference at this point in Mauss's text to Rivers's essay on the genealogical method (Rivers [1910] 1914), and to Richards's article on the village census (Richards 1935). The history of the group could be reconstituted by compiling the biographies of other members. Furthermore, precious details of property transmission and inheritance could be obtained through this method.

It is instructive to contrast the context and manner in which Mauss introduces the genealogical method with the way it is presented in *Notes and Queries*. The fifth edition of *Notes and Queries* (1929) devotes ten pages to it (pp. 44–54), and it is quite central to the methods of Part II (Cultural Anthropology/Socio-logy). The sequence runs *from* social groups and groupings, through the life history of the individual, economic life, political institutions, and thence to material culture, arts and sciences and so on. Mauss, on the contrary, begins briefly with *morphologie sociale*, but gives considerable attention to technology (46 pages), aesthetics (30 pages), rather less to economic matters (9 pages), before discussing juridical phenomena which, as mentioned above, included the family and marriage. Thus, although it is there, the place of the genealogical method cannot be compared with that of *Notes and Queries*.

Although Cresswell and Godelier complained, in 1976, that the questions asked in the old-style research manuals were precondi-tioned by our own notions of such categories as 'economics', 'technology', 'kinship', 'politics', 'religion' and 'art', it is worth noting the reflexive use to which Griaule suggested such a 'draw-back' might be put.[12] Griaule's *Méthode* was published a decade after Mauss's *Manuel*. Griaule's contention was that although it might initially seem desirable to try to suppress one's European mentality (if such a thing exists in the singular), this is in fact impossible when confronted by cultures of a different hallmark. It is better to face up to one's biases and even try to make use of them. Astonishment at the spectacle of foreign customs can indeed act as a spur to curiosity, and even lead to discoveries (Griaule 1957, p. 10). A 'morbid tendency to introspection' could, in fact, assist the observation of certain kinds of unconscious facts (*ibid*, p. 11). Griaule underlined the need for tact on the part of the ethnologist by evoking the image of a Mangbetou asking questions about the preparation of a corpse and modes of succession at a Burgundian funeral (*ibid*, p. 13). While Firth certainly urged that the bias of personal interest should be consciously faced (Firth [1936] 1983, p. 488), he scarcely advised its incorporation into methodology.[13]

In his *Esquisse d'une théorie de la pratique*, Bourdieu examines the disparity between the practical relations of kinship and the official definitions which anthropologists assimilate to their rule-bound accounts of kinship systems. He contrasts the logical relationships constructed by anthropologists with those which are continuously practised, maintained and cultivated. These two orders of relationship can be compared with the theoretically possible roads and routes on a map, as opposed to the actual network of beaten tracks and paths which are in constant use. The genealogical tree compiled by the anthropologist is a spatial diagram that can be taken in at a glance, *uno intuito*, and can be scanned indifferently from any point in any direction. This means that the entire network of kinship relations over several generations exists only as a theoretical object: it is a *tota simul*, a simultaneously present totality (Bourdieu [1972] 1977, pp. 37–8).

As a footnote to these remarks, Bourdieu recommends a social history of the genealogical tool, with particular attention to the functions which have produced and reproduced the need for such an instrument. This means rendering 'completely explicit the implicit demand which lies behind genealogical inquiry, as it lies behind all inquiries'. He asserts that it is in fact the problems of inheritance and succession which have given the genealogy its particular position within the anthropological tradition. The relationship between 'social' and 'scientific' uses of the instrument would be a central issue.

43

But the most important thing would be to carry out an epistemological study of the mode of investigation which is a precondition for production of the genealogical diagram. This would aim to determine the full significance of the ontological transmutation which learned inquiry brings about simply by virtue of the fact that it demands a quasi-theoretical relation to kinship, implying a break with the practical relation directly oriented towards functions (*ibid*, p. 207, n. 71).

It is possible to speculate on why the genealogical method has not been subject to such inquiry.[14] One reason may be that it was 'imported' from British social anthropology, as Mauss's references to Rivers and Richards suggest. Genealogical 'trees' and pedigrees have existed in France, as elsewhere, for centuries. The transformation of pedigree into a scientific methodology was, however, a specific invention made at the inception of twentieth-century British social anthropology.

Parler famille

The originality claimed by Cresswell and Godelier for their approach lay not so much in the questions it posed as in the efforts required to learn how to answer them. This response clearly did not depend on separating France from the rest of the world – as seems to have happened with certain aspects of English life in British social anthropology. Two important essays concerning kinship and marriage illustrate this point. The first of these was written by F. Héritier (1976) and concerns processing extensive African genealogical data by computer.[15] The second is by Zonabend (1976) who discusses the study of kinship in French peasant society. The very existence of such a methodological treatise in a volume like this emphasises two important points. Firstly, there was expertise, material and demand for such a paper at the beginning of the seventies in France. Secondly, the inclusion of a chapter on research techniques for the study of kinship in French peasant society in a general work on anthropological methodology, evinces communication between those involved.

Zonabend examines three ways of approaching the topic: through written documents, oral sources and 'talking family' (*parler famille*). Her focus is principally on the last two categories. Genealogies are among the most significant oral sources through which it is possible to explore the field of kinship for each individual. 'Talking family', on the other hand, allows one to grasp relations and protocol through spontaneous discourse (cf. Jolas, Verdier and Zonabend, 1970). Zonabend observes that it is necessary to compile genealogies in order to circumscribe the field of kinship, to get to know the links which unite inhabitants of the same village, and to perceive specific marriages. A sample can be drawn according to the demographic importance of the village, using criteria such as profession and age – or simply taking all the adult inhabitants of a commune. The process of making a genealogy requires several interviews: the first to make an initial schema on the basis of which kin can be put in place. Subsequent interviews can then be used to complete and specify information about each kinsperson.

The information to be collected for each person comprises (sur)name and first names; date and place of birth and (where applicable) marriage and death; place(s) of residence; profession; godparents. The information will be more or less readily available according to collateral distance and to how far back in time it refers. There may be long biographies to record for close kin, while only the place of residence (for example) of more distant relatives may be known. It is also important to record the modes of address ('*tu*' or '*vous*') and reference for each relative, and to discover something of the content of the relationship: whether it involves visiting, commensality or whatever. Although genealogies can be 'completed' by consulting State archives, information acquired in this way should be recorded separately so that the limits of a person's knowledge are quite clear.

Kin relations, conduct, terms of reference and address may appear spontaneously during the course of the interview. Zonabend emphasises that where kin ties are significant, a person's identity is always formulated in genealogical terms: one is a father, son, spouse, or brother before all else. This is an opportunity for hearing family talk. Another excellent way of conducting such an interview, she suggests, is by discussing kin portrayed in wedding photographs. Genealogical inquiry, she observes, allows the researcher to perceive the continuity or persistence of kin groups through time. But these facts of kinship are organised according to an ethic of family relations, which people express in their discourse. Although written sources enable the researcher to imbue informants' discourse with historical depth and to produce statistical analyses, it is this discourse which ultimately orients the analysis.[16] There is a telling contrast here with Barnes's article published some nine years earlier. Barnes advocates recording whatever information about his kinsfolk an informant thinks important, in the form in which he presents it, before beginning the sequence of inquiries structured by the ethnographer (Barnes 1967, p. 106). How this indication of the informant's perception of his kinsfolk and the names, status, numbers and relationships he wishes to present to the ethnographer might be used, we are not told. He does not suggest that this discourse might in fact provide the interpretative key. Later on, Barnard and Good come much closer to the 'parler famille' position, although significantly enough they make no reference to that article nor to other work by the ethnologists of France (Barnard and Good 1984, p. 26).

The difficulties of *'parler famille'* as a research method should not be underestimated, as Segalen has vividly summarised. Research on family and kinship, systems of inheritance and devolution, are less neutral than certain other general social phenomena. 'Talking family' is charged with latent violence quite as much as affectivity, even if the ethnologist claims to stick to the *terra firma* of kinship terminology, relations between those connected by marriage, and wedding ceremonies. It is a discourse that deserves comparison with sorcery which, as Favret-Saada shows, is about power rather than knowledge or information (Favret-Saada 1977, p. 21). Segalen became aware of this aspect of the topic through reactions to her questions, her very presence in southern Brittany, and comments made about her and carefully repeated in her absence. She recounts that she sometimes had the sensation of having burst into some forbidden zone, forcing an intimacy in which she did not participate. This intrusion appeared to deprive the person with whom she was speaking of part of his or her identity. The situation was exacerbated by a sense that Segalen had somehow taken it over. Reactions covered the entire spectrum from rather feeble exhortations not to 'write that down' ('you will make my mother look ridiculous'), to more violent letters of protest, or being brusquely shown the door. Segalen describes how she found herself slipping imperceptibly from obtaining information to acquiring power, to the extent that she was dealing with knowledge about others (Segalen 1985, p. 10).

The comparison between kinship and sorcery as potentially

explosive research topics in France is a striking one. The refuge taken by many researchers in the mass of historical material at their disposal is one way of deflecting the unacceptable face of their inquiries, both for the population being studied and for the person conducting the research. How do you, asks Segalen, report on those who have taken you in, fed you, enfolded you in their affection and become good friends? Working as a member of a group of researchers may, to some extent, assuage the sense of isolation experienced by an anthropologist on home ground, but the dilemmas and ambiguities are still there. The Minot project in the Châtillonnais area of Burgundy, involving four researchers over the period 1968–75, presented similar difficulties. Zonabend comments that she and her colleagues (Tina Jolas, Marie-Claude Pingaud and Yvonne Verdier) had to take their 'irruption into this reality', and the distortions brought by their very presence, into account (Zonabend [1980] 1984, p. x). Zonabend and her colleagues developed the *'parler famille'* technique in the course of their Minot studies. In spite of the difficulties associated with it, the technique modifies the genealogical method in a quite distinctive way.

The emphasis on *talking* family is one to which we shall return in the chapters on Portuguese kinship. It illustrates one way in which the genealogical method has been practically modified within another European tradition of social anthropology. The fact that this modification did not take place on British home ground is particularly significant. There is no parallel to the directions taken by the ethnology of France in British 'anthropology at home'. The respective disciplinary and intellectual histories are quite different.

Concluding remarks

The ethnographers responsible for the British vision of anthropology have not always been very explicit about the tools of their trade. Fortes, in a confusing metaphor, stresses the 'materials' upon which a 'journeyman' sets his sights: wood, stone or steel. But he fails to discuss the 'axe', 'hammer' or 'anvil' by which such materials are presumably extracted and worked (Fortes 1978, pp. 1, 24). Such selective metaphors only work if everyone understands the references. As British anthropology texts, translated or untranslated, become standard works for non-native English-speaking students, the matter of making the hidden contents explicit becomes more than an 'academic' exercise. Readers are at two removes, one conventional and the other quite unorthodox, from the acknowledged contents.

The aetherialisation of anthropological texts has encouraged the present back-track to what is conceptualised as one of the flashpoints of British kinship theory: Rivers's genealogical method. The genealogical method is a sensitive register of hidden assumptions precisely because it is seen as a methodological rather than a theoretical instrument. The hypothesis is that the ease with which Rivers interchanges the terms 'pedigree' and 'genealogy' reflects the proximity between a cluster of folk notions (pedigree) and one of the enduring methods of anthropology. This proximity needs attention since it may explain some of the difficulties experienced by non-native English speakers (not to mention native English-speakers!) with the 'language' of early-twentieth-century British anthropology, as well as problems associated with studying English kinship.

The following chapter will examine the proposition that genealogies played a central role in establishing the characteristic discourse of early-twentieth-century British social anthropology. They were critical in two respects: firstly, as a means of collecting data, and secondly as a way of presenting materials in the publications which ensued. Genealogical charts and diagrams are supposed to 'illustrate' texts. Genealogies are, in fact, a kind of 'language' in themselves which, running parallel to the texts, function as 'concrete evidence' for the conceptual abstractions of British kinship theory.

Notes

1 The toing and froing between 'English' and 'British' which goes on in *Families and Their Relatives* is not, as far as one can tell, conscious. I return briefly to the 'Englishness' of 'British' social anthropology later on in this chapter when discussing Rivers's 'background', and in more detail in Chapter 5.

2 Although see Firth, 1975 – and, indeed, the passage cited at the beginning of this chapter.

3 Although one of the points of this book is to endorse the view that anthropology means different things in different national traditions.

48

4 See, for example, the category 'fieldwork' in the *Annals of the Association of Social Anthropologists of the Commonwealth and Directory of Members.* The lack of an additional category means that here, for example, I had no alternative but to cast the four years spent in Portugal as 'fieldwork'. I am of course sceptical about this.

5 The 'Dutch angle' already supplies fresh refractions on the Portuguese, as the examples of Rentes de Carvalho and Komrij, discussed in Chapter 4, indicate.

6 My rather peripatetic trajectory has continued this pattern.

7 I am speaking here from experience. This volume was recommended reading material before going up to Cambridge in October 1974.

8 Mair states her preference for 'Maine or even Morgan' when tracing her own intellectual paternity, rather than Tylor, who is often described as the father of British social anthropology.

9 Contrast with what Pulman does with the same set of signposts: 'Comment pourrait-on ne pas relever d'emblée que cette double ascendance forme comme une sorte de creuset généalogique des interrogations de Rivers concernant les rapports entre la vie ecclésiale et le savoir anthropologique?', (Pulman 1989–90, p. 74).

10 See, for example: Cuisenier and Segalen 1986; Segalen and Zonabend 1987; Segalen 1989; Segalen, Lenclud and Augustins 1990; Cohen 1990a,b; Chiva 1987a,b; Jamard 1985.

11 Contrast with Britain where, as Fenton puts it, 'social anthropology in universities did not come to open its doors to folklorists' (Fenton 1990, p. 180). And writing of the late twentieth century: 'It is as if anthropologists, ethnologically-orientated museum staff, and adherents of other related disciplines, were running along parallel roads with high walls between', (*ibid*, p. 186).

12 Griaule and his associates studied the Dogon during the 1930s.

13 Although see Firth 1975, p. 9.

14 Although see the exhibition, *Liens de famille*, (especially the section on l'arbre généalogique), at the Musée National des Arts et Traditions Populaires, 1991. Interestingly enough, there was no account of the genealogy *qua* method in French anthropology and ethnology. See also the accompanying publication, *Jeux de Familles*, especially the article by M. Segalen and C. Michelat, 'L'amour de la généalogie', 1991.

15 Héritier first did genetic-demographic work on the Samo. Later, she was to ask, 'In contemporary, numerically populous western societies, which do not appear to be organised on the basis of kinship, does kinship nevertheless play a role in the choice of spouse' (Héritier 1981, p. 137). Zonabend raised a similarly intriguing problem by

turning around one of Lévi-Strauss's remarks. Lévi-Strauss commented that social and political manoeuvres are frequently disguised beneath the cloak of kinship in so-called archaic societies (Lévi-Strauss 1979, p. 179). Zonabend's question is whether our supposedly modern societies do not attempt to disguise the genealogical imperatives of marriage beneath the mantle of politics and the economy (Zonabend 1986, p. 46).

16 See, for example, the kinship zones identified by Jolas, Verdier and Zonabend: 'les cousins', 'les parents à la mode de Bourgogne', 'les propres' and 'le chez' (1970, p. 7).

CHAPTER TWO

THE LANGUAGE OF GENEALOGY. A 'BOTTOMLESS PIT OF ANALYSIS'?

A brief complaint by Phyllis Kaberry in her 1939 monograph expresses uneasiness with the 'British' way of going about things. She refers, in fact, to those two aspects of the genealogical method identified in the previous chapter as subjacent to how British social anthropologists went about collecting and organising their materials:

The anthropologist works on genealogies, sifts and winnows data, delves into the technicalities of adjustments in kinship terminology and discovers principles. In the process, the day-to-day existence in the camp with its play of temperament, the foraging for food, the discussions of scandal that are rarely virulent and generally tolerant, the moments of excitement and tension – all these tend to recede into the remote background. The dust and heat of native life are replaced by the somewhat sterile atmosphere, precision, order, and cloistral quiet of the laboratory. Natives are gradually denuded of their humanity as the anthropologist strives to cut to the bone of truth; vital personalities are reduced to skeletons to give *an almost diagrammatic representation of the principles enunciated*. Unfortunately the attempt to explain occupies more time and space than the bare description. It is one of the penalties that the scientist has to pay that he cannot take statements at their face value, but must endlessly seek to burrow to their inner significance. In so doing he is likely to be plunged into a bottomless pit of analysis and never touch reality again (Kaberry 1939, p. 134, emphasis added).

The sense of 'reality' receding into analysis is probably shared by many who study social anthropology. Kaberry's remarks express similar feelings on the part of the anthropologist as author. The view that there is a 'reality', external to the ethnographic texts which seek to 'describe' and 'analyse' it, was a basic premise of

British social anthropology during the first decades of the twentieth century. The genealogical method was among the instruments for prising 'principles' from 'reality', as Kaberry's extract indicates. It was both a means of collecting and of presenting data. Predating the Malinowskian fieldwork 'revolution' as it did, it was to prove a remarkably resilient component of the methodological battery.

This chapter considers how what is known (or not known) about the English 'background' to British social anthropological discourse, might be crucial for readers who are historically and/or 'culturally' removed from the source of these texts. That would seem to apply to just about everybody who begins to read social anthropology in the 1990s. There is no pretence at exhaustive coverage, just a few examples.

The 'flesh and blood' of kinship à la Malinowski

Rivers died in 1922, the year in which *Argonauts of the Western Pacific* was published. Malinowski had accompanied Marrett to Australia, and he began fieldwork in southern New Guinea after the outbreak of the First World War. Armed with the 1912 edition of *Notes and Queries*, Malinowski began collecting genealogies. Rivers, as noted in the previous chapter, was one of the principal contributors to the large section on sociology where he stresses the importance of methodology in the collection of material, of learning the local language and taking notes and drawings. Although Malinowski was very dissatisfied with the results of this first sortie, the experience seems to have to have been valuable preparation for the Trobriand fieldwork. In 1935 he wrote, 'I still believed that by the "genealogical method" you could obtain a foolproof knowledge of kinship systems in a couple of hours. And it was my ambition to develop the principle of the "genealogical method" into a wider and more ambitious scheme to be entitled the 'method of objective documentation' ([1935, p. 326] cit. in Urry 1972, p. 52). Fieldwork in the Trobriand Islands lasted for two years (1915–16 and 1917–18), and then, the First World War also over, Malinowski returned to the London School of Economics, where he was to spend the next fifteen years.

It is beyond the scope of this book to go into the Polish 'background' to Malinowski's anthropological vision (see Paluch 1981), although it may be important for understanding his marginality to the line later developed in British kinship studies.[1] Malinowski refers to the genealogy in his famous description of the methods he used in collecting ethnographic material in the Introduction to *Argonauts*. It was, he wrote, 'nothing else but a synoptic chart of a number of connected relations of kinship' ([1922] 1983, p. 14). It did not differ, in this respect, from the charts or synoptic tables he proposed for studying almost any aspect of native life. 'In the investigation of kinship, the following up of one relation after another in concrete cases leads naturally to the construction of genealogical tables. Practised already by the best early writers, such as Munzinger, and, if I remember rightly, Kubary, this method has been developed to its fullest in the works of Dr Rivers' (*ibid*).

Malinowski relativised the importance of the genealogical material, placing it alongside other kinds of material collected in equally systematic ways. Economic transactions, for example, could be analysed just as carefully: Seligman's tables of how valuable axe-heads circulated were a source of inspiration for settling 'the more difficult and detailed rules of the Kula'. Malinowski did not privilege genealogical material as providing direct access to the hidden form of social organisation, as Rivers had done. He had another message concerning fieldwork: you had to go and pitch your tent in the midst of a village, learn the local language and take part in events in such a way as to be able to bring home the intimate touches of native life (Gellner 1986). He makes a contrast between the 'excellent skeleton' of the tribal constitution recovered by 'survey work', but firmly assured his readers that it was lacking 'flesh and blood' (Malinowski [1922] 1983, p. 17). These were found in the imponderabilia of actual life, facts which he felt 'can and ought to be scientifically formulated and recorded' (*ibid*, p. 19). They were to be found in daily routines of work, care of the body, preparing and eating food; conversation and social life around the village fire, friendships and hostilities, passing sympathies and dislikes between people; the way in which personal vanities and ambitions of the individual are reflected in the emotions of those around him:

if we remember that these imponderable yet all important facts of actual life are part of the real substance of the social fabric, that in them are spun the innumerable threads which keep together the family, the clan, the village community, the tribe – their significance becomes clear. The more crystallised bonds of social grouping, such as the definite ritual, the economic and legal duties, the obligations, the ceremonial gifts and formal marks of regard, though equally important for the student, are certainly felt less strongly by the individual who has to fulfil them (*ibid*).

Malinowski's insistence on the importance of daily life for scientific ethnography, and his forthright and personal way of expressing this conviction, contrasts sharply with Rivers's approach. Instead of a 'body of dry facts' we are urged to get to grips with the 'flesh and blood' on the skeleton. Nor did Malinowski hesitate to apply his insight 'to ourselves':

we all know that 'family life' means for us, first and foremost, the atmosphere of home, all the innumerable small acts and attentions in which are expressed the affection, the mutual interest, the little preferences, and the little antipathies which constitute intimacy. That we may inherit from this person, that we shall have to walk after the hearse of the other, though sociologically these facts belong to the definition of 'family' and 'family life', in personal perspective of what family truly is to us, they normally stand very much in the background' (*ibid*).

It is significant that inheritance, rights and duties are the 'background' of 'family life', for Malinowski, while for Rivers they were the crucial social functions which distinguished 'our own' systems of relationship from classificatory ones (Rivers [1914] 1968, p. 46). This led Rivers to stress difference ('the great paucity of definite social functions associated with relationship, and ... the almost complete limitation of such functions to those relationships which apply to individual persons and not to classes of persons' (*ibid*). Only in the cases of the transmission of hereditary rank and the property of a person dying intestate, were social regulations embodied in the law. Malinowski, by contrast, stressed the atmosphere and emotions associated with family and home, and was certain that '[e]xactly the same applies to a native community'. While Malinowski's approach to empirical fieldwork became the hallmark of the British School, his ideas on kinship were shelved as unsystematic (cf. Kaberry 1957; Fortes [1957] 1970).

What did Malinowski mean by the 'flesh and blood' of kinship? In the first place he rejected the emphasis which had been devoted to studying kinship terminologies, particularly as a means of reconstructing historical kinship and marriage regulations. Yet he himself regarded the few words printed in capital letters on the only genealogical diagram to appear in *The Sexual Life of Savages* as providing 'the key to the whole terminology of kinship and ... the foundation both of the sociological system within native culture and ... its linguistic expression' (Malinowski 1929, p. 436). His jibes at classificatory and descriptive systems in the article 'Kinship', published in 1930, make the evolutionary preoccupations of Morgan and Rivers (in an early phase of his career) look absurd and irrelevant. He was equally scornful of the 'concrete method of questioning' (1929, p. 426). Since ethnographic fieldwork revealed the truth of contemporary, extant savage society, why rake through dull, second-degree material such as kinship terminologies to such questionable ends?

The emotions and sentiments of family life interested Malinowski. *The Sexual Life of Savages* was, as far as he was concerned, his study of kinship. He reported, amongst other things, on relations between the sexes in tribal life; prenuptual intercourse, love-making and the psychology of erotic life; erotic dreams and fantasies; and a savage myth of incest. Small wonder the book achieved a measure of popular notoriety – enough to have it classified 'ARC' by the Cambridge University librarian, which meant that it could only be read with special authorisation from a senior college tutor! (Leach 1984, p. 8). The single genealogical diagram included (Figure 2.1) concerned in fact terms (of kinship, marriage and in-laws). Kinship to Malinowki was something which 'grew out of' domestic family life. Writing about the Trobriands he asserted that all the sociological divisions, local communities, clans, sub-clans, and classificatory kinship groups were rooted in the family. It was only possible to grasp the native kinship system by studying how the earliest bonds between parent and child were formed, following their gradual development and growth, and ever-widening extension into bonds of local grouping and clanship (1929, p. 433). A year later, writing on kinship in more general terms, he depicted the 'initial situation' of a child within the supposedly universal nuclear family, gradually extended through the addition of further kinship relations. Each person thus constructs kinship for him- or herself; there was no notion of Rivers's covert, enduring system of socially recognised relationships which precede and supercede the individual. The 'biographical method' was considered particularly suitable for studying the 'extension' of kinship from the initial (domestic) situation outward to such extra-domestic institutions as the clan and tribe. Exactly

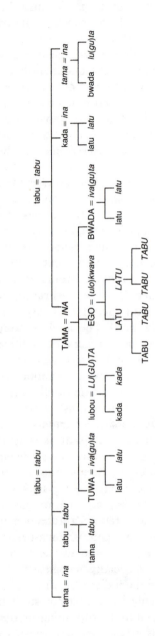
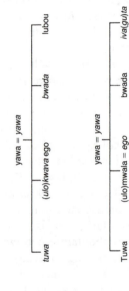

Figure 2.1 Genealogical diagram of relationship.

how this was to be done we are not told, although he does emphasise the 'distortion' implicated in this process (Malinowski 1930).

Malinowski did not subordinate his use of English language to the analytical strictures against which Kaberry railed. Late-twentieth-century students who read his prose alongside Rivers's or Radcliffe-Brown's are often struck by its literary qualities. Malinowski's metaphors certainly involve their own difficulties, as we shall see in the second part of Chapter 3, but these belong to another order. Crucial 'background' to the novelty of Malinowski's writing for the late-twentieth-century reader, includes the differences between post-1924 Cambridge and London (and later the triangle Oxford–London–Cambridge) anthropological circles (cf. Leach 1984). Rivers's trajectory took him from Kent, via London to the 'stifling Cambridge social atmosphere' and its 'conformist' anthropology. In the next generation, Malinowski came from Poland via London and Melanesia back to London, where his seminar attracted a number of ex-Cambridge anthropology students (Leach *ibid*). 'Outsiders' included not simply anthropologists of other nationalities, such as Malinowski, but also women anthropologists. There were those 'internal' outsiders whose responses to 'the system' sometimes included theoretical conservatism. Leach clearly placed both Rivers and Radcliffe-Brown in this category: although English, both remained marginal to the 'intellectual aristocracy' which dominated Oxbridge.

Radcliffe-Brown: corporate descent groups

Malinowski's approach to kinship contrasts sharply with that of his near contemporary, Radcliffe-Brown, the Cambridge-trained student of Haddon and Rivers. A.R. Brown was born in Birmingham in 1881, and had a very different kind of 'background' to either Rivers or Malinowski[2]. Leach observes that he 'tried to give the impression to the more gullible members of the non-English audiences that he was usually addressing that he was, by lineage and upbringing, an English country gentleman. The fact that in 1926, on moving from Cape Town to Sydney, he should have taken the trouble to change his name from Brown to Radcliffe-Brown gives an indication of the value he attached to such matters. In actual fact he was not born into the English social class which reacts favorably to hyphenated names. His education started at the

Royal Commercial Travellers School at Pinner in Middlesex' (Leach 1984, p. 21). Leach describes his own comments as arrogant and prejudiced, but nonetheless a faithful reflection of what he felt.

Leach's passage is, in fact, a precious piece of supporting English ethnography for those who are expected to study Radcliffe-Brown – and indeed Leach himself, and the various other anthropologists he mentions. This text, like Adam Kuper's history of the British 'School', is an indispensable guide to the anthropological classics. Non-English audiences are less gullible than Leach seems to have imagined in matters concerning English social class. Many are aware of its importance to the English, even though they might not be able to specify exactly how. The lack of explanation as to how this English 'platform' somehow intervenes between the reader and the 'societies' and 'kinship systems' which are being presented, may well be confusing but it is not necessarily mutely accepted.

Brown was persuaded to change from reading the Natural Sciences to Mental and Moral Sciences at Cambridge. Rivers and Myers were among those who taught him, but from about 1910 onwards he was attracted to the 'sociological' ideas of Durkheim (Stocking 1985, pp. 144–5). Kuper suggests that the attraction lay in its optimistic vision of the possibility of man's self-realisation in a properly ordered society. Durkheim's socialism did not emphasise the class war (Kuper 1983, p. 39). What may seem rather 'personal' motivations for intellectual development to an English reader may be vital clues about an unfamiliar world to others. Some see Radcliffe-Brown's gravitation towards Durkheimian ideas as an early instance of the love–hate relationship between French and British anthropologies. The 'personal', from this perspective, is anything but 'individual': it documents image and counter-image production between two 'metropolitan' anthropologies.

The same applies to spatial mobility. Radcliffe-Brown's trajectory was even more geographically mobile than those of Malinowski and Rivers. Unlike Malinowski, who returned from fieldwork in the Trobriands to establish himself in London, Radcliffe-Brown went to the South African University of Cape Town in 1920, where he remained until 1926. He then spent five years in Australia (Sydney); and a further six in Chicago, before returning to

Oxford in 1937. The following year, Malinowski left the L.S.E. for the United States. Radcliffe-Brown 'reigned' in Oxford until 1946. It is probably more difficult for many readers to grasp an idea of stability, where persons remain all their lives in one location. Nonetheless, the variety of these trajectories provoke many questions, certainly abroad, about the sense of calling this 'British' anthropology. The adjectival use of 'British' does not seem to be based on 'soil' or 'blood' in any straightforward way. Such questions are not simply 'background noise' for large numbers of contemporary readers. Later chapters of this book will go into some of these observations in greater depth.

Radcliffe-Brown's first monograph, *The Andaman Islanders*, was published in the same year as Malinowski's (1922). The book was based on research carried out on the Andaman Islands between 1906 and 1908, and written up only in 1914. Radcliffe-Brown's account of kinship is rather thin (there are no genealogies), the main focus of his analysis being on the meanings and functions of rites and myths. He admitted, 'I collected a number of genealogies from the natives, but unfortunately my own inexperience in the use of the genealogical method, and my consequent inability to surmount the difficulties with which I met, made this branch of my investigations a failure' (Radcliffe-Brown [1922] 1964, p. 72, n. 1). Although he dedicated the book to Haddon and Rivers, it is clear from his Preface that his main methodological inspiration came from the French sociologues (there is a lengthy citation from Hubert).

It was in his paper on the mother's brother in South Africa (1924), that the differences between Radcliffe-Brown and Malinowski regarding kinship begin to emerge – despite the fact that Brown still uses 'extensionist' vocabulary. He emphasises the importance of studying the behaviour characteristically associated with a relationship, and discusses the case of the Bathonga mother's brother and sister's son. The Bathonga were first studied by Junod, who interpreted the relationship in evolutionary terms. Although now patrilineal, he saw this relationship as evidence for an earlier matriarchal stage. Radcliffe-Brown rejected this interpretation, stressing instead the need to contextualise it among other relationships in that society, and then to compare them with patterns of conduct in other societies.

While both Malinowski and Radcliffe-Brown stressed the importance of contemporary empirical research, the comparative emphasis given by the latter depended on a systematic view of the functioning of kinship within any given society, very unlike Malinowski's generalisations. The underlying notion of 'systematisation' is perhaps what most distinguishes the respective approaches of Radcliffe-Brown and Malinowski. Radcliffe-Brown believed that more or less definite patterns of behaviour are associated with recognised relationships. He thought that genealogical relationships constitute the basic means of regulating social relations, and that kinship is bilateral in all societies. The distinction between 'genealogical' and 'social' is an important one: there are clearly two orders, one more 'social' than the other, involved. Like Rivers, Radcliffe-Brown believed that kinship ties are the basis of social organisation, and hence social structure, in primitive societies. His hypothesis was that there is a tendency in primitive society to merge the individual with the group to which he or she belongs, and that this implies extending a certain kind of behaviour to all members of a group which has its origin in a relationship with one member of the group. Thus care and indulgence between one particular Bathonga mother and her son is generalised to all maternal kin; whilst obedience and respect between father and son is extended to all paternal kin.

Although Radcliffe-Brown disagreed radically with Rivers's general theoretical position, he built directly on concepts and methods developed by Rivers. 'His concept of social structure, his notion of the relation between genealogical connection and the kinship system, his approach to the analysis of descent groups, all benefited from Rivers's lead' (Fortes 1969, p. 43). Kuper has argued that Radcliffe-Brown returned to Rivers's concept of descent, and infused it with new justification in his 1935 paper entitled 'Patrilineal and matrilineal succession' (Kuper 1982, p. 77). Kuper traces the thematic link with Rivers even further back, to Maine and his discussion of corporateness in Roman law. Maine's concept of 'corporation' seems to have made way for a more clearly structural view of the 'individual'. The corporate role of descent groups as an emergent 'British' theme, is complemented by a submerged notion of the 'individual'. The stability, continuity and clarity of social organisation was thought to depend on the existence of corporations which transcended individuals. Such corporations might be either kinship- or territory-based. The approach was by now explicitly juridical: rights in persons and property, and duties between individuals and groups were central. Radcliffe-Brown's emphasis on the rules of descent, inheritance and succession addressed the problem of assuring continuity and avoiding conflict among close kin.

This 'natural science of society', with its systematic definition of concepts for a theoretical understanding of how societies 'functioned', contrasts sharply with Malinowski's conviction that social institutions 'hang together' – as if this were the logical outcome of competent ethnographic description.

Radcliffe-Brown's comparative perspective on kinship and social structure can also be seen in the 'Introduction' to *African Systems of Kinship and Marriage* (1950). Here the idea that kinship was historically important in England, is supported by many examples from the Anglo-Saxon period. The significance of kinship in modern England, on the other hand, was thought to have been steadily eroded ([1950] Kuper 1977, p. 256). The reader is confronted by a curious equation between the importance of kinship in historical England and in contemporary primitive societies. It is as if the emphasis on synchronic studies of primitive societies had the effect of temporally distancing any observations which might, for comparative purposes, be made about the anthropologist's own 'society'. Fabian has analysed how the ethnographic present tense severed primitive societies from history (Fabian 1983). The English past perfect deserves equal attention, however, as one of the means of keeping the wolf from the home front door: things relevant for comparative analysis seem relegated to history.

Radcliffe-Brown underlines his equation between kinship and social structure in primitive societies by referring to the passage of persons through the social structure which they enter by birth and leave by death, and in which they occupy successive positions' (*op. cit.*, p. 217). He identified two structuring principles in the alternating relations between generations, and sibling solidarity. Within these parameters, '[e]very kinship system provides each person in a society with a set of dyadic (person-to-person) relationships, so that he stands as it were, at the centre of a narrower or wider set of relatives' (*ibid*, p. 230). Thus, while 'actual structure' changes (persons are born and die), 'structural form' remains more or less constant ([Radcliffe-Brown 1965] Kuper 1977, pp. 28–9). The kinship systems of many societies include a further type of structure,

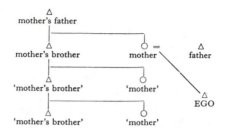

Figure 2.2 The principle of the unity of the lineage

beyond this 'structural form': these are separate groups comprising persons who are or who regard themselves as being a unilineal body of kindred (Figure 2.2). Some societies, it seems, are more kinship-based than others in the sense that they include these wider groups of unilineal kin. British anthropologists began to argue that such groups could form the basis of political organisation in certain acephalous societies in Africa (Fortes and Evans-Pritchard 1940). This seems to reduce the importance of kinship in 'advanced' or 'modern' societies, or at least to remove it from the public, political sphere. If this was only one of the avenues for exploration on the basis of Radcliffe-Brown's theoretical work, it is remarkable that it proved so influential to a generation of British anthropologists. For if those who attended Malinowski's seminar were initially inspired by his 'revolutionary' approach to ethnographic fieldwork, many seem to have gravitated towards Radcliffe-Brown when it came to analysis and drawing theoretical conclusions. Radcliffe-Brown's theoretical position could have inspired empirical research in other directions. The fact that it did not, particularly during the 1930s and 1940s, is of course significant. The very terms of the theory suggest a certain inevitability to the relative neglect of contemporary Britain as fieldwork terrain. The question is complicated, however, by the origins of the vocabulary and its associations in the English language: 'social structure', 'person', 'individual' – none of these concepts are conjured out of thin air, however carefully they may be tailored to a specific intellectual project. For those who do not belong to 'the system', there is once again the sense of a hidden ethnography to these terms.

Radcliffe-Brown saw social structure as a concrete arrangement of persons, human beings. The orderliness of that arrangement was institutionally defined and regulated. He distinguishes between *social structure*, as the arrangement of persons in institutionally controlled or defined relationships (a system of social positions); and *social organisation*, as an arrangement of activities or a system of roles. The person is thus thought to be universally subject to (unruly) emotions. These are brought to heel by institutional constraints which adhere to the successive positions occupied by the person in the social structure (Kuper 1977, p. 265). The logic of the emotions is 'inborn, not acquired'. The separation between *self* and *role* implicit in Radcliffe-Brown's notion of a person's social position (within the social structure) is far from obvious. The 'self' somehow contrives to be both 'more' and 'less' than the sum of his statuses. 'More' in the sense that this is presumably what permits the 'playing of roles'; 'less' in that this person is constantly under threat from his emotions and only a fully *social* person as a part of something greater (cf. Strathern 1992). Compare this extract from Fortes:

'Person' ... comprises a variety of statuses. In any given situation or social relationship, he employs one or some of them, while others remain potentially available for conducting himself in other situations. The ensemble of statuses corresponds to what Radcliffe-Brown at one time called the 'social personality' (Fortes 1969, pp. 95–6).

The person here is faceted, and plural, and yet still somehow contained ('ensemble'). It is significant that the plurality of the 'social personality' is not systematically related to the 'self'. Another direction was taken.

Radcliffe-Brown clearly saw descent as the basis of social structure. Marriage was regarded as a 'rearrangement' of this structure, a dubious process full of stresses and strains, which had to be brought under control. He emphasised the unusual (and probably recent) prerequisite of romantic love for modern Anglo-American marriage. The frequency of Hollywood-style divorce was scarcely surprising given this explosive combination of emotion and structural rearrangement. The contrast between kinship and affinity is very clear. Kinship is based on descent, and the kinship system is determined by the way descent is recognised and reckoned ([1950] Kuper 1977, p. 200). The orderliness and sense of continuity associated with descent, is disrupted by the chain of events unleashed by marriage: 'In the new structural situation resulting from marriage there are possibilities of conflict' (*ibid*, p. 250); 'A marriage produces a temporary disequilibrium situation' (*ibid*, p. 251). This is so much so that affinity is at best only a 'kind of reverse kinship': 'We think of kinship only as a relation between two persons who have a common ancestor. But there is a kind of reverse kinship between two persons who have a common descendant, and it is relationships of this kind that are created by marriage conceived as a process' (*ibid*, p. 247).

One of the most notorious relationships produced by the rearrangement of marriage is that between mother-in-law and son-in-law, although Radcliffe-Brown is careful to point to father-in-law/daughter-in-law parallel. It is the transference of control over the daughter from 'the person most intimately connected with the wife before marriage', together with sexual rights over her, which makes the relationship so sensitive. Mother-in-law jokes clearly separate these two potentially hostile persons, in their curiously similar roles, with respect to the daughter/wife. Such jokes allow the husband to vent his feelings about his mother-in-law's continuing influence over his wife. The mother-in-law should not take offence at such jokes since they are only 'sham hostility'. It seems as though such role-playing somehow preserves the essential person from a tumult of emotions. These are pitched very high where romantic love is a supposedly vital component to marriage.

Radcliffe-Brown's own marriage seems to have been a failure, and in this respect descent may have seemed a safer bet. Yet to reduce his theoretical views to his personal situation trivialises their wider significance. There is a striking parallel here with Rivers. Both Rivers and Radcliffe-Brown were 'born' Englishmen, and although from different 'backgrounds' and generations their paths crossed in early-twentieth-century Cambridge. Neither belonged to the intellectual aristocracy, and yet both drew upon a notion of descent as a means of anchoring the unfamiliar. Corporate descent seems to have struck some kind of chord among early-twentieth-century 'British' anthropologists when they conducted and wrote up fieldwork among primitive peoples. Where did these images and ideas come from and what did they mean?

We, The Tikopia is a key text for understanding how British social anthropologists came to look at kinship. Raymond Firth came to London from New Zealand in order to study the new-style anthropology with Malinowski. He became one of the leading figures in the discipline and, as one of the first to study English middle-class kinship, he occupies an important position in this account.

Raymond Firth: from 'ramage' to lineage

Firth acknowledges both Malinowski and Radcliffe-Brown in *We, The Tikopia*, and their respective influences can be discerned in the monograph. Firth was born in New Zealand in 1901, and was one of the first students from Malinowski's L.S.E. seminar to carry out fieldwork: this he undertook in 1928–29 (arranged by Radcliffe-Brown, who was then in Sydney), with return visits in 1958, 1966 and 1973. Malinowski described Firth as his 'best pupil' (Stocking 1985, p. 162).

We, The Tikopia is a sociological analysis of family life and kinship. Firth explained, much as Malinowski might have done, that later publications would deal with other institutions. This was an analytical study of kinship with empirical generalisations founded on data and presented in the most objective form possible. Malinowski wrote the Preface, praising the book as a model of anthropological investigation. It was, he said, genuine scientific scholarship based on real experience, and particularly welcome at a time of pretentious new anthropological theories. He nonetheless took the opportunity of disagreeing with Firth's caution about the 'biographical model'.

Firth's main criticisms were directed at Rivers, who had spent a single day on Tikopia producing (as Firth put it) a useful report but scarcely reliable ethnography. But he does also point to the antiquity of empirical studies, which go back to Morgan at least, thereby qualifying some of Malinowski's claims about fieldwork. The basic kinship unit of study for Firth, as for Malinowski, was the family. He was interested in household organisation and the ways in which recognised genealogical ties emerge in concrete domestic activities: production and food consumption, upbringing, care, and conversation.

Firth was also concerned with the activities of individuals in associated units beyond the family, who were related by consanguinity or marriage. The first eight chapters of *We, The Tikopia* deal with 'the salient principles of Tikopia kinship ... considered primarily with reference to the way they work in the lives of individuals, especially in the immediate family circle'. The remaining part of the book described 'larger groups', and aimed through their analysis to contribute to a 'general theory of kinship aggregations' (Firth [1936] 1983, p. 298). These larger groups were the 'house' (*paito*), 'definitely of the patrilineal type', and clan (*ibid*, p. 299). This is how Firth introduces the *paito*:

Every individual family of father, mother and children is part of a larger group known as the *paito* and composed of similar families, tracing their relationship ultimately to a common male ancestor through male forebears in each case. Each *paito* bears a proper name. The head of the *paito* is, in theory, the senior male descendant of this ancestor, though circumstances may have introduced a representative from a junior branch for the time being. The *paito* as the incorporation of a number of individual families is itself the outgrowth of such a single family in past time; there is, in fact, a continuous process of fission at work in Tikopia society ... The position of the individual as a member of a *paito* is one of the most crucial factors in his social status. From it, through his father, he receives guardianship from others of the group in his young days, rights to the produce of lands and a share in them and other property, a house-site and an associated name when he marries, economic and ritual assistance on the necessary occasions, and privileges in the use of religious formulae and in appeal to the principal ancestral deities. Wealth, rank and clan membership are all primarily determined by the *paito* into which he may be born (*ibid*, p. 300).

Firth uses genealogies to concretise his description of the 'house' as, for example, in presenting the chiefly houses of Kafika, Tafua and Taumako. Figure 2.3 *is* the 'Chiefly house of Kafika'.While the cohesion of the house 'depends primarily on the tie of recognized descent from common ancestors' (*ibid*, p. 309), the degree of corporate unity within such groups varied considerably. Firth acknowledged the difficulties of drawing the line clearly between separate units since they are formed by a process of branching (*ibid*, p. 310).

The terminological difficulties experienced by Firth in describing the Tikopian *paito*, document the sharpening and focusing of British anthropological interest in descent. His initial proposal of ramage as the technical term for the *paito* is justified in terms of the 'tree metaphor ... actually used by some native peoples in describing their social organisation' (*ibid*, p. 328). The etymologi-

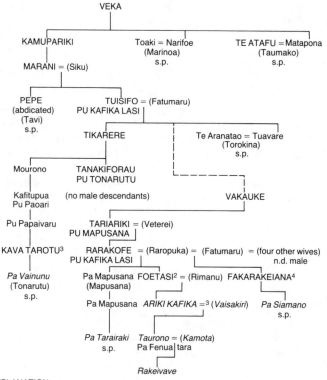

EXPLANATION:
These genealogies are skeletal, omitting many polygynous marriages, offspring without modern descendants, junior members of families, etc.
Chiefs in capitals, thus: TUISIFO.
Numbers indicate order of succession in the last few generations.
Houses (ramages) in brackets thus: (Siku).
s.p. − still proceeding.
n.d. − no descendants.
Names of living persons italicized.

Figure 2.3 The Chiefly House of Kafika

cal advantage of 'ramage' is that it evokes the branching process: groups attain individuality and yet remain connected to the parent stem. Firth remarks that it is also consistent in metaphor with the expression 'genealogical tree'. The exact significance of such metaphorical consistency is left unsaid. The important point, then, was to find the correct term. Firth decided that this was ramification.

By the time he came to write the Introduction for the Abridged Edition in 1963, the terminology had changed. He would not substantially alter or modify his treatment of kin groups and their residential distribution, although he might go into more detail about them 'in order to conform to a modern trend of interest'. He would, however,

modify the expression in one respect. Instead of using the term 'house' – the translation of the Tikopia term *paito* – for the patrilineal descent group, I would term it lineage in accordance with what has now become general usage. The term 'ramage' which I tentatively applied to the 'house' I would now reserve for other Polynesian descent groups which are not unilineal but in respect of which the factor of choice is built into their structural principle (*ibid*, p. xiii).

Firth insists in his concluding chapter that 'kinship behaviour and not kinship sentiment is the study of the anthropologist' (*ibid*, p. 482). His generalisations were, he said, empirical ones based on material actually observed. Informants' statements were used as commentaries on a range of topics, rather than evidence of what actually occurs:

I have tried to reduce assumptions to a minimum, and in particular to discuss what the Tikopia do rather than what they think or feel. In the psychological field, more than anywhere else in the study of uncivilized people, unverifiable postulates are apt to be introduced so subtly that they pass unnoticed by the ordinary reader, and no attempt to justify them is made, or even to admit that they are present (*ibid*).

The idea that observable behaviour might be interpreted in a more straightforward way than people's statements about their actions, resembles but qualifies Malinowski's stipulations. The convergence lies in the emphasis on observation; the divergence in the focus on behaviour rather than sentiments. The meaning of kinship, for Firth, is

fundamentally a re-interpretation in social terms of the facts of procreation and regularized sex union. The complex series of social relationships formed on this basis comprises activity of a residential, an economic, a political, a juridical, a linguistic order, and constitutes a primary system of integration in the society. A scientific definition of a kinship tie between individuals means not only a specification of the genealogical bond between them and the linguistic term used to denote that bond, but a classification of their behaviour in many aspects of their life (*ibid*, p. 483).

This passage spells out in empirical terms what Rivers and Radcliffe-Brown had been writing in more explicitly theoretical terms. The consequences of this type of formulation can be seen in subsequent empirical work. The assumptions constitute a kind of common basis for discussion. Firth can confidently write,

The fact that there is no society without a kinship system of some kind means that in the first place there is overt allowance made for sentiments generated by parturition, sex union and common residence (to put it at its lowest, even where male procreation is not understood); in the second place that these physical phenomena provide a simple base, usually easily recognizable and usually unchallengeable, on which other necessary social relationships may be erected. Moreover, the kinship tie is permanent until death – unless diverted by the fiction of adoption. In small societies such as Tikopia, then, it can be readily grasped why kinship is at the root of much of the social structure (Firth [1963] 1983, p. xiii).

We, The Tikopia has been characterised as typical of British functionalist monographs published in the 1930s: long, discursive books often echoing discussions which had taken place in Malinowski's seminar a decade earlier. Participants in that seminar had included E.E. Evans-Pritchard, Raymond Firth, Isaac Schapera, Audrey Richards, Camilla Wedgwood and Hortense Powdermaker (Kuper 1983). Firth supervised Phyllis Kaberry's thesis. They all undertook participant observation lasting between one and two years, working in the vernacular, out of touch with other Europeans so that (in theory, anyway) the people studied became 'we' instead of 'they'. Starting from a single institution, studies like Fortune's *Sorcerers of Dobu* (1932) and Richards's *Land, Labour and Diet in Northern Rhodesia* (1939), moved through the entire culture. There are, however, some interesting internal differences not least in the use of diagrams. Apart from *We, The Tikopia*, which is replete with genealogies, Fortune used a simple diagram to 'summarize' his argument about the marital grouping and the *susu* (Fortune [1932] 1962, p. 8); Richards included diagrams of the matrilineal extended family and the matrilineal descent group to 'represent' a headman's 'relationship to the members of the two groups' (1939, p. 117), and appended kinship charts to show the composition of Kasaka village in 1933 at the end of the book. Although Schapera's *Married Life in an African Tribe* dealt (like *We, The Tikopia*) with the social functions of the family, there is not a single diagram!

Kuper has identified the main difficulty with all these late-1930s monographs as distinguishing between analytical relevance and empirical connection. He also claims that they lack a theoretical framework and are therefore old-fashioned and undisciplined. My contention is that there *is* a theoretical framework, but that it is *implicit* in what appear to be reams of empirical description. It is particularly striking that such framework as can be discerned in *We, The Tikopia* also informs work on English/British kinship, of which Firth was a prime mover during the 1950s and 1960s. We shall return to this later in the chapter. There is, however, another counter-example which may serve to underline the point.

Bateson's aside on 'fraudulent heraldry'

Radcliffe-Brown's sociologically elegant approach significantly influenced those casting about for theoretical direction in the late 1930s. Bateson published an experimental work on the central Sepik Iatmul people of New Guinea in 1936. It was to the pretensions of this book, with its three analytical points of view, that Malinowski made disapproving reference in his Preface to *We, The Tikopia*. Radcliffe-Brown, on the other hand, was full of praise for Bateson's achievement.

A series of studies published during the 1940s were inspired by Radcliffe-Brown. The focus of geographical interest shifted away from the small groups of South Sea islanders to large-scale African societies with complex political institutions. Bateson's book was marginal to the direction taken by the majority of British social anthropologists after 1940. Despite a number of 'ruptures' with Malinowski, British anthropologists kept faith with his ethnographic empiricism. Bateson approached the fantastic behaviour associated with the *naven* ceremony, which included transvestitism and other dramatic reversals of normal behaviour, from three explanatory perspectives: sociological, logical and psychological.

Every aspect of the *naven* ceremony was subjected to analysis in terms of social relationships between those involved. Bateson approached the *lau/waua* relationship (mother's brother/sister's son) as Radcliffe-Brown might have done: placing it in its patrilineal context. He also analysed cultural structure: the logical relationships between the premises of Iatmul culture, such as head-hunting and male violence. Finally, he considered the emotional needs of individuals, the details of cultural behaviour, and the way in which the emotional emphases of the culture as a whole mediated the two.

Bateson's use of diagrams within the text deserve attention. The first shows the genealogical position of *wau* and *laua*, together with three arrows representing the three identifications on which the behaviour of *wau* and *laua* is based. The diagram (Figure 2.4) is used to summarise the principal characteristics of the *wau*'s (structural) position. Although Bateson used the 'traditional symbols' for males and females (Barnes 1967, p. 114), also used to indicate the planets Mars and Venus respectively, rather than triangles and circles, his underlying notion of genealogical connection remained very 'British'. This comes out in his discussion of Iatmul ancestral naming practices: 'The Iatmul totemic system is enormously elaborated into a series of personal names – spirits, birds, stars, animals, pots, adzes etc. etc. – of his or her clan – and one individual may have thirty or more such names' (*ibid*, p. 127). Erudite men may retain between ten and twenty *thousand* ancestral names in their memories. Iatmul ancestral names are used strategically in competitive oratory. They can be stolen and shifted around in ways which affect the prowess and power of those who

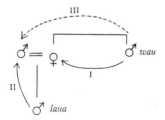

Figure 2.4 The *wau*'s kinship position

71

wield and yield them. Bateson's reference to a 'mass of fraudulent heraldry' (*ibid*, p. 128) reflects a (very English!) ideal of authentic pedigree as inalterable.

Bateson realised as he wrote the Epilogue that the various analytical concepts were not somehow inherent in the data, as Malinowski and Radcliffe-Brown apparently believed. They were simply useful for organising data. Bateson went from New Guinea to the U.S.A., where he remained largely outside the mainstream developments which took place in Great Britain. Although certain ideas, such as schismogenesis (the idea that oppositions are continually and dialectically accentuated once initiated) filtered through into Evans-Pritchard's analysis of Nuer feuding and Gluckman's theory of conflict, it was scarcely in the spirit of Bateson's formulation. The experimental potential of Bateson's work was left unexplored in the 1940s and '50s. British social anthropologists seem to have been more concerned with consolidating and elaborating upon that part of Radcliffe-Brown's legacy which concerned corporate descent groups.

The domestic and the political: Fortes and Evans-Pritchard
Radcliffe-Brown's influence is clear in the 1940s publications of several anthropologists who worked in Africa. Evans-Pritchard's *The Nuer*, and *African Political Systems*, under the joint editorship of Fortes and Evans-Pritchard, both appeared in 1940, setting the course for what was to come (Fortes 1969, p. 72). In addition to the geographical shift of emphasis, the analytical dichotomy between descent status and familial kinship, which had arisen in previous decades, was now combined in a single scheme.

Social structure had become political and juridical in character. Interest now focused on 'the rules and sanctions that lie behind kinship relations and institutions everywhere ... [which] ... cannot be understood without regard to the political and jural constraints that are generated in the extra-familial domain of social structure' (*ibid*, p. 71). Fortes saw this direction in the study of kinship as the 'renewal of a dimension of kinship structure not systematically investigated since Morgan and Maine' (*ibid*, p. 72). He insists that the 'structuralist' approach he adopted in association with Radcliffe-Brown and Evans-Pritchard at Oxford, 'grew directly out of repeated, objectively presented field observations' (Fortes 1978, p. 9). Radcliffe-Brown only later distinguished between the jural dimension of kinship and descent institutions, which were supposedly confined to the lineage, and personal relations of affection, esteem and attachment (Radcliffe-Brown 1950, p. 78).

Fortes considered the analytical separation of two 'domains' – one politico-jural, the other familial – within the total social universe of 'what have been clumsily called kinship-based social systems', as the single major advance since Radcliffe-Brown. Later, Fortes was to declare, 'human social organization everywhere emerges as some kind of balance, stable or not, between the political order – Aristotle's polis – and the familial or domestic order – the oikos – a balance between polity and kinship' (Fortes 1978, p. 14). He held that kinship and polity could be distinguished, analytically and indeed empirically, even when the two orders appeared to be fused together in a single kinship polity, as among the Australian aborigines.

However clumsy the epithet 'kinship-based social systems', it is clear that the contrast to which it refers was unquestioned by a large number of British anthropologists. This contrast, between apparently kin-dominated non-Western and pragmatic Western societies, is one to which Langham draws attention (Langham 1981, p. 1). Yet it is an ambiguous distinction. Some societies appeared to be more kinship-based than others due to their wider unilineal descent groupings, and yet it was assumed that all societies had a kinship system of some kind or another. Bilateral *kinship* seems to be universal, while *descent* seems to be more restricted in its distribution. Barnard and Good, summarising this position, write: 'Kinship – that is, the ego-centred sphere of domestic life and marriage – is here treated as merely the "functional by-product" of the descent system. Affinal links are ego-centric, ephemeral, and therefore structurally unimportant' (Barnard and Good 1984, p. 74). Descent was limited to people who were not very much 'like ourselves': such people were distant either in time (the Romans, the Anglo-Saxons) or in space, as were contemporary primitive societies. Kinship in Western societies therefore existed, but as an internal, non-political phenomenon – a watered-down version of the non-Western world.[3]

Fortes mentions *The Nuer, We, The Tikopia* and *The Web of Kinship*, when distinguishing between the 'internal' and 'external' aspects of structure. Fortes himself distinguished between filiation and descent as domestic and jural concepts respectively. *Filiation* referred to the fact of being the legitimate child of both one's parents, and was thus an aspect of 'kinship' in the restricted sense. Descent, on the other hand, was 'socio-centrically' defined: the connecting link between external, or political and legal aspects of unilineal descent groups, and the internal domestic domain. Descent is transitive, having or containing a direct object, and extends step-by-step through Ego's lineal ancestors to form his *pedigree. Complementary filiation* therefore becomes the relationship an individual has towards the side of the family through which descent is not traced.

Evans-Pritchard presents the corporateness of the Nuer descent group as a function of its external relations with similar units in a lineage system, which was the overarching political armature of the society. The metaphorical use of 'armature' for political structure is a significant addition to the more organic images of the 1920s and '30s – such as Malinowski's 'flesh and blood' and Firth's 'musculature'. The organic and more specifically vegetative imagery did not, however, disappear in the 1940s. The new images translated the idea that there were now two parts, an inside and an outside, to social structure.

Evans-Pritchard begins his chapter on 'The lineage system', with a diagram illustrating the segmentary nature of one of the clans. The hierarchical order 'descends' from the most inclusive level (that of the clan), through maximal, major, minor and minimal segments (1940, p. 193). Next he presents 'three trees of clan descent ... in a form conventional to us, and which would also commend itself to Nuer, who sometimes speak of the lineage as *kar*, a branch, as illustrations of the way in which lineages split up, each being a branch of a larger one' (*ibid*, pp. 196, 197,198). Here the hierarchical order is reversed: the clan level is at the 'base' of the tree, while the minimal lineages are the 'twigs' at the uppermost level. Then there is a diagram illustrating structural distance, as distinct from structural form (presented as trees), between lineages depending on their relative positions in clan structure (*ibid*, p. 201). But most revealing of all is the last illustration in the chapter which shows 'how the Nuer themselves figure a lineage system' (*ibid* p. 202):

When illustrating on the ground a number of related lineages they do not present them in the way we figure them in this chapter as a series of bifurcations of descent, as a tree of descent, or as a series of triangles of ascent, but as a number of lines running at angles from a common point. Thus in Western Nuerland a man illustrated some of the Gaat-gan-Kiir lineages, using the names of their founders, by drawing the figure above on the ground. This representation and Nuer comments on it show several significant facts about the way in which Nuer see the system. They see it primarily as actual relations between groups of kinsmen within local communities rather than as a tree of descent. For the persons after whom the lineages are called do not all proceed from a single individual ... The Nuer outside certain ritual situations, evaluate clans and lineages in terms of their local relations (*ibid,* p. 203).

The anthropologist's representation of lineages for British colleagues (Figure 2.5) was clearly made in an idiom comprehensible to them. The question of whether either representation or idiom would have made sense to Nuer themselves is not the issue here. We may safely assume that it was scarcely an issue for them! It is rather the fate of the various illustrations presented. Although Evans-Pritchard investigates the spatial and temporal coordinates of the Nuer social system, what passes into the literature for broader discussion or comparison are of course *his* theoretical proposals. The Nuer sketch itself is only used to make a point about the importance of locality in social organisation. What, then, of the 'hierarchical order', 'trees of descent' and 'structural distance'? If, as Bateson discovered, they are part of an analytical language, then where can that language be pinned down?

By 1945 Fortes had consolidated a diagrammatic 'paradigm of the lineage system', in *The Dynamics of Clanship* (see Figure 2.6). The diagram looks authoritative in its stark simplicity. How could such an artefact be other than 'correct'? How could it do anything other than support the written account of descent it illustrated? Again, the point here concerns the cumulative effect of the discourse of which this diagram was a part. Old-fashioned genealogical charts with named persons had given way to much more abstract feats of draughtsmanship. This quiet revolution in the genealogies is telling. Indeed, it is a vindication of Rivers's objective of abstraction through the concrete. 'Pedigree' seems to have made way for 'paradigm'.

In 1958, Fortes went on to elaborate on 'internal' and 'external' aspects of lineage and domestic group in his Introduction to a

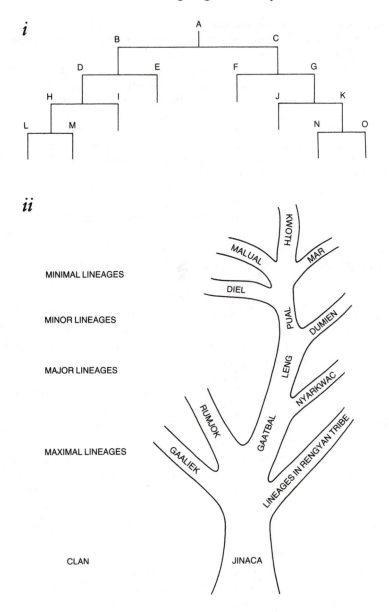

iii

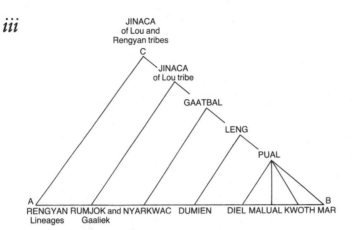

iv

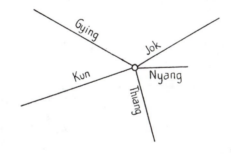

Figure 2.5 Four representations of Nuer social structure:
(i) the genealogical structure of a Nuer clan
(ii) the Jinaca clan tree of descent
(iii) structural distance between lineages of the Jinaca clan
(iv) the Nuer view of their lineage system

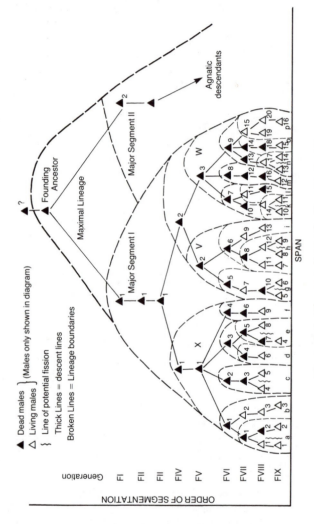

Figure 2.6 The paradigm of a lineage system

volume edited by Jack Goody entitled *The Developmental Cycle in Domestic Groups*. Although designed for analysing non-Western social organisation, the developmental cycle of domestic groups proved inspiring for those who later began to study kinship in Europe (e.g. Laslett and Wall 1972; Netting, Wilk and Arnould (*eds*) 1984; O'Neill 1984).[4] The 'domesticity' of the domestic group was to prove troublesome from the 1970s onwards when feminist scholarship began to elucidate the political nature of much that had previously seemed beyond the purview of such analysis (cf. Barnes 1980, p. 300).[5]

The 'paradigm' was already under attack by the 1950s. *Pul Eliya*, published by Edmund Leach in 1961, is one of the most interesting 'internal' critiques.[6] Leach completely rejected the notion that kinship could be analysed as a thing in itself. He meticulously documents the environmental constraints on social organisation (including kinship) in the Sinhalese village of Pul Eliya. Corporate descent groups simply did not exist in this society, he argued. It was the ideology of lineality, rather than some empirical 'fact', which required explanation. Leach provided plenty of genealogical 'evidence' aimed at convincing sceptics of the sort who had found *Naven* 'thin' on ethnography. Perhaps the genealogies were just *too* detailed (Figure 2.7). Portuguese students were bewildered that this (untranslated) Leach monograph, with its insistence that 'kinship systems have no "reality" at all except in relation to land and property' (Leach 1961, p. 305), could have been written by the same author as (say) 'Magical Hair', which *is* translated (Matta 1983, pp. 139–69). 'Glimpses of the Unmentionable' provides the kind of insight needed to make sense of what they were reading. Significantly enough, Leach himself did not dismiss background, training (his was in engineering), and taste (he preferred Baroque architecture to Romanesque and certainly Gothic), as factors in the kind(s) of anthropology he produced. Yet these are indeed 'glimpses' into a world which British anthropologists assume to be part of the reader's general knowledge.

English middle-class kinship: an analytical cul-de-sac?
There was a certain inevitability to the eventual appearance of English middle-class kinship on the British anthropological research agenda (cf. Barnes 1980, p. 296). The British position, that bilateral kinship was universal, while descent had a more limited

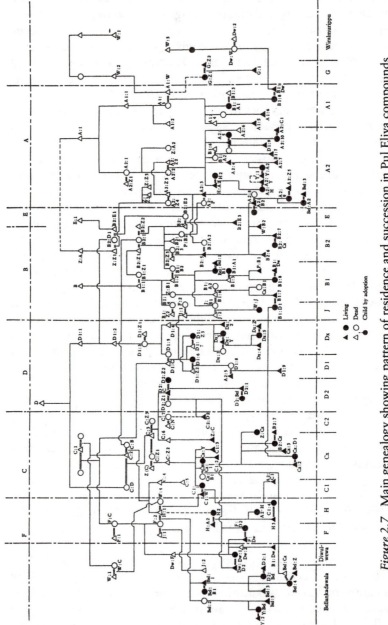

Figure 2.7 Main genealogy showing pattern of residence and succession in Pul Eliya compounds

distribution, meant that English kinship would be identified later rather than sooner as a legitimate problem for empirical investigation. The residual nature of the category 'bilateral' (cf. Lancaster 1961), and the fact that its conceptualisation occurred in tandem with lineal kinship (cf. Strathern 1992a), were two factors in the delay. The appearance of *Families and Their Relatives* is nonetheless a kind of watershed. History seems to have come full circle. The prospect of fieldwork among people from much the same kind of 'literary', 'intellectual' background, speaking English with much the same accent as the anthropologists themselves, has a paradoxical allure. The suggestion that there is something 'new' to be discovered about that which is familiar is eminently intriguing. The paradox is that there is no longer a frontier across which to 'translate', if it is assumed that the readership will also largely share the same background. That is, of course, a big 'if'; yet since the text was indeed written in English, it seems a fair assumption. Despite the transatlantic comparison with Chicago, *Families and Their Relatives* does not set out to explain the English middle classes to American readers.

Almost a decade before, Firth and Schapera had organised a joint conference of the Association of Social Anthropologists and the British Sociological Association, on kinship in Britain. A number of the papers were published in the *British Journal of Sociology* that same year. Firth's Introduction sums up the situation as it was then:

Kinship in Britain, pervasive, intangible, still largely unstudied, with its significance either not appreciated or in danger of being over-estimated – such was the background to this conference. It is only during the last few years that the subject has received systematic attention from social scientists.

As far as I know, though University seminars have been held on this theme, this is the first time that a full-scale discussion has taken place on the materials available and the problems involved. The decision to call the conference on studies of kinship in Britain was taken with the knowledge that such materials are still relatively unsystematic, of uneven quality, and sporadic in their regional distribution (1961, p. 305).

I have argued that British social anthropologists learned to look at kinship in a highly specific manner over the first half of the present century. I have suggested that the British social anthropologist's voice was decidedly middle-class, and that the enormous interest in the kinship of others fits uncomfortably with an image of middle-class 'kinshiplessness', such as that present in Robin Fox's introductory textbook, *Kinship and Marriage*, which also dates from the sixties. Fox writes:

even in our own enlightened and rational society the web of kinship and marriage around our 'great families' – the Cecils, Devonshires, Churchills, etc. – spreads into most corners of political life. In some working-class enclaves, also, kinship seems to be important. *It is in the less conservative and more mobile middle-classes that kinship now seems to be of little relevance beyond the level of parent–child relationships, and even these have a looseness about them which would shock many of our primitive contemporaries.* That old parents should be left by their children to live and eventually die in loneliness – or be put in homes – would seem to many to be the depths of immorality; but our whole system of architecture and social welfare is geared to the elementary family of parents and dependent children. We may be a relatively 'kinshipless' society (although sociologists have probably exaggerated this tendency) but the sentiments of kinship still linger on ... Blood, as the old adage has it, is thicker than water (Fox 1967, pp. 14–15, emphasis added).

If middle-class British social anthropologists were mainly indifferent to their own kinship, why were they so fascinated by that of other people?

The originality of Firth, Hubert and Forge's lengthy text (460 pages) partly consists in posing middle-class kinship as a question rather than a foregone conclusion. But in what sense is this an 'empirical' study? Numerous contrasts are drawn between the north London middle class and the 'classical' field of 'comparative' anthropological studies. The emphasis on the importance of kinship to social organisation, or social structure, was decidedly 'British'. The results of the Chicago end of the Anglo-American collaborative study appeared two years earlier than *Families and Their Relatives*. Schneider's slim 'cultural account' of American kinship deftly evinces how differently American and British anthropologists approached the 'same' topic.

The north London study problematises the comparative claim made for the earlier British studies. In what sense were these studies 'comparative', when such 'comparison' presupposes a contrast rendering certain societies analytically out of bounds? The authors of *Families and their Relatives* were faced with a taxing version of this problem in north London. For if the association between kinship and primitive societies relies on a more or less implicit contrast with 'modern' ones, how can this contrast (and hence the whole approach) be sustained when anthropological comparison is extended to these 'modern' societies?

There are a number of complicated manoeuvres involved. Primitive and civilised societies were formerly opposed to one another using the significance of extra-familial kinship and the elementary family respectively. Yet methodological procedures developed for studies 'elsewhere' were nonetheless deemed applicable 'here'. One of the major hypotheses of the north London study was that families in industrial societies are not in fact isolated from their kin, and that kinship has important positive functions. Extra-familial kinship ties were thought to condition the interplay of intra-familial roles, as well as providing individuals with sources of social support outside the family (Firth *et al.* 1969, p. 29).

Several studies, of working-class kinship (Young and Willmott [1957] 1967), and kinship in rural British communities (Williams 1963; Littlejohn 1963), had already made it clear that the contrast between primitive and civilised was more complicated than originally thought. The north London study went much further in that the anthropologists involved found themselves facing people who were not only like themselves, but occasionally considerably more sophisticated in anthropological and social scientific argument than the interviewers themselves (Firth *et al.* 1969, p. 53). The mini-contrasts between anthropologists and working-class people, or rural populations, were more or less flattened in Highgate and on the Greenbanks estate. The authors drew particular attention to the 'literate, intellectual quality of middle-class culture', and they saw this as influencing patterns of kinship behaviour. Despite considerable variation, 'many had been brought up in an atmosphere of books and general discussion about social issues, and were accustomed to a somewhat self-conscious analytical attitude towards their social relationships with their kin' (*ibid*, p. 460).

This intellectual, reflective attitude to kinship, together with its 'flexibility', 'articulate conceptions of morality', and 'the habit of letter-writing'[7], was tempered by a remarkable lack of interest, however, in systematic documentation of family pedigrees (*ibid*, p. 125). Thus, despite the importance of a literary and intellectual culture, most kinship knowledge was in fact transmitted orally. Indeed, Firth and his colleagues compare this mode of kin knowledge with peasant and other non-literate societies. The similarities in 'background', or intellectual field, between the anthropologists and their informants in this study poses another intriguing problem. If their literary and intellectual leanings did not materialise in lengthy pedigrees and documentation of their own families, why did Firth and his colleagues collect genealogies 'as soon as possible and, if it could be managed, before kin were discussed at all' (*ibid*, p. 33). If it is a puzzle that this artefact should have been considered a suitable means for studying the kinship of others, then it is doubly puzzling that it was deployed in this way in the London study. One possible explanation could be that even if there was no straightforward transference from middle-class background to anthropological methodology, there was nothing to prevent a kind of 'hypergamous' borrowing of a technique vaguely associated with 'great families' who *did* have an interest in recording lines of transmission for property or office.

The curiosity of 'pedigree' translated into the 'scientific' idiom of the genealogical method, in the 'stifling' social atmosphere of early-twentieth-century Cambridge depicted by Leach, has already been mentioned. Rivers's method raised knotty epistemological problems when turned back upon post-1945 English middle-class people. Although participant observation, field-notes, and talking family may have modified perceptions, genealogical connectedness (as might be expected from the previous chapter) still 'set the scene' for middle-class kinship.

Reading between the lines

The focus of British anthropological attention had long been directed primarily to *other* societies. The 'comparative study of human societies' actually refers to what were then called primitive societies, without inverted commas. There are all kinds of synonyms for referring to these objects of study.

Firth *et al.*(1969) contrast English society with 'human societies', 'a great range of societies' (p. 4), 'societies traditionally studied by anthropologists' (p. 11), 'the classical anthropological field', 'a kin-oriented society' (p. 35), 'primitive fieldwork', 'a completely strange society' (pp. 56–7), 'societies of a pre-industrial kind', and so on. Synonymous with (modern) 'English society', on the other hand, are 'modern British society' (p. 3), 'modern, western, industrial society' (in its 'great complexity', p. 153), 'any modern, western society' and, somewhat confusingly, 'indeed any society at all' (p. 7); 'metropolitan environment' (p. 11), 'a country of complex, industrial development such as Britain' (p. 18), a 'modern urban community', 'own culture' (pp. 56–7), 'north London middle-class people' (p. 87), and a 'modern, highly differentiated type of society' (p. 231).

There can be little doubt about the general focus of 'comparative' studies in the classical era of anthropological fieldwork: 'completely strange', 'primitive', 'kin-oriented', 'pre-industrial' societies dominated the ethnographies. They illustrated a range of organisational possibilities, conceived in many instances as being under duress from modern civilisation. The ethnographer's duty was to document these endangered species, paradoxically viable-as-revealed-by-the-ethnographer.

Versailles and house names

Translation requires bringing the unfamiliar into some kind of relation with the familiar. There are some illuminating examples of references to 'own' society in the early ethnographies of Malinowski and Firth. Malinowski, for instance, contrasts the benighted 'authority' on natives who remarked, 'Customs none, manners beastly', with the 'modern Ethnographer', whose picture of the native code of behaviour and good manners make life at the court of Versailles or Escurial seem free and easy (Malinowski [1922] 1983, p. 10). Firth, describing house-names in Tikopia, declares 'these are not mere casual appellations given for show, according to a rather stupid European habit, but are intimately related to the native social organization'. In a footnote to this remark he concedes, 'The Scottish custom of calling a landholder by the name of his holding has much in common with the Tikopia usage, see for example, 'Grippy', 'Plealands' etc. in John Galt's *Entail*' (Firth [1936] 1983, p. 83).

In Malinowski's example, the image selected is historical, and Continental: the ultimate in extravagant foppery – for a British readership. The wisdom of the modern Ethnographer not only revealed the complexity and propriety of savage life, but even made Versailles pale in significance! It was, perhaps, a double coup for a Polish anthropologist to be writing (savage) and rewriting (European) histories in English – the language of wartime victory.

Firth's example concerns the more mundane middle-class practice of house-naming. European house-naming was dismissed as 'rather stupid', while on Tikopia it was 'intimately related to native social organisation', and therefore worthy of ethnographic attention. Although he concedes the comparative interest of a Scottish custom, 'European' habits of house-naming were not generally seen as serious ethnographic material for British trained anthropologists in the 1930s. This attitude persisted, oddly enough, in the 1969 study where, although fieldwork was mainly carried out inside houses. (Firth *et al*, p. 47), the significance of the house for extra-familial kinship, as conceivably expressed in the name, is not considered.[8] The idea that there might be more to house-owning than the accommodation of relatives if the need arose was simply not on the north London research agenda. Empirical studies of kinship and social organisation were remarkably thin on material culture and its interpretation.

London and Chicago

Something clearly changed between the British ethnographies of the early-to-mid twentieth century and those which began to appear in the sixties and seventies. However, although a few anthropologists began to turn their attention to matters closer to home, this change should not be exaggerated. The question, 'What is now the position in modern English society?' is significant as much for the empiricist thread of continuity with the earlier studies as for the relative tardiness with which it was posed. Firth had become interested in studying bilateral, cognatic kinship systems under urban conditions as early as 1947. His Tikopian work had surely made him curious about it. Twelve years later, in 1959, he discussed the possibility of a comparative project on the structure and meaning of kinship in modern, Western society, with David Schneider. Since most British studies had been carried out, as already mentioned, among rural or working-class populations, the aim was to look at extra-familial kin ties in middle-class sectors of London and Chicago.

Differences of approach are clear from the opening sentences of each of the studies, *Families and Their Relatives* begins with the question 'How important is kinship in modern Britain?' *American*

Kinship, A Cultural Account begins with the declaration 'This book is concerned with American kinship as a cultural system; that is, as a system of symbols'. For Firth and his colleagues, 'Kinship is a set of ties socially recognized to exist between persons because of their genealogical connection, that is, in terms of relationships thought to be created between them by marriage and/or the procreation of children' (Firth *et al.* 1969, p. 3).

This contrast reinforces the point already made about the focus of British social anthropological interest. Firth and his colleagues' approach rides atop a historically crafted field of empirical studies. There are several references to Firth's work on Tikopia, to Malinowski, and other work from the classical era of anthropological field studies, in *Families and Their Relatives*. In an early chapter on 'Kinship ideology', for instance, the authors ask whether English middle-class ideas about kinship are 'expressed in speech and action as a coherent whole, and are so interrelated that one kind of idea depends in some logical way upon the others'. The question is immediately followed by the observation, 'This is so in most societies of a pre-industrial kind, where kinship is commonly one of the major organising principles of the social order'. Trobriand material is brought to bear in a footnote:

In a society such as the Trobriands, for instance, a classic matrilineal form, the ideas of descent in the female line, responsibility for economic support of a married woman and her children by her brothers, authority of the woman's brother over her children, and even denial of physiological paternity in favour of a theory of impregnation by matrilineal spirits, are all linked together in a series of principles which are treated as interrelated and as empirically demonstrable as such, by the people (*ibid*, p. 87, n. 1).

The reference to Malinowski's work on Trobriand kinship reiterates the book's methodological prediction: 'The ideas of north London middle-class people about their kin, we can predict, will be found almost certainly not to be of such a clear-cut, systematic kind'. But even so, the empirical justification for pursuing the matter is unquestioned: of course we ought to know *more* about it. Although kinship and primitive society were seen as practically indissociable, clearly nobody was trying to argue that north London had suddenly become savage. The point is 'merely' an empirical one:'granted this, what *are* the ideas which people do have about kinship, the pattern of behaviour characterizing it, and the responsibilities attaching to it?' (*ibid,p. 87*).

Although Tikopia is not discussed in the main body of the text, there are several references to it scattered throughout *Families and Their Relatives*. One such reference is to the essay, 'Bond-friendship in Tikopia', which appears in the discussion of 'kin and friends':

This aspect of the social role of friend invites comparison with conditions in societies where friendship is institutionalized, and has as one function the provision of an alternative mode of social relationship and support to that provided by kin ties. In such societies, bonds and obligations of kinship and descent are often highly formalized. What ties of bond-friendship do is to help to give an individual some wider field of choice, some greater flexibility in social arrangements, and even at times some avenue of escape from the demands of kin [ref. to the Tikopian article]. The kinship and friendship system of London middle-class people is not of this formalized character. But it is interesting to note that even here relations with friends do to some extent fill a similar antithetical and complementary role to those of kin (*ibid*, p. 117).

The lack of formal arrangements in English middle-class kinship is stressed throughout the book by means of such contrasts. They re-emerge in the discussion of affinal relations, and the thorny question of mothers-in-law: 'A man in our society has only one mother-in-law – he would look with horror at, say, the Tikopia custom of having a whole group of them' (*ibid*, p. 412). Apart from the constraints on behaviour, there is the difficulty of what to call in-laws: 'The so-called primitive societies manage things much better; as anthropologists know, most of them lay down quite definite ways of addressing mothers-in-law and fathers-in-law' (*ibid*, p. 418). In the north London context, however, 'people got up to some odd dodges in this naming of in-laws', including using no term of address at all, or (with the arrival of children) using the grandparental terms (*ibid*, p. 423). As an aside to the main discussion, the possibility of 'generation differences' is raised: 'There was probably more formality in the mother-in-law-son-or daughter-in-law relation in Victorian times in England than today, and the problem of what to call mother-in-law would then have been less acute – the Mr and Mrs terms would probably be the common solution' (*ibid*, p. 424).

1960s informality

Several examples of this kind have an ambivalent effect on the reader. On the one side they dilute any suggestion that English middle-class kinship might be directly comparable with the formal 'systems' encountered in other societies. Yet the suggestion that the sixties 'revolution' was removing formality implies that there had been greater formality in the past (cf. Radcliffe-Brown 1950). Formal displays of wedding presents at marriage receptions had, for example, disappeared:

Former standard middle-class custom was for the present to be sent before the wedding, and to be displayed ceremonially. Modern custom seems to dispense with formal display. It still seems customary to send the present in advance, though in line with *the general trend to greater informality in social matters* the present is sometimes given to the married pair at the wedding reception, as would appear to be an American custom (Firth *et al.* 1969 p. 240 n. 10, emphasis added).

The demise of formality seems to have brought a measure of uncertainty to interpersonal relations in the 1960s. The publication of an analysis of middle-class kinship at such a moment almost certainly reflects worries about what was to be done now that 'doing the done thing' was no longer 'in'.

Another preoccupation, touched upon earlier in the quotation from Fox, was the substitution of State care for the elderly and sick – services formerly performed by kin. Fears about the quality of interpersonal relations at a time when the Welfare State was relatively strong were perhaps understandable. Such consternation was, nonetheless, qualified by the observation that kin services during women's confinement probably saved the 'national accounting system' considerable expenditure (*ibid*, p. 383).

It was a problem to connect two major social issues of the day, sixties 'permissiveness' and the provision of State welfare, with an anthropological approach emphasising continuity rather than rupture. However thorough Firth and his colleagues undoubtedly were in assembling and organising their considerable materials, they interpreted them within the parameters of earlier British work on descent and kinship as the basis of social organisation. Metropolitan middle-class kinship, in these terms, boils down to specific interpersonal relations. It then becomes difficult to do much more than present exemplificatory, variable cases. These fall into a theoretical vacuum because 'comparison' was, by definition, impossible. The book flounders. Fox suggests that the materials were difficult to handle with descent theory or even its residue, and suggested experimenting with alliance theory. But this does not seem to have happened.

Kuper has observed that the history of anthropology was neglected in Britain during what he calls the 'lean years' (1972–82), in contrast to both France and the U.S.A. (Kuper 1983, p. 189). The very notion of taking stock of claims to knowledge about kinship in other societies does not seem to have figured on the agenda at that time. This produced a hiatus between the world of primitive kinship and kinship in the modern world which could not be bridged by 'more of the same'.

Interest in surrogate motherhood, incest, and child abuse have made the headlines in Britain since about 1983. What anthropologists call 'kinship relations' have become matters of public debate, via the mass media, as well as academic debate (e.g. Wolfram 1987; La Fontaine 1990). It is a sign of the times that the Royal Anthropological Institute of Great Britain publishes *Anthropology Today* alongside *Man*, in an attempt to provide anthropologists with a platform to reflect on current issues in accessible language. Interest in post-modernist debates filtered through into British anthropology during the 1980s (cf. Strathern 1987, 1988; Caplan 1988). 'Personal' issues are finally surfacing, at least in certain areas. It was acknowledged at the 1989 A.S.A. conference on anthropology and autobiography that 'the personal is also theoretical and should not be relegated to the "merely" anecdotal on the peripheries of a positivistic social science (Judith Okely)' (Rapport 1989, p. 25). Some, including Kuper, were 'less consensual': it was not possible, he thought, to be reflexive in a social structural mode. Rephrasing the statement as a question, how is it possible to be reflexive about a social structural mode?

If the Dogon ...

Kaberry's pit of analysis is not, in fact, a bottomless one. Almost thirty years after Kaberry's monograph, Mary Douglas published a thought-provoking exercise in imaginative anthropology. What would our image of the Dogon be if they had been studied by Evans-Pritchard, instead of the French Missions Griaule? Had the Nuer lived in French Sudan, and the Dogon on the banks of the

White Nile, what would we now know of them? She remarks on how 'unmistakably French the Dogon seem: they are so urbane, articulate, and with such philosophical insight. Nuer myths, by contrast, are as crude as their way of life. They are rude, and their cosmological ideas are confused' (1967, p. 659). Douglas seeks to demonstrate that British and French anthropologists are following different trails, and using different techniques to pursue different kinds of quarry (*ibid*, p. 670). Among the British techniques are genealogies.

Douglas writes that the British reduce the universe to 'small-scale, abstract models, such as genealogies and tables of village composition. These do not serve a love of genealogical lore for its own sake' (*ibid*. p. 669). 'Thus while the Dogon seem pre-eminently susceptible to the literary and aesthetic investigation at which the French excel, the Nuer seem only apt for the discoveries in primitive politics and kinship which interest the British' (*ibid*, 660). British anthropologists are nonetheless 'passionately interested in getting behind the screen of appearance', and in this they have an affinity with the truth of the Pale Fox of the Dogon (*ibid*, p. 665). 'All our professed interest in kinship and politics is an interest in the machinery that casts the shadows on the wall', which might also be called pre-cosmology.

The stylistic differences between British and French approaches serve to highlight what has been referred to variously as 'background', 'implicit theory' and 'hidden ethnography' in this chapter. Malinowski played down the importance of the genealogical method. In refurbishing Rivers's concept of descent with corporateness, Radcliffe-Brown effectively reinstated the stock-in-trade status of the genealogy. While it is indisputably one among many techniques, it nonetheless retains the curious allure of concreteness – whether as a means of collecting the kinship system data, or as a way of presenting and explaining arguments in the text. The passage from pedigrees, such as those presented by Codrington and Rivers, to Fortes' paradigm of a lineage system makes this point. Genealogical diagrams look concrete and straightforward enough. They are in fact, as Douglas put it, 'small-scale abstract models'.

The problem is, to what 'concrete' reality might they refer? The standard answer has mostly been an 'external' one. Fortes, for instance, insists that the 'structuralist' approach he was to adopt in association with Radcliffe-Brown and Evans-Pritchard at Oxford 'grew directly out of repeated, objectively presented field observations' (Fortes 1978, p. 9). Does the rubric of 'descent', under which '[l]ineage theory, or rather the theoretical and empirical evaluation of the nature and function of the rules, ideologies and social arrangements were etically grouped' (*ibid*, p. 12) only refer in a one-way direction to empirical reality? Firth maintained that there was a need 'to devise systematic methods for differentiating perceptions and for controlling if not reducing the subjective component in observation and interpretation' (Firth 1975, p. 12). The problem is that the rubric of descent, for example, is not simply a 'subjective' meaning. It does refer to something quite specific within the English language. The persistent sense of a hidden ethnography which besets the contemporary reader trying to understand what these texts convey, concerns precisely these English notions.

Firth *et al*'s north London study, provide certain clues about that occulted ethnography. The following chapters explore the notion further by means of the 'case study', to which reference has already been made. The attempt to use British kinship theory texts, from Rivers to Leach, as teaching materials for second-year Portuguese anthropology students brought difficulties, such as those discussed theoretically in the present chapter, into the practical foreground.

Notes

1 Leach describes him as a 'permanent Central European ... [who] ... liked to claim that he was a Polish aristocrat' (Leach 1984, p. 16). Malinowski was born in Cracow in 1884, the son of a professor of Slavic philology. He began by studying physics and mathematics at the Jagellonian university, before gradually switching to philosophy. At some time during his studies in Cracow (1902–08) he read, and was much impressed by *The Golden Bough*. He studied cultural psychology at Leipzig, and was influenced by Wundt. In 1910 he moved to the London School of Economics where he worked with Westermarck. He published *The Family among the Australian Aboriginals* in 1913; this study reflects both the evolutionary primacy attached to the monogamous family, and the interest for the Australian material in the intellectual circles in which Malinowski was then moving.

2 Kuper reports that his father died when Brown was still very young, leaving his mother destitute. The children were brought up by their maternal grandmother, while their mother worked as a 'companion' (Kuper 1977, p. 52). In Kuper's account, Brown was educated at King Edward's School in Birmingham. His later studies were funded by an elder brother before winning an Exhibition (a kind of scholarship) to Trinity College, Cambridge.

3 Firth, for example, writing of the conversion of bilateralism to multilineality, concedes: 'What is difficult, however, is to ascribe the term descent to this process ... By descent is implied the limitation and recognition of the continuity of kinship ties for certain social purposes (in particular, membership of continuing named groups) and the accent is on the notion of continuity. In many of the societies studied by anthropologists, these continuing groups are unilineal in descent principle. Membership must then be traced genealogically, but the genealogical tie may be through either mother or father, or indeed in some cases through either a male or a female more remote ancestor. Such is the type of descent group, corporate in its activities, which has been described as bilateral' (Firth [1956] 1971, p. 386).

4 The 57 diagrams of *casa* structure in O'Neill (1984, pp. 420–6) are a case in point. Segalen has more recently sounded a cautionary note (Segalen 1991; see, also, Pina-Cabral 1990.

5 It is impossible to do more than mention the existence of this literature. Its significance in providing new positions or vantage points from which to survey the ethnographic literature, as well as the inherent limitations have been considered in depth by M. Strathern (1988), see especially Chapter 4; and La Fontaine 1990. For a particularly fascinating analysis of 'farm families' from a feminist perspective, see Whatmore 1991.

6 Barnes's 1962 article on the applicability of African descent models in the recently discovered New Guinea Highlands populations was, arguably, more influential in undermining that view of kinship and descent which had held sway for several decades. Network theory, which Barnes also helped to pioneer, provided another influential source of critique for descent theory (cf. Barnes 1954, 1968).

7 Compare with Firth's remarks on his first bout of fieldwork:'on Tikopia, from July 1928 to July 1929 ... my chief desire was for the letters of friends rather than for the company of Europeans as such' (Firth [1936] 1983, p. 5).

8 One of the many contrasts with the way ethnologists of France went about their studies: naming, including house-naming, is considered by Bromberger (1982) and Zonabend (1980), amongst others.

CHAPTER THREE

TRANSPOSING BRITISH KINSHIP THEORY TO 1980s PORTUGAL

I. Reading lists and teaching programmes

The purpose of history may then be to make the practitioner conscious of these constraints, of the forces which shape practice ... I see the history of anthropology as offering the possibility of a really challenging reflexivity (Kuper 1991, pp. 138–9).

Traditions of anthropological thought and their perpetuation
The history of the anthropological approach discussed in the foregoing chapters is not, of course, a thing of the past. Some of the studies considered have become 'classics', occupying venerable positions on contemporary bookshelves.[1] These classic works form the pedagogical bedrock of the academic discipline, often in the synthesised form of introductory texts. 'Reading' anthropology (like any other academic discipline) involves a lengthy process of assimilating what has already been written: effectively, the history of the discipline. The problem is that many of the setbooks emphasise fieldwork as the centre-piece of anthropology – either directly (monographs) or indirectly (various kinds of anthologies and introductions). This impression is often fuelled, however inadvertently, by those responsible for teaching when they try to define what is distinctive about an anthropological perspective, and when they discuss their own research.

A current, small-scale debate on the place of fieldwork in undergraduate anthropology in Britain underlines how reading anthropology and conducting anthropological research can appear to be at odds with one another to students. Reading seems to make them impatient for what they see as the 'real thing'. This is the would-be anthropologist's view on conciliating the weight of a tradition with the practice of ethnographic research. The discussion of Firth and his colleagues' north London study, in the previous chapter, considered the problem from the practitioner's point of view.

Fieldwork seems to hold out the promise of immediacy, a direct route into understanding through contact with the 'real world', for many students (cf. Lie 1990, p. 22 Shore 1990, p. 22;). Reading theoretical and ethnographic texts can appear to represent only delay, however persuasive arguments to the contrary by established academics (cf. Ingold 1989, 1991). The very term 'fieldwork' suggests physical labour 'outside' the academy: 'in the field' means 'elsewhere', doing the 'work' of participating and observing. This opposition has been structured by the deferral of field experience until after reaching a desired level of theoretical competence – usually marked by completion of the undergraduate degree. This orchestration faithfully reflects the way that anthropology has been institutionalised as an academic discipline in Great Britain, creating expectations not necessarily shared by those responsible for designing and teaching courses.

Sharma contests as 'spurious' Ingold's opposition between 'books' and 'projects' (Sharma 1989, p. 3), emphasising the way in which such work can improve appreciation and understanding of the way in which social scientific knowledge is constructed (*ibid*, p. 4). Yet since an opposition between reading and fieldwork is embedded in the very texts which are studied, it is not difficult to see how this has been translated into that of 'books'/'projects' at the level of undergraduate study – whatever one may think of that.

The lack of consensus about how anthropological knowledge is best imparted in British universities gives pause for thought about the use of the anthropological classics as pedagogical material outside their native context. The narrative shifts now from considering the kinship classics in and of themselves, to considering their place in the reading lists and teaching programmes that reproduce, propagate and transform anthropology as an international academic discipline. The discussion will consider some effects of transposing such works from their British setting to mid-1980s Portugal. Kuper's remarks about the reflexive possibilities of history (*op. cit.*) assumed a very concrete sense when I found myself caught up in the 'export trade'.

The carrot and the stick: studying anthropology at
undergraduate level in Britain

A recent flurry of exchanges among British anthropologists on the place of fieldwork in undergraduate studies bridges the gap between the first and subsequent parts of the book. Earlier chapters have shown that while Radcliffe-Brown galvanised the theoretical development of kinship studies until mid-century, the radical empiricism of Malinowski continued to influence the exercise and style of ethnographic fieldwork. These two dispositions are both perhaps intrinsic to the genealogical method, providing a thread of continuity between the historical texts – as we have seen. This thread of continuity may also be transcribed through these texts into the way anthropology is taught and understood.

The hypothesis that kinship was significant in spite of the (Welfare) State and the de-formalisation synonymous with which the 1960s, is closely tied up with the empirical premise that it should be investigated anyway (cf. Firth, Hubert and Forge 1969). The rather anticlimactic resulting ethnography fuelled the notion that kinship was somehow 'less significant' among ourselves than among (especially 'primitive') others. The underlying presuppositions of kinship theory have subsequently faded from polemical foreground into routine background: although the primary focus for relatively few, an adequate description of the kinship system remains a *sine qua non* for any British anthropologist returning home from the field (Barnard and Good 1984, p. 1). This requirement assumes that 'Kinship' will be a compulsory part of the teaching that precedes empirical study. Competent descriptions of kinship systems require more than technical instructions about how to collect and present data (cf. Ingold 1991). Students will need to have internalised much of the orientation which connects them to a quite specific tradition.

The debate which has been taking place in the *B.A.S.A.P.P. Newsletter* (Summer 1989) and, subsequently, *Anthropology Today*, reflects the quandary of teaching anthropology in a tradition which has placed so much emphasis on 'fieldwork'. The polarisation referred to above is immediately visible in the original problem discussed at the A.S.A./G.A.P.P./S.A.S.C.W. conference in 1989: how to highlight the practical relevance of anthropology for students in the teaching of the mainstream concepts and concerns of the discipline. This 'practical relevance' is portrayed as being somehow beyond or in excess of the business of teaching, and therefore learning. Tim Ingold vigorously challenged this assumption, evoking both practical and more 'principled' dissuading factors (Ingold 1989, p. 2). Time was one limitation: both staff and students (in three-year undergraduate courses) have limited time available and competing claims on it. This means there is not enough time for adequate supervision, for carrying out research, or for analysing the field material. Learning the extent of the gap between raw field material and ethnography as presented in books was, he found, an essentially negative one. More fundamentally, 'doing anthropology is not, as many students seem to imagine, the same as doing fieldwork ... Students learn from lectures and tutorials, but above all from reading books' (*ibid*).

Ursula Sharma took a different perspective, emphasising how projects can help students develop a practical understanding of social science methodology: not just through the collection of data, but by learning how to pose relevant and soluble problems, evaluating data and reasoning from it (Sharma 1989, p. 3). Whereas Ingold refers to 'participant understanding in a cultural milieu that is not one's own' (1989, p. 2) Sharma mentions that Keele students are encouraged to choose a milieu with which they are already familiar. Ingold appears to assume that such project work would be done individually, whereas Sharma describes projects jointly undertaken as a way of maximising the use of time and different abilities. Sharma lists the advantages of experience gained in formulating sensible sociological or anthropological questions and attempting to answer them; experience in observation, reasoning, generalising, recording and presenting data are all positive – even if not entirely successful. Difficulties may, indeed, prove stimulating.

First-hand field experience must be deferred, according to Ingold, partly because of the time it takes to set it within the proper perspective. That perspective is achieved primarily by reading books, and by lectures and tutorials. Accompanying student projects can be very time-consuming. Indeed, as Hanley points out, one of the advantages of studying in Scotland is the four-year Honours degree which allows for immersion in 'practical' situations where students are 'socially slightly out of depth' (Hanley 1989, p. 4). Strict deadlines are nonetheless imposed on the Edinburgh students of whom Hanley writes: 'removing the dissertation from students to prevent them endlessly twiddling with it, to the detriment of their other work' (*ibid*). Like Sharma's, Hanley's assessment of the value is positive, however costly: '[h]aving tried it themselves they are in a better position to judge how others have done it' (*ibid*).

This is an important point. Undergraduate projects are clearly distinguished from fieldwork proper; their purpose is to promote an understanding of fieldwork as presented in texts. The various positions on reading anthropology as a necessary preliminary to undertaking fieldwork, expose the problem of empirical research literally (and pedagogically) constructed as a 'lure'. Transposing these teaching materials outside the British context, even within western Europe, raises important issues. These include the meaning of empirical understanding for theoretical knowledge; personal power and compassion as against an impersonal 'system' in the pedagogical context; and consequently differing notions of time and space in study.

Understanding British kinship theory circles around the genealogical method, for reasons that have been discussed at length in Chapter 2. This presentiment was almost certainly expressed in the decision to introduce a second-year anthropology course (based on that material), in Portugal, by asking students to collect a genealogy. The Portuguese context will be deliberately minimised, for the moment, in order to focus upon the process of transferral.

Out of the British context: studying anthropology in Portugal after 1974

The Revolution of 1974 meant, *inter alia*, a period of expansion and popularity for the social sciences in general, just as they were falling from grace elsewhere in western Europe, notably Britain. Boaventura de Sousa Santos describes the fifteen years between 1975 and 1990 as one of vigorous individual and collective affirmation for the social sciences in Portugal (de Sousa Santos 1990, p. 10). Many Portuguese intellectuals had lived in exile during the Salazar regime. When they returned home after 25 April 1974, they brought with them the experience of studying and working in various European and other countries. The dramatic ruptures brought about by the April Revolution, no less than certain continuities with the former regime, transformed Portugal, for a while, into an intriguing laboratory of social action and innovation. The situation was difficult to understand, according to de Sousa Santos, in terms of sociological theories developed in other times and places. Yet these were the theories, 'foreign' and out of focus, with which social scientists were equipped, either through clandestine autodidactic study, or in exile (*ibid*, p. 9). How was this general situation translated into the field of anthropology?

Portuguese students wishing to read social anthropology at university level can choose between three different departments established in Lisbon between 1974 and 1983, another in Coimbra, and several other anthropology courses in different departments (sociology, psychology, economics, fine arts, biology, dance, theology etc.) at other universities[2] (Fernandes-Dias 1991, p. 12). Fernandes-Dias considers the most significant innovation (since 1974) to have been the appearance of social and socio-cultural anthropology, brought in from Belgian, French and British national traditions. Vale de Almeida even refers to Britain and France as 'central factories' in which most Portuguese anthropologists were raised (Vale de Almeida 1991a, pp. 19–20).

The composition of the teaching staff at the Instituto Superior de Ciências do Trabalho e da Empresa (I.S.C.T.E.) in Lisbon in 1983[3] reflected this mixture of intellectual backgrounds. The lecturers and assistants in social anthropology included persons with, or working for, higher degrees from universities in Belgium, France and Britain; and with field experience in Africa, India and Portugal itself. A number of these anthropologists took initiatives, in the early 1980s, to begin a degree course in social anthropology at this Institute, where until then anthropology had been an ancillary course within the sociology degree curriculum. Those involved were then mostly under 40 years of age, and were dissenters (cf. Fernandes-Dias *op. cit.*) – personal, political or intellectual – from the existing Anthropology departments of I.C.S.P.U. and the Universidade Nova (New University), where many had either studied or taught. Some held research positions in institutions such as the Gulbenkian Institute of Science or the Museu de Etnologia.

The initiative, taken by relatively junior anthropologists, of establishing a separate course in social anthropology at I.S.C.T.E. deserves comment on several scores. Firstly, the desire to professionalise anthropology and to mark it off from sociology is especially remarkable given the fact that many Portuguese sociologists carry out ethnographic-style fieldwork in their empirical research[4].

The popularity of ethnographic fieldwork within the Portuguese context is closely associated with the general expansion of the social sciences in the post-1974 period, and the wish to conduct empirical research on multiple aspects of Portuguese life. Secondly, the return of many young intellectuals made expansion outside the established institutional framework a necessity. There was no room for them, literally and intellectually, within existing institutions. Fernandes-Dias suggests that there were in fact two successive waves of 'dissenters': those who left I.S.C.P.U. for the Universidade Nova; and then those who left the Nova for I.S.C.T.E.. Thirdly, the I.S.C.T.E. group of anthropologists decided, after lengthy discussion, that fieldwork should be reserved for the post-graduate phase. Undergraduate projects, such as those carried out in the final year at the Universidade Nova, would be discouraged although it was also decided that some smaller, empirically based *trabalhos* (i.e. pieces of written work) would be allowed as part of specific *cadeiras* (courses). One of the reasons for allowing some form of empirical work at undergraduate level in I.S.C.T.E., was pressure from students, many of whom had been inspired to read anthropology as an effect of the post-Revolutionary enthusiasm for studying different aspects of Portuguese society. It was difficult to rationalise the fact that sociology students were allowed to undertake empirical projects with an 'ethnographic' component, while they were not. The (sometimes) conflicting staff and student definitions of what reading anthropology in post-1974 Portugal was about, deserve brief contrast with the situation in a British university at about the same time.

Anthropology not at home in Cambridge in the 1970s

Mainstream interests, certainly in Cambridge towards the end of the 1970s and early 1980s, did not really include 'Anthropology at Home', and certainly not as the first piece of research[5]. Although a number of us were working in Britain, the tenor of departmental Friday seminars was still strongly 'overseas'. It was less a question of whether this was south-east Asia or north-west Italy, except in financial terms (and these certainly became important in narrowing the scope of fieldwork possibilities); the distinctive criterion was still 'foreignness'. While much lip-service was paid to the importance of doing research in Britain, the impression given off was of rhetoric inspired by hard times rather than

101

intellectual conviction. All in all, anthropology at home was not, then, an inspiring option.

English, or British, material was, of course, sometimes discussed with enthusiasm; but this was mostly confined to historical (e.g. Macfarlane 1970), or 'minority' (Okely 1983) or other non-English groups. Only later, when anthropologists who already had field experience overseas brought fresh insight to bear on the familiar (Richards 1981), was anthropology at home really launched.

It seemed extraordinarily difficult to say anything that was not trivial, let alone original, about English farmers to an audience for whom these were basically 'familiar' people. As Segalen found in Brittany, it is all too tempting for various reasons to take up the historian's problem of change through time (Segalen 1985). Not only can people in the field become impatient with questions concerning routines which ought to have been obvious and banal (cf. Bankes 1991); similar problems can arise when trying to present the material to fellow anthropologists. How can one tell 'tales of the field' to those for whom this is also a field of background reference?

Nothing could have been further from the attitudes of young Portuguese anthropologists towards studying aspects of Portuguese society in the early 1980s.

Post-1974 anthropological diversity in Portugal

Portugal has become a holiday destination for many northern Europeans, and a fieldwork location for increasing numbers of northern European and American anthropologists. The kinds of stereotypes which frame tourist perceptions range from the positive attractions of climate and Portuguese politeness towards foreigners, to the 'shocking' spectacle of human poverty and refuse on the streets of the capital (cf. Silva Dias 1989, pp. 12–13). Destitution and disease openly displayed for alms on the streets of Lisbon *are* profoundly disturbing: this is Europe, but not our Europe. The theme of Portuguese peripherality to Europe goes back hundreds of years. Portuguese have been called the 'Indians of Europe', and Byron referred to them as 'slaves' (*ibid*).

Consciousness of foreigners' views about them conditions both Portuguese attitudes towards that which is external (*o estrangeiro*) and themselves. The importation of various foreign versions of social anthropology after the 1974 Revolution might even be interpreted as a case in point. Fernandes Dias describes the dominant pre-1974 paradigm, centring around Jorge Dias and a small group of collaborators, as 'a rather personal and eclectic view, articulating a German-biased cultural and geographical–historical anthropology (diffusionist) with the central notion of the old American Culture-Personality school' (*op. cit*). They were left somewhat isolated as new clusters formed around those who returned or arrived from France, Belgium and Britain. Teaching of (and perhaps 'in') the 'British tradition' must be understood against this background of post-1974 Portuguese diversity.

The enthusiasm of those involved in anthropological research or teaching in the early 1980s was striking, despite a dearth of basic resources (such as books) certainly at the outset, which would probably have meant no course at all in a northern European context. Formidable obstacles, such as the lack of course books, were routinely overcome by massive annual photocopying operations, carried out by the Students' Association using texts provided by teaching staff.

Fieldwork as a genre

This chapter and the next are based on four years' teaching social anthropology to Portuguese students. As I have already stressed, it was not a premeditated experiment. I did not set out to do 'fieldwork' on the hidden content of classical British social anthropology texts concerned with kinship. It is of course possible to write it up as if it were a piece of fieldwork. This genre is difficult to avoid and I do, indeed, often revert to it. Some clarification of the substantial differences from fieldwork as traditionally conceived is, for this very reason, in order.

Anthropologists do not, or should not, go into the field with the object of 'teaching' their 'informants' (cf. Pulman 1989–90, p. 73). The posture they adopt is, on the contrary, that of a humble 'student of the culture', requiring elementary instruction. That they later become 'expert' on this 'society' in the context of their own has, in recent years, become the catalyst for debates ranging from the problem of time or coevalness (Fabian 1983) to the nature of ethnographic authority (Clifford 1988). Teaching early-twentieth-century British social anthropology involved the assumption that this material ought to form part of Portuguese undergraduates' training in the discipline. This is the first fundamental difference from orthodox fieldwork.

Another important contrast is that anthropologists mostly go to 'the field' as well prepared linguistically, bibliographically and otherwise, as possible. This groundwork may scarcely equip them for the experience they undergo, but is at least an institutionalised form of preparation. It also 'saves time', as Fabian has pointed out (1983, p. 107). Having forgone these ritual preliminaries 'at home', the first nine months living in Portugal were spent acquiring the rudiments of the language. Apart from living and teaching English in the suburban village of Parede, west of the city of Lisbon along the Tejo estuary, I spent a total of about three months in a peasant village in the central northern province of Beira Alta (Bouquet 1984). The conventional divisions between pre-fieldwork training, 'being there', and writing-up, are therefore much less clear-cut in this trajectory.

Finally, labour-market considerations should not be underestimated. There was shortage of qualified staff at I.S.C.T.E., in the early 1980s, for teaching certain courses of the *licenciatura* (undergraduate degree) in Social Anthropology. (For an outline of the degree course as it had evolved by the early 1990s, see Appendix.) This was the case, for example, with a second-year course (Social Anthropology I), which was principally though not exclusively based on British approaches to kinship, marriage and the family during the first half of the twentieth century. It was a positive asset to be English, with degrees in social anthropology from a British university, and to have carried out research on family farmers in England, in this particular Portuguese setting.

Teaching Social Anthropology I

Among those responsible for the initial impetus and organisation of the I.S.C.T.E. degree course in social anthropology, was João de Pina-Cabral[6]. I worked as his assistant in teaching (and to some extent planning) the second year course, Antropologia Social I (Social Anthropology I, hereafter ASI), during the initial year of 1983–84. The 'Britishness' of our respective anthropological backgrounds, although certainly not identical, was to affect the early shape of the course and the way it evolved. Some of the differences can be deduced by juxtaposing my own biographical notes included in Chapter 1, with the following excerpt from the Preface to Pina-Cabral's *Sons of Adam, Daughters of Eve. The Peasant Worldview of the Alto-Minho*:

even though I am by birth and by education Portuguese, I grew up in Africa as an Anglican. In the summer of 1977, when I first started to prepare for fieldwork, the staunchly Catholic world of provincial Portugal represented to me a largely novel experience ...

... only later ... I became aware of a problem ... This was the progressive discovery of my identity as a member of the urban élite ...

At the time, this struggle was largely unstated and unconscious. It was only in the process of writing up the material that I became aware of how important my personal experience of the conflict between the bourgeoisie and the peasantry had been for my understanding of local society. I believe my perception of the struggle was increased by my being a native Portuguese. Fewer expectations would have been placed on a foreigner, particularly one who did not speak Portuguese fluently.

This study was written as a D.Phil. thesis for the Institute of Social Anthropology of Oxford University ... (Pina-Cabral 1986, pp. vii–viii).

Responsibility for ASI was handed over to me at the start of the academic year 1984–85, allowing my colleague to concentrate on the third-year follow-up course, Social Anthropology II (hereafter ASII), which was mainly concerned with the work of Murdock and Lévi-Strauss and their followers.

There were about a dozen second-year students in the academic year 1983–84. It was hoped to build up to a maximum of twenty students in succeeding years. Going back to the course outline with which we began in 1983, the image of the course was largely a 'British' one – both in terms of the literature used and the methods of evaluation adopted. This Britishness was to some extent qualified by references to one or two translations, and several American and French writers.

ASI, with its two main themes of family and kinship and ethnographic analysis, was conceived as a key (*charneira*) course in the four-year Anthropology degree. The first term was to be concerned with kinship analysis prior to Lévi-Strauss; the second with questions of marriage and the family, especially in the contexts of Europe, Melanesia and in matrilineal central Africa. Finally, special attention would be devoted to two central life-cycle events: initiation and death. A small 'practical' project – the making of a genealogy – was included right at the outset of the year. This was less a piece of research than an exercise in consciousness (*consciencialização*) a break with the mirage of 'normality' and the tendency not to see the nose on one's face (*a tendência de 'não ver a ponta do nariz'*. It was viewed as a practical way of introducing the topic of kinship as well as calling students' attention to its actual significance and forcing them to take a more distanced, objective view of the social relations in which they themselves were involved.

It is interesting to note that there has been no direct reference to the genealogy to date in the current British debate about undergraduate projects in teaching anthropology. Why has the genealogy failed to materialise as a suitable possible 'practical' topic among those concerned in Britain with fieldwork in undergraduate studies? Would it be considered merely a 'technique', scarcely worthy of elevation to the status of a 'project' in and of itself? Or would it, on the contrary, be seen as too 'advanced' for undergraduate use? Why did it seem such an appropriate entreé for a second-year course based largely on British kinship studies in the Portuguese context? The contrast which underlies these questions is fundamental and will be explored from various angles in the following chapters.

The introduction to kinship

It is retrospectively startling to see what we considered as 'introductory' to kinship in the first term of the academic year 1983–84: kinship terminology, the genealogical method, descriptive and classificatory systems, Malinowski on kinship and the family, and Radcliffe-Brown on descent and lineage. They seemed reasonable enough points of departure at the time. The texts were mainly 'British', apart from the Portuguese translation of Alain Marie's introduction to kinship terminology (in Augé [1975] 1978), and the classic American articles – by Kroeber and Lowie – on classificatory and descriptive kinship. Many important articles by Rivers, Radcliffe-Brown and Malinowski were then untranslated, and students were expected to read them in the original English, with guidance provided during lectures and tutorials.

A number of major publications were available in translation: for example, *Sex and Repression in Savage Society* (available in a Brazilian translation); similarly, *African Systems of Kinship and Marriage*, whose 'Introduction' (by Radcliffe-Brown) students were supposed to read. The availability of French translations of Radcliffe-Brown's articles on the mother's brother and the study of kinship systems, reprinted in *Structure and Function*, were considered godsends by many students more familiar with that language than with English. The existence of Evans-Pritchard's *Nuer* in Spanish, and Fortune's *Sorcerers of Dobu* (in Portuguese), made these two monographs almost compulsory essay material.

The topics for the second term ranged through exchange relations, local groups and kinship groups. Considerable use was made of Fox's *Kinship and Marriage* for classes on local groups, segmentation and complementary filiation, cognatic descent, and ego-centred groups. Students were expected to prepare Murdock's (1949) article on 'The nuclear family'. They were also supposed to be able to follow discussions like the one between Leach on 'Polyandry' (1955) and Gough (replying to him) on 'The Nayars' (1959). The subjects of family and marriage were brought from what must have seemed rather 'distant' (both in time and space) anthropological debates to the European context by way of Hajnal's 'European marriage patterns in perspective' (1965), and Davis's *People of the Mediterranean*. Southern Europe became the focus of attention through publications by Pitt-Rivers (1971) and Campbell (1964), Peristiany (1966) and Bourdieu (1980). Kinship in northern Europe was approached through Arensberg and Kimball (1940), Firth (1956), Schneider (1968), Strathern (1981) and Fox (1982). Apart from Europe, two other ethnographic areas were selected for discussion during the second term: matrilineal central African societies and Melanesia.

The final part of the programme, on the life cycle – initiation and death – began with Van Gennep (in translation), and was to proceed through African, Melanesian and South American examples.

The plan was ambitious, and by May 1984 it became apparent that it was also ill-conceived. We were trying to squeeze more material into a single year than there was time or human capacity to accommodate. There were complaints from the students about the amount they had to read in English, about the exam, and about my problems with teaching in Portuguese. (There was no option of beginning by teaching in English as there is, for instance, in Holland.) We were, of course, rather inexperienced at that stage, although this is the common lot of all who begin a teaching career. Our situation was distinguished by the lack of a long-term institutionalised structure for the anthropology we were teaching. Such structures can serve, ideally anyway, to ease the paths of younger staff members when they begin their careers. Any structure that could be mustered when building up from scratch in Lisbon at that time, was inevitably drawn from elsewhere. Lack of the experience makes it more difficult to distribute teaching materials equitably – particularly when student throughput has only reached the second year! It is all the more interesting, for that very reason, to observe how we reacted to the challenge of designing and teaching an anthropology course. We drew, of course, upon what we 'knew'. While there were obvious differences in our experiences and interpretations of the 'British' anthropological tradition, we shared the basic assumption that studying this theory of kinship was centrally important for second-year Portuguese undergraduates. One of João de Pina Cabral's innovations was locating the genealogical practical at the beginning of the year.

The British tone (or tones) muffled beneath the neutral-sounding title, 'Anthropologia Social I', must nevertheless have been confusing for students. An incipient perception of this intervening Britishness intrigued and disturbed me – perhaps because of my rather narrow British background (which contrasted with the more varied trajectory of my colleague). When full responsibility for the *cadeira* was transferred to me at the end of the year, I tried to include the problem as an explicit part of the course.

The second programme: 1984–85

Thinking about the Britishness of the course raised more problems than it solved. First there was the issue of language. Things that seemed obvious when expressed in English had to be explained when rendered in Portuguese (see Part II). Then there was the question of 'flow'. It seemed essential to try to establish connections, logical or otherwise, between the authors of the set texts. The course objective was redefined as tracing a line of anthropological thought concerning units of social organisation, within the British school. 'Kinship' and 'family' could, for example, be seen as special cases of group formation: a process conceptualised and reconceptualised within several anthropological paradigms (cf. Verdon 1981).

The content of the course was thus narrowed to rather fewer, almost exclusively British authors, with the emphasis placed on comprehending the development of selected ideas. This narrowing also involved restructuring and redistributing the main course units over the year. There were now six units of different kinds: one practical, one 'continuous', and four theoretical blocks. The genealogy was relocated to the beginning of the second term, when the students had already assimilated two theoretical units. The 'continuous' section consisted in reading three ethnographies alongside the theoretical material being covered.

When the revised programme was finally ready, the Students' Association requested some kind of graphic design to serve as a cover (*capa*) – as was customary at I.S.C.T.E. My response was a collage comprising several cut-out images of the anthropological ancestor figures involved (top left, Malinowski leaning on a ship-rail, cigarette in hand; somewhat to the right, on a level with Malinowski's torso, the head and tie of Radcliffe-Brown; the same parts of Fortes; Evans-Pritchard's printed name only; Goody, seated with his legs crossed, shoes and socks visible, beneath R.-B. and Fortes; and the head of the smiling, bespectacled Leach, with part of his raised right hand visible, bottom left. The message was clear: bring the actors back into the history of anthropological thought on kinship and, with them, the 'Britishness' which was becoming so painfully apparent.

Time and the assessment of persons

It was my belief that putting things down on paper at the outset would provide a charter to keep things moving according to certain basic rules throughout the year. The quantity of pedagogical matters seemingly open to negotiation and renegotiation at I.S.C.T.E. had come as a surprise to me during the previous year. It was surprising, of course, only insofar as it contrasted with another way of doing things. The implicit standard, here, was 1970s Cambridge, where 'the system' had appeared totally inflexible.[7] At I.S.C.T.E., by contrast, continuous assessment was a matter of principle: formal examinations were regarded as anachronistic and authoritarian, except in subjects like mathematics. The business studies students also sat exams but, since the majority were identified with the political right, this was somehow seen as consonant with their image. Continuous assessment was regarded by most sociology and anthropology students as a symbol of the new order, and openly contrasted with pre-1974 evaluation in higher education. The value of continuous assessment (*avaliação contínua*) was seen as its flexibility, a critical factor for part-time students who often combined study with work and family commitments. One of the aims of post-revolutionary educational reforms was to encourage workers to study in their spare time, thereby raising the general level of education, and the (real) need for flexibility had become almost an article of faith by the early 1980s.

Time acquires different qualities, of course, when exogenous factors can be brought to bear on deadlines and timetables. Constant requests to hand work in later than the deadline effectively shift the locus of power from an impersonal 'system', to a very personal process of bargaining. The lecturer may find him-or herself with a revolt on their hands if they do not show the required measure of pliancy. Inflexibility on this point was regarded as a serious failing in understanding (*compreensão*) and in the highly prized quality of *simpatia*: 'niceness' which specifically takes account of other people's circumstances, conditions or state of mind. A person with *simpatia* might also be referred to as *porreira*, a colloquial adjective referring to being on good form. A stubborn, rule-abiding person who insists on deadlines and refuses to hear and respond to excuses, is a *chato*: thoroughly unpleasant and disagreeable, lacking compassion and humanity. These qualities will receive more detailed discussion in the second part of the following chapter.

Like time, the written word acquires a different sense when it is structured through continual, personal negotiation. Much more value is attached to command of the spoken word in Portuguese intellectual circles than in British ones. Verbal eloquence and duelling are the order of the day on the (very public) occasion of doctoral thesis examinations. Lectures follow a similar pattern. The most respected lecturers were those able to hold their audience's attention for 90 minutes in a verbal performance that one (anthropological) colleague likened to 'shamanic'. Knowledge does not simply stand for or by itself: the lecturer must summon it as a living presence into the classroom. The successful mediation of knowledge by the lecturer should inspire and enable the student to learn.

Although the prospect of carrying out fieldwork appears to have been among the most compelling reasons for studying social anthropology in post-1974 Portugal, the 'attraction' differs from that voiced by British students (cf. Lie 1990). Student resources seem to have been drawn upon quite extensively in social science research, sometimes as part of the degree course, in the aftermath of the Revolution. The notion of a common undertaking partially explains the power but also the compassion expected of the teacher. And what is a deadline when those concerned are engaged in such a momentous undertaking? Something of this sentiment carried over in a more general way to other areas of the pedagogical system a decade after the Revolution. Requests for leniency regarding the completion of work were part of the currency of exchange between the parties involved.

Frenzied attempts at defining and clarifying the whole course on paper – before it had even begun – were little more than straws in the wind. Students did not read anthropology 'by the programme': such declarations seem to have had no finality for them. The real world was subject to constant verbal re-creation. There were, of course, proper channels for registering grievances, and students made use of them. They found, for example, my six proposed moments of assessment, corresponding to each of the course units, excessive – and said so in Conselho Pedagógico (pedagogic council). My argument that four of these 'papers' were merely one or two pages (maximum) in length, cut no ice. Statistically, and politically, they looked like six on paper, and might be used as a precedent by other lecturers to demand more work. At the same time, they felt slighted (one young man went as far as to say 'castrated') by the brevity of the work prefigured in the new ASI programme. The virtues of being succinct were lost on them – not surprisingly, when oral elaboration and embellishment were so highly prized. Time *and* space were both required to write in the way that many wanted to write, reflecting perhaps the written analogue to the verbal prowess of the lecturer in this pedagogical system.

One effect of this configuration was almost constant anxiety about amounts of work set by lecturers. The degree to which students complied with or contested those requirements reflected varying esteem for different members of teaching staff – as much a function of verbal accomplishment as publication record. Reputation among colleagues was also partly determined by reported classroom skills and the ability to inspire students to produce work. These were favourite topics for the rather ample *conversas* (conversations) among colleagues, in what were literally the corridors of power of the labyrinthine I.S.C.T.E. building[8]. Converse will be dealt with much more extensively in Chapter 4.

It became clear, during the course of 1984–85, that a programmatic approach to the problems of ASI was inappropriate. Fundamental differences showed up in the values attached to time (punctuality/flexibility), to verbal and written eloquence, and to the lecturer as a person in whom both power and compassion should converge (as opposed to 'the system').

The third programme: 1985–86

Instead of trying to plan ahead exhaustively within the programme issued at the beginning of the following year, the general course objective was compressed into a single sentence: it would look at the ideas of certain British social anthropologists, concerning kinship and family, from Malinowski to Barnes. The year's work was divided into four blocks. The first of these considered questions such as 'Why study kinship?' and 'Why study the British School?'. The second examined the cultural study of kinship alongside its study as the basis of social structure. The third unit dealt with kinship as ideology. The fourth section, dealing with the practical study of kinship, was now positioned at the end of the year. Apart from the classical literature used in the first two blocks, I added some more recent English, French, Portuguese and Dutch (in English translation) references in the third and especially the fourth sections.

The practical work associated with making a genealogy completely changed its position and also its meaning in the course over these three years. It started out as a way of introducing students to the study of kinship; it gradually evolved as a means at their disposal. The emphasis on the genealogical method embodied in this book is partly an acknowledgement of that 'empirical' shift. The relocation reflects a process of rethinking the purpose of anthropological knowledge in a country like Portugal. How could one 'explain' the British passion for studying kinship without summoning the fundamental means for studying it into the 'presence' of the students? It no longer seemed self-evident that Portuguese students should have to study British ideas and their authors as a priority in their anthropological training. Pina-Cabral's (highly original) initial perception that making a genealogy might provide students with critical distance on issues close to hand, had some problematic implications. Despite the implied centrality of the genealogical method to British thinking on kinship, how central was it to Portuguese notions of kinship?

The notion of using anthropological thought/analysis as a tool for gaining distance on one's own society could (it seemed to me) be accomplished in other ways. Why not try reading fiction from an anthropological perspective? As an opening shot to the year, students were set Marguerite Duras's novel, *O Amante* (*The Lover*) to analyse in terms of Malinowski's (1930) approach to kinship. The exercise appeared to capture their imaginations in the way that was hoped. Portuguese students of anthropology and sociology were often fascinated by aspects of their own society and culture, particularly its emotional and amorous tenor. *O Amante* was a good choice, for this reason, while the practical exercise of identifying the 'initial situation', extensions and so on (in Malinowski's terms), gave them a concrete idea of how anthropological analysis could be used.

Fascination with their own culture, as already mentioned, had everything to do with the 1974 Revolution, and the revitalisation of the humanities which came with it (cf. Santos 1990). It was as if it suddenly became possible for the Portuguese to see themselves for the first time. There is, of course, a long tradition of Portuguese Ethnology (e.g. Dias, 1948, 1953; Ribeiro 1945; Leite de Vasconcellos 1958). But the sociological and anthropological approaches which seemed to interest students introduced a new theoretical impetus. The desire to learn about intellectual developments elsewhere in Europe, through which Portuguese social transformation might be understood differently, was very marked. So, too, was the wish to comprehend the difference made by the revolution to their own and their compatriots' lives.

These considerations were all the more immediate since a number of students and colleagues had been actively involved in the 1974 Revolution. They gave accounts of what it was to live through such a time: the examinations, the restrictions on political activities, the secret police. Intellectual vitality owed much to a sense of having been culturally isolated from the rest of Europe for decades, and an imperative to re-establish contact and make

113

up for lost time as quickly as possible. This out-going tendency was, on the other hand, qualified by a pride in their own intellectual and cultural tradition, despite the isolation and the decadence of a glorious past.

The fourth programme: 1986–87

The last programme, devised for the academic year 1986–87, was another reformulation. While the course continued to examine the approaches and analyses of certain British authors, it also tried to consider how they wrote and their ways of representing kinship material. There was clearly an attempt to understand the literary craftsmanship as well as (or as part of) the ethnographic contents of the texts studied.

The first term was primarily concerned with studies of kinship made in the first part of the twentieth century by Rivers, Malinowski and Radcliffe-Brown. Fortune's, Firth's and Bateson's 1930s ethnographies were also brought into the discussion as examples of the work of participants in Malinowski's seminar. This section was now provocatively titled 'Ethnography, Literature and/or Science'. The aim was to make students think about Rivers's, Malinowski's and Radcliffe-Brown's respective claims to scientific status for social anthropology. Rivers's genealogical method aimed to establish ethnology as a science as exact as physics or chemistry. Malinowski's preoccupation with the scientific methodology of ethnography is clear from his 'Introduction' to *Argonauts*. Radcliffe-Brown was interested in developing a natural science of society, defining the sociological laws which structure the functioning of society. The aim was to force students to confront received wisdom simply by questioning the scientific or literary status of ethnography. It was, in retrospect, less successful than the use of some of Malinowski's ideas to analyse a novel had been making a very similar point.

The second term was concerned with kinship understood as the basis of social structure and political organisation, beginning with selected readings from *African Political Systems* and *African Systems of Kinship and Marriage*, and followed by a number of critical approaches to Radcliffe-Brown's theoretical legacy on kinship: Leach (1961), Evans-Pritchard (1961) and Barnes (1962).

The final part of the course dwelt even longer on the tools for studying kinship – genealogy, autobiography, biography, and life histories – and used a number of recent non-British authors besides those with which the students were already familiar. Readings from Bertaux and Ferrarotti, for example, were included. The aim was to place the collection, representation and interpretation of kinship 'data' in a broader perspective. We also discussed some artefacts of family life, including photographs and domestic architecture, as well as fictional portraits of family life (particularly in Latin American novels, such as Isabel Allende's *House of Spirits* and Gabriel Garcia Marquez's *One Hundred Years of Solitude*). The aim was to try to use the ideas and ways of thinking about kinship studied during the first two terms to discuss different kinds of 'family' materials.

The basis for refraction

The Portuguese context has so far been introduced in a deliberately minimalist fashion. This sketchiness reflects where the original emphasis lay: on British texts and British ways of doing things. The four programmes delineated document a gradual apprehension of constraints and forces shaping pedagogical practice (cf. Kuper 1991, pp. 138-9). A number of assumptions were challenged and reworked in the course of teaching more or less the 'same' material from 1983 through to 1987. The contrasting notions of fieldwork in British undergraduate studies (as seen in a recent mini-debate), and in the Portuguese undergraduate setting, underline the way context can affect teaching what seem to be 'the same' anthropological materials. The process of reorientation embodied in the programmes was of course a response to the reception(s) they were getting. This is one way of introducing a much wider process of reconceptualisation which started to unfold. It was an experimental situation in many respects. Hidden assumptions about time, about dealing and conversing with other people, were being drawn into discussions apparently concerned with a corpus of British anthropological texts. What had they to do with one another?

The second part of this chapter proceeds with the central issue in rewriting the programmes: the interplay between English and Portuguese ideas about relatedness.

II. Between English and Portuguese understandings

English ideas about social relationships, in Portuguese

It is one thing to develop a teaching programme, another to teach it. A clear cultural divide between the classical British texts and their Portuguese readers became increasingly obvious with time. Agreement about the 'obvious', which underwrites pedagogical authority when docent and alumni share a common language, was also missing. The familiar English frame of reference started to become strange for me too. My attempts at mediating understandings brought two orders of problem to the fore. The first consisted of *students'* perplexity with the English language usage in their anthropological set texts. The second involved my own bafflement with the interpretative procedures required for seeing both English and Portuguese meanings simultaneously and attempting to mediate them.

Two examples from these respective domains will be discussed in this chapter. The first is located in the classroom and concerns the use of metaphor in ethnographic texts. Malinowski's reference to the 'flesh and blood' of kinship, in his 1930 article, provoked wide-ranging discussions about anthropological intentions and linguistic assumptions. The second is situated in the shady area of publishing texts designed for a student readership where decisions about language use can have long-term effects for what is 'understood' of a subject. The English concept of *descent* in English, is rendered as *filiação* in Portuguese, apparently due to filtering through French (*filiation*).

These examples illustrate the kinds of discussions that developed in the teaching context. They indicate both the potential and the limitations on drawing inferences from linguistic usage in texts. It is necessary to proceed beyond this kind of literary mediation to unravel the conundrum of these texts in that situation. The final section of the chapter marks a switch of perspective by briefly introducing the Portuguese perspective (to be more fully developed in the following chapter) through the concept of corporation. The Revolution of 1974 resonated in the meanings attached to studying anthropology by many Portuguese students during the 1980s. Some reacted with hostility to the notion of 'corporation' in Radcliffe-Brown's theorisation of unilineal descent. The echoes

116

of Salazar's *Estado Novo* – the corporate State – which some 'heard' in Radcliffe-Brown were grounds for a discussion which would have been unlikely in Britain. That discussion emphasises how anthropological knowledge cannot be regarded as neutral. The kinds of ideas that are seen as dangerous or derisive vary cross-culturally.

Metaphors of flesh and blood

Malinowski, trying to describe his place in British anthropology, compared it with Joseph Conrad's position in English literature. The vivid quality of Malinowski's ethnography has received much comment (e.g. Stocking 1983). No less vivacious is his use of language in what are explicitly theoretical texts. The article 'Kinship', published in *Man* (1930), is a case in point. This was one of the readings used in the second-year teaching programmes under consideration. Students were presented with this text in the first part of the year (the term before Christmas), which may account for the strength of their reactions to it.

Malinowski begins by asking, 'Must kinship be dehumanized by mock-algebra?', and opens forth with what is a self-confessed 'florid metaphor':

Much ink has flowed on the problem of blood – 'blood' symbolizing in most human languages, and that not only European, the ties of kinship, that is the ties derived from procreation. 'Blood' almost becomes discoloured out of all recognition in the process. Yet blood will rebel against any tampering, and flow its own way and keep its own colour. By which florid metaphor I simply mean that the extravagantly conjectural and bitterly controversial theorizing which we have had on primitive kinship has completely obscured the subject, and all but blinded the observers of actual primitive life.

He then criticises those conjectural theories of kinship, from Bachofen, Morgan and McLennan to Rivers and his school (Radcliffe-Brown, Deacon, Barnard, Hoernlé, Seligman, Malinowski himself, Kroeber, Lowie and Gifford):

The handful of us, the enragés or initiates of kinship, are prepared to wade through the sort of kinship algebra and geometry which has gradually developed; memorize long lists of native words, follow up complicated diagrams and formulae, sweat through dry documents, endure long deductive arguments, as well as the piling of hypothesis upon hypothesis (Malinowski [1930] 1971, p. 95).

117

On the other hand the 'average anthropologist' remains on the outside of all this esotericism: somewhat mystified and a little hostile. This average anthropologist has doubts about the 'bastard algebra of kinship', feeling instead that kinship is a matter of flesh and blood, the result of sexual passion and maternal affection, of long intimate daily life, and of a host of personal intimate interests (*ibid*).

Malinowski's rhetoric involves creating two imaginary anthropological camps: the kinship esotericists and the average anthropologists. Malinowski places himself among the first, as kinship initiate *enragé*, and uses that as a position from which to champion the second. The literary device is a clever one for designing a way out of what he calls the 'impasse' of kinship. First he establishes his authority, as one of the devotees of the inner circle; then he rejects the basis of that position and presents an iconoclastic alternative. That alternative is in harmony with the sentiments of the average anthropologist: kinship is a matter of flesh and blood, and so on.

A number of students had difficulties with in-jokes about Rivers's 'school', but more especially with the sense of the flesh and blood metaphor. Malinowski states first that there has been so much theorising on 'blood' that it has become almost unrecognisable. Next, that 'blood' itself has a way of getting its own back: that the flesh and blood of primitive kinship holds more interest for contemporary anthropologists than do the abstractions of their predecessors. Malinowski's first reference to blood alludes in English to the semantic cluster of relations by descent through a common ancestor; to kinship in general; to descent through parents of recognised blood or pedigree. Next he plays with the primary meaning, of red fluid, which gets 'discoloured' as the ink flows about it. Then he adds a third sense, where blood is regarded as the seat of the emotions or temper: one of the four humours of medieval physiology believed to cause optimism or cheerfulness. It is as a 'humour' that blood will rebel. And the moment for rebellion within anthropology had arrived with the doubts expressed by the average anthropologist. The need to master the bastard algebra of kinship was questioned by this person. Kinship, he feels, is after all a matter of flesh and blood. Flesh and blood refer here to human nature, but also to what is of the essence: that which is beyond dispute. The heart of the matter, for Malinowski, was the result of sexual passion and maternal affection, of long intimate daily life, and of a host of personal interests. Such concerns simply cannot be reduced to symbols, formulae or equations. It is the fleshing out of ideas which is important, according to Malinowski, rather than their desiccation into algebraic expressions. The phrase 'flesh and blood' captures that imperative while succinctly condensing an impressive array of connotations – at least, in English.

The problem in Portuguese is that the common expression is not *carne e sangue* (lit. flesh and blood), but *carne e osso* (lit. flesh and bone). This difference is not trivial. *Sangue* has the same connotations in Portuguese (blood, progeny, offspring, family, temper, disposition) as does blood in English. But the sense of the 'essential' which 'flesh and blood' conveys in English, translates in Portuguese as *carne e osso* [*em pessoa, na realidade*]. The semantic field covered by *osso* in Portuguese includes a notion of difficulty as, for example, in the idiomatic expression, *não há carne sem ossos*: literally, 'there isn't any meat without bones' or, more generally, 'everything has its problems'. *Carne sem osso* (meat without bone) is indeed a figurative way of referring to a bargain or a godsend. While there is certainly something of this in 'picking a bone' with someone, a 'bone of contention', or 'making no bones' about something, the specific alliance between flesh and bone does not exist in English. It is possible to feel something 'in one's bones': to feel something intuitively. Or something may be 'close to the bone': it may be risqué or slightly indecent. But these senses of intuition and sailing close to the wind are quite distinct from the problems attached to Portuguese *ossos*. Blood and bone are, in English, very different[9]. Blood is a brightly coloured fluid; bone is dry and solid. The optimism, warmth and cheerfulness associated with this humour contrasts with the dry coldness and dismal white–grey–brown colour of bones. 'Blood-red' and 'bone-dry' borrow the respective emotional contents to make common metaphors in English. When Jack climbed the beanstalk and surreptitiously entered a miraculous land, the giant detected him:

Fee! Fi! Fo! Fum! I smell the blood of an Englishman!
Be he alive or be he dead, I'll grind his bones to make my bread!

Only in the fairytale world of magic beanstalks and giants would English bones be associated with blood rather than with flesh, and for transformation into bread!

Apart from the verb 'to bleed', for which there is a Portuguese equivalent, *sangrar*, there is another English verb 'to blood', meaning to stain, wet or mark, especially the cheeks of an inexperienced hunter with the bloody stump of the dead fox's tail.

The different emphases given by using bodily substances to refer to basic notions of life, such as relatedness, are neatly summarised in the two contrasting pairs: flesh and blood, *carne e osso* (flesh and bone). Flesh and blood, it seems to me, is wet but essentially warm; *carne e osso* tends towards solid and dry, so that although *carne* generally includes *sangue* this content is played down by accentuating the *ossos*[10]. The first has an optimistic emotional colouring in referring to cultural essentials; the latter tends towards another, as yet unspecified, direction. They are a first concrete indicator of the problems with the assumption that European kinship ideas are more or less equivalent. The impact of Malinowski's succession of ink/blood metaphors is lost when *carne e osso* is the cultural rendering of 'flesh and blood'. Unimportant in itself, the illustration nevertheless illuminates distinctive emphases and meanings attaching to such basic substances as flesh, bone and blood.

This will scarcely come as news for Europeanist anthropologists, who are probably wondering what all the excitement is about! But the gist of my argument is not about simple difference. Instead, it concerns how difference is revealed as anthropological knowledge. The mechanism under examination is an anthropological text in English; a native English-speaker is at an advantage regarding implicit meanings in that text; conversely, non-native English-speakers can be bewildered by such imagery. It could be said that the problems of reading this text were largely due to localised senses embedded in the respective languages, which compromised strictly anthropological ones.

The first example has been unabashedly metaphorical, and florid at that. It is ironical that the author was a non-native English-speaker. Was he trying to be more English than the English? Or was this Polish imagery sounding through English? Anthropological texts, like any others, rely to greater or lesser degrees on metaphor as vehicles for scientific argument. One of the problems they present is where these metaphors lead if we care to follow them. Most English-speakers find the senses too self-evident and too lateral to the anthropological purpose to do more than skip over them. But they are stumbling-blocks of a provocative order for non-native English-speakers and, if one cares to see them that way, rich sources of the implicit meanings being considered.

The correctness or otherwise of giving such a text at the beginning of a second-year course is a different issue. My interest here lies in the linguistic obstacle course unleashed. This amounts to admitting that the English cultural notion of 'blood' is as problematic as Portuguese ideas about *ossos*. This reading uncovers a mechanism resembling a two-way mirror: in it we see Portuguese students (with their assumptions, of course), confronted by certain English assumptions when they attempt to read certain 'British' anthropological texts in the 'original'. This device sets English-speakers on the unfamiliar darkened side of the glass, observing a previously unknown linguistic area through the aperture of Portuguese. I have unearthed a metaphor of my own[11] to try to express what Portuguese students' perplexities made me aware of, in questioning one of Malinowski's metaphors.

Lest the Malinowskian example be brushed aside as too extravagant and not, in any case, 'truly British', the next section will examine the more measured language associated with the all-too-English A.R. Radcliffe-Brown, as presented in Fox's modernist synthesis. Here the problem is cast in rather different terms. It is tempting to see in translations the solution to predicaments of reading set texts in the original language. Translation, however, brings its own set of quandaries – such as the discrepancies between 'original' and translated versions, and the commentaries given (or omitted by translators).

Translation and drawing upon the known

Early in 1986, I was asked to write an afterword (*posfácio*) to a Portuguese translation of Robin Fox's *Kinship and Marriage*. The book had been pending for quite some time, and there seemed to be problems with the translation. There was little choice about accepting the task given the obvious difficulties of studying anthropology with so few translations, especially from English. The precise nature of the translation problems were also intriguing. *Kinship and Marriage* has a central place on many course reading lists, and it was instructive to return to the original alongside the Portuguese translation by J.C. Rodrigues.

The translator's two dozen or so annotations give an insight into what required explanation or comment in his view. Rodrigues comments, for example, on Fox's reference to the substitution of bottles for mothers in Huxley's *Brave New World*. Fox was arguing that no society so far had ever managed to dispense with a minimum of kin-based social relationships, however little emphasis there is on kinship in certain (advanced industrial, and other) societies. Rodrigues comments that although there is as yet no society emanating from test-tube babies, the image is today much less futuristic than it was – either in Orwell's time or Fox's.

Both author and translator appear to associate test-tube babies with a lack of interest in kinship, concurring in this with Malinowski's 'flesh and blood' of sexual passion and maternal affection. The desire to 'have children' seems to be so strong, however, that people have recourse to *in vitro* fertilisation, artificial insemination or surrogate motherhood, to overcome obstacles such as infertility or lack of a male partner, which would formerly have left them childless. The fact that such issues are publicly debated as, for example, in the B.B.C. television series, *Family Matters* (January 1990), suggests that social concern with what anthropologists call 'kinship' may in fact be enhanced by the various forms of 'technical' intervention[12].

Rodrigues does not, on the other hand, explain Fox's reference to Bertie Wooster, whom he uses to introduce the idea of claims on aunts and uncles even in our 'relatively 'kinshipless' society' because, '[b]lood, as the old adage has it, is thicker than water' (*o sangue, como diz o velho adágio, é mais espesso do que a água*). This notion of blood would not seem to present the reader with difficulties. But the upper-class buffoon, Bertie Wooster, and his aunts and uncles could well have done with some elaboration. The example is much less famous than others, such as some animals being more equal than others, and yet it is these well-known illustrations which are 'explained'. A comment on Bertie Wooster would require a thorough understanding of how class concerns infiltrate the English language and ideas about relatedness. The reference also underlines the dubiety of presenting England as a relatively 'kinshipless' society, effectively compromising the contrast with 'Mediterranean countries' where 'unthinking, familistic, kinship-centred loyalties run in opposition to the laws of church and state and the demands of an expanding, industrial society'

(Fox 1967, p. 15). Even if kinship sentiments 'still linger' among the aristocratic and working classes, it is an idea of middle-class England which sustains the image of low-key kinship. It is clearly easier to comment upon the internationally known examples of test-tube babies and the (in)equality of animals, although the first of these is less clear-cut than it may once have seemed. The second, as we shall see in Chapter 5, is also far from obvious.

In a similar vein, Rodrigues elaborates on Fox's dismissal of 'Rumpelstiltskin philosophy' of 'name it and nail it', with a reference to the dwarf in German folklore who helped a miller's daughter to transform flax into gold and marry a king, on condition that he would receive her first-born child. When the child was born, the queen was so desolate that the dwarf agreed to relent in the unlikely event that she should guess his name within three days. She did not succeed on the first two days, but on the third a strange voice was heard singing,

Little dreams my dainty dame
Rumpelstiltskin is my name.

When this was reported to the queen, she saved the child by 'guessing' correctly. The dwarf stamped his foot, and killed himself in rage. Fox was deploring anthropologists' idle belief that by discovering a name for something, you bring it within your power. Hence their interest in coining natty Latinisms. Fox thoroughly disapproved of making conceptual distinctions in place of making discoveries: 'Much modern kinship analysis is not analysis at all but an exercise in bad etymology. This fools other social scientists into thinking that the subject is 'very mature and complex' with a highly developed technical vocabulary' (*ibid*).

The partiality of Fox's use of the Rumpelstiltskin story is flagrant. He might, for example, have chosen to underline the accidental nature of the discovery of Rumpelstiltskin's name by the queen's servant, which saved the life of her child. This could have illustrated good detective work rather than 'name it and nail it'. The fact that it was a German popular fable might make the details a little more vague for an English reader. But the sense Fox wants to convey is the affected arrogance of (British) anthropologists with their concepts of 'descent', 'lineage', 'matrilineal', 'patrilineal', 'agnatic' and 'cognatic'. He is as impatient with these Latinisms as he is with undue respect for them. There was little more to be done about such confusions, he had to admit, than to 'note them and warn the reader' (*ibid*). Rodrigues scarcely hints at this; his concern is for the reader's appreciation of the story.

Descent and *filiação*

It (almost!) goes without saying that what starts out as 'confusion' in English becomes still more convoluted in Portuguese. This is especially so when a French authority is used to clarify English concepts. Rodrigues drew upon M. Augé in translating Fox: the Portuguese version of *Les Domaines de la parenté* (edited by Augé in 1975), was translated by Ana Maria Bessa, and published in 1978 as *Os Domínios de Parentesco (Filiação, Aliança matrimonial, Residência)*. It was a logical choice on the translator's part: scores of Portuguese anthropology students were already familiar with Augé as one of the few reference works on kinship translated into Portuguese. The notational systems and glossary of kinship vocabulary (*sistemas de notação, introdução ao vocabulário de parentesco*) are among those most frequently consulted in the initial years of study. One of the most systematic confusions can be traced to p. 65, in the following entry: 'Descent, *filiação, filiação unilinear, unifiliação*; common descent, *filiação comun, a mesma ascendência*; descent group, *grupo de filiação (unilinear)*. On the following page, under Filiation: 1 *descendência*; 2 *filiação*; complementary filiation, *filiação complementar*'.

The origin of the English/Portuguese glossary in Augé (1978) is still more complicated. The translator elaborated it on the basis of Gulbenkian Foundation publications and 'Portuguese university practice, also taking into account the French translation of M. Aghassian and Christine Mesiant' (1978, p. 11)! The Gulbenkian publications referred to are presumably the translations by Teresa Brandão of *African Systems of Kinship and Marriage* (1950), which was published under the title, *Sistemas Políticos Africanos de Parentesco e Casamento*, in September 1974; and *African Political Systems* (1940) was also translated into Portuguese, and published in January 1981. The Portuguese addition of the adjective 'political' (*políticos*) to the title of the first publication (making it *African Political Systems of Kinship and Marriage*), is a telling commentary on the intellectual atmosphere immediately following the April Revolution. The coup was sparked off by a revolt against the conditions under which the armed forces were expected to fight the colonial wars of the 1960s in Mozambique, Angola and Guinea-Bissau. The ramifications of the Revolution upon the educational system will be discussed in somewhat more detail in the following chapter. It is sufficient here merely to note the discrepancy in a translated title.

In *Sistemas Políticos Africanos de Parentesco e Casamento*, 'descent' is sometimes translated as *filiação*, sometimes as *descendência*, giving the impression of interchangeability. The Portuguese translation of Augé's *Domaines de la parenté* in 1978 supports Rodrigues's rendering of descent as *filiação*, descent groups as *grupos de filiação*, unilineal descent as *filiação unilinear*, and so on. On the other hand, the English 'filiation' becomes *afiliação*; while complementary filiation becomes *filiação complementar* (Augé [1975] 1978, pp. 65, 67; Fox [1967] 1986, pp. 159, 160, 281, 282, 284). The last two Portuguese translations are 'technically' inconsistent since 'complementary filiation' is a specific form of the more generic 'filiation'.

It is sometimes interesting to speculate on the sense of linguistic inconsistencies (cf. Bouquet and Freitas Branco 1988, pp. 131–44; Bouquet 1990). The present example looks at first like a simple case of English terminology infiltrated by French terms when expressed in Portuguese. The problem of discrepancy between English and French renderings of the concept of descent is discussed by Goody (1983). In a lengthy footnote on Guichard's 'system of descent', he draws attention to the distinction between English 'descent' and 'filiation', and the French 'filiation':

I have translated the French term 'filiation' by the English 'descent'. In English anthropological usage the two terms have been distinguished, descent referring to eligibility to membership of a kin group (following Rivers) and hence to its genealogical framework. Some writers have confined the usage to unilineal descent groups (to clans and lineages), although others, taking the term more literally, have applied it to 'descending kindreds' and similar groupings that are recruited and organised around both paternal and maternal filiation. In English the term 'filiation' refers to parent–child links that are necessarily 'bilateral' in virtually all societies (Goody 1983, pp. 12–13, n. 2).

Translating *directly* from the English original into Portuguese, it might have been possible to use *descendência* for 'descent'. According to Almeida Costa and Sampaio e Melo, *descendência* refers to a series of individuals springing from a common trunk (*série de indivíduos que procedem de um tronco comun* [Lat. *descendente, que descende*]). *Filiação* could then have been reserved for 'filiation': *'acto de filiar; descendência de pais para filhos* (the act of incorporating (persons) as members; descent between parents and children). Certainly this would have avoided the inconsistency between *afiliação* for 'filiation', and *filiação complementar* for 'complementary filiation'.

The words in themselves, it could be argued, are not obsessively important. This is perhaps what Fox meant with his scathing remarks about a Rumpelstiltskin philosophy, replete with 'natty Latinisms' (1967, p. 50). It would also seem to be Goody's position when he writes,

These usages are not standard; but the distinctions to which they refer (not necessarily the terms) are essential (indeed are minimal) if we are to understand the variety of human organisations and the way they have changed over time. A significant number of problems in the analysis of family and kinship could be cleared away by more careful distinctions, definitions and usages. Many existing controversies and hypotheses are generated by ambiguities inherent in terms like 'patriarchal' and by the tendency to deal crudely in the presence or absence of qualities (affection etc.) when it is more subtle ways of discrimination that are needed (*loc. cit.*).

Goody is suggesting that kinship terminology is not in itself important, but that the underlying distinctions to which it refers are for comparative purposes. His presupposition is that 'these links with kin are used across a wide variety of contexts of social action (eligibility to kin groups, succession to office, transmission of property, all kinds of behaviour between kin'(*ibid*). Goody opts for his own set of definitions to refer to the differential stress placed on links to and through males and females: paternal or maternal for immediate links of filiation; masculine or feminine for those to males and females; and agnatic or uterine for those through males or females.

The question is whether the underlying distinctions to which Goody refers are any more universal or useful for comparative purposes than the terminology. Or, put rather differently, whether the terminology itself may not be more closely tied up with local (i.e. English) idiosyncracies than either Fox or Goody would care to admit. What seem to be linguistic muddles, needing a good spring-clean, may turn out to reflect significant differences in emphasis among Europeans. The problem with the nattiness of the Latinisms scorned by Fox is the assumption that they refer to a pan-European ('Western', even) scientific reality, when in fact they are subject to syncretism from the moment they enter a language. The hegemony of English, relative to certain other European and world languages, in the diffusion of anthropological knowledge, fosters the vague assumption that its Latinisms somehow express distinctions which are equally sensible in other languages. English 'descent' may not in fact be best translated by Portuguese *descendência*; the verb *filiar*, with its notion of incorporating persons as members, may actually capture the Riversian preoccupation with eligibility to membership of a kin group, and hence its genealogical framework, better. But is this the main point?

The conceptual distinctions wrapped up in descent and filiation, however they are rendered in French or Portuguese, basically refer to a deeply rooted English concept. The dilemma facing the various Portuguese translators who have been mentioned here is clear enough: how best to represent a foreign concept when, paradoxically, its Latin 'vehicle' refers to a different cultural reality than their own! *Descendência*, in referring to a series of *individuals* descending from a common trunk, may not include the ideas of conditional entry to a group, and the notions of social replacement or substitution involved in this (English) notion. So specific is the English anthropological notion of 'descent' that Portuguese translators have tended to accommodate it in what appears to be the most contradictory way. In fact they were working in a culturally consistent way (cf. Overing 1989). This contradiction can nevertheless cause considerable insecurity, even though it may be more apparent than real. Being confronted by two versions of linguistic signs can bewilder, especially in an early phase of studying anthropology. And when corresponding degrees of credibility and authority attach (as they do) to the 'original' and 'translations', this can be particularly disorienting.

Our second example, then, has juxtaposed 'descent' and *filiação* rather differently from the way 'flesh and blood' was ranged alongside *carne e osso* in the first. The first illustration led into a thicket of bodily notions and metaphors; the second into the jungle of natty Latinisms. English notions of 'flesh', 'blood' and 'bone' are more easily enjoined to yield up their cultural contents when considered through the *carne*, *sangue* and *osso* of Portuguese, than

127

through the medium of English itself. This device provides leverage by which that 'strangeness' which has often passed for authority, can be detached.

The hesitation afflicting those trying to translate these hidden assumptions, points up a deference to the English language which undoubtedly contributed to the world position of British social anthropology (cf. Asad 1986, p. 157). This hidden content may only become visible out of the British context. Out of that context, 'blood' and 'descent' become English problems for exploration, points of ethnographic departure rather than literary sophistries or terminological 'givens'.

Parts of translated texts which call for attention, confuse, or are rejected out of hand by readers in specific historical periods, provide important clues to these local sensibilities. Attention to such detail is not 'introverted', in the sense that foreign meanings stay or are kept out of reach. Instead, they reflect upon 'original' meanings, showing them up in a different light; recasting them for interpretation. In the final part of this chapter, I shall consider the meaning of 'reading time(s)' for texts, and for the other ethnographies they contain.

Reading times and places: corporations that never die ...
Apart from the linguistic difficulties associated with reading British social anthropology that have been discussed so far, there was also resistance to studying certain texts that had to do with an image of kinship as 'reactionary' in post-Revolutionary Portugal of the mid-1980s. This idea was accentuated by a vision of Britain as the original class-based society, hereditary privilege or deprivation, and the stiff upper lip. The Thatcherite decade did much to affirm that view: de Sousa Santos, indeed, compares *cavaquismo*[13] with Thatcherism (1990, pp. 187–9, n. 8). British anthropological kinship theory, dating from the inter-war years, before the Welfare State and socialist reform, was seen by some Portuguese students as an 'irrelevance'. Irrelevant, that is, to understanding contemporary Portugal. The point is mentioned here since it underlines the apparent obscurity of the texts they were being asked to study. Fixation on Portugal as an object of study should not be overdrawn. Many found Griaule and his associates' work on the Dogon more congenial than the mires of structural–functionalism.

Resistance to descent theory, and more particularly to the notion of 'corporation', illustrates the importance of what might be termed 'reading time'. Developments in British social anthropology between 1935 and 1954 were mainly taken up with exploring the nature and significance of unilineal descent groups (Leach 1961). Radcliffe-Brown (1935), Evans-Pritchard (1940) and Fortes (1953) were the chief exponents. Continuity of societies with a lineage structure was thought to reside in continuity of the system of lineages, each of which was a 'corporation', independent of any individual member's life. The thesis generated its own antithesis, as Leach demonstrated in *Pul Eliya*. The problem he posed, within the parameters of the theory, was what kind of 'corporation' provides inter-generational continuity in societies which do not have unilineal descent groups? An over-emphasis on lineage-based societies left those with other kinds of social organisation remarkably thinly described.

Pul Eliya was one of the ethnographies set with the aim of providing students with an 'internal' critique. The book marshals a large amount of empirical material to show that 'kinship as a thing in itself' could not explain the continuity of Pul Eliya. Leach cites Fortes at length as 'a text for my whole investigation':

We see that descent is fundamentally a jural concept as Radcliffe-Brown argued in one of his most important papers (1935); we see its significance, as the connecting link between the external, that is the political and legal aspect of what we have called unilineal descent groups, and the internal or domestic aspect. It is in the latter context that kinship carries maximum weight, first, as the source of title to membership of the groups or to specific jural status, with all that this means in rights over and toward persons and property, and second as the basis of the social relations among persons who are identified with one another in the corporate group. In theory membership of a corporate legal or political group need not stem from kinship, as Weber has made clear. In primitive society, however, if it is not based upon kinship it seems generally to presume some formal procedure of incorporation with ritual initiation ... Why descent rather than locality or some other principle forms the basis of these corporate groups is a question which needs more study. It will be remembered that Radcliffe-Brown (1935) related succession rules to the need for unequivocal discrimination of rights *in rem* and *in personam*. Perhaps it is most clearly connected with the fact that rights over the reproductive powers of women are easily regulated by the descent group system. But I believe that something deeper than this is involved, for in a homogeneous society there is nothing which could so precisely and incontrovertibly fix one's place in society as one's parentage (Fortes 1953, p. 30, cit. by Leach 1961, p. 7)

Leach set out to show, with the kind of ethnographic minutiae his British colleagues could accept as evidence, that it was locality rather than descent which formed the basis of corporate grouping. Leach understood by 'locality' a 'particular man-made ecological environment ... the inflexibility of topography – of water and land and climate' (1961, p. 9). He insisted that the constraints of economics are prior to those of morality and law.

The corporate group identified by Leach was a compound group – the *gedara*. It was corporate not in the Weberian sense of *Verband* (1947, p. 133), but rather in Maine's sense of a 'corporation aggregate' (1883, p. 187). It was a continuing entity with certain types of ownership right relating to the estate as a whole rather than to any particular part of it, and vested equally in all individuals who acquired rights therein.

Leach resisted calling the compound group a descent group for, even though membership depended on successfully asserting a claim based on pedigree, this form of recruitment was not automatic (1961, p. 101). Despite the material reality of the compound group, however, people did not conceptualise 'their society as being composed of compound groups' *ibid*, p. 104). Indeed they discussed aggregates of people using the term *pavula*, which has much the same range of meanings as the English term 'family' (*ibid*, p. 105). Leach distinguishes between 'ideal' and 'effective' *pavula*. But his main concern was to show that even though people might think in these terms, there was no justification for analytical blindness to the concrete basis of corporate groups. Locality and not descent was the basis of corporate grouping. There followed a series of exchanges between Leach and Fortes in *Man*.

These discussions had seemed at best dull (and strategically avoidable under an exam regime), at worst almost incomprehensible, in England. 'Corporation' provoked little resistance in 1970s Cambridge – it had never seemed remotely connected with local, empirical reality[14]. Some Portuguese students' reactions could not have been more different. Having grown up in the final phase of the Salazarist corporate state, they did not experience the notions of corporation present in descent theory in a pacific way. Classes were constantly interrupted, especially in the academic year 1984–

85[15]. There are two important points here. Firstly, the important part enacted by schoolchildren and students in the making and aftermath of the 1974 Revolution[16]. A twenty–year–old student in 1984 would only have been 10 in 1974. However, many Portuguese are mature students – well into their twenties or thirties. A thirty–year–old would have been twenty at the time of the Revolution – quite old enough to play an active part in it. Although much radicalism had been eroded in the course of ten years, people do not simply 'forget' something as momentous as a revolution through which they themselves have lived, and to which they may have actively contributed.

So what was so offensive about corporatism in that Portuguese context? The *Estado Novo* (1926–74) had been based on the idea of a Portuguese economy protected from the international depression of the 1930s, with all national activities controlled by centralised, corporate bodies. Under Salazar, who became Prime Minister in 1932, the corporate State became authoritarian, xenophobic and introverted, attempting to seal itself from the effects of the outside world[17]. Corporatist institutions had dominated the industrial sector since 1924. The only political party, the Party for National Action, was called a civic association. Only national trade unions (*sindicatos*) whose leaders were approved by the government were allowed. If disputes arose, these were to be settled harmoniously with State intervention through government-appointed labour courts whose decisions were final and binding. It was supposed that the employers' guilds' (*grémios*) interests were not in conflict with those of the unions, and strike action was illegal. The P.I.D.E. (secret police), together with the censors, enabled Salazar to establish and maintain social order and to put down opposition.

Apart from these structures, there was a Control of Industry Act (*Lei de Condicionamento Industrial*) which effectively chained industrial development to government direction. Permission was needed to begin a new industry, to build a new factory or to change or extend an existing one. This fostered large and powerful private monopolies, each in the hands of a small number of extremely rich families. These business empires[18] supported the regime in exchange for state protection from foreign investors (until the 1960s) and from small businessmen. By the 1960s, however, mounting costs of the colonial wars had made it increasingly clear that the corporate State formula no longer functioned.

Salazar refused to countenance the loss of what he saw as the extension of Portugal itself into the African colonies of Mozambique, Angola and Guinea-Bissau. Colonialism came to substitute corporatism as the central nucleus of the regime (de Sousa Santos 1990, p.25). Waging these wars caused immense economic distortions between 1968 and 1974, without the gratification of military success. The policy continued, despite this, even after Salazar's death in 1968. This resulted in the majority of the armed forces becoming politicised: the Armed Forces Movement began in 1973.

By April 1974 there was a 30% inflation rate, rising unemployment, the worst-ever balance of trade, and industrial unrest despite the illegality of strikes. Salazar had rejected liberal capitalism at home, and tried to keep foreign liberal-capitalist influences at bay. The timid reforms made in 1970 were insufficient. The system had 'worked' insofar as there was political, social and economic stability – even if that was achieved by keeping a large proportion of the population uneducated (there was over 33% adult illiteracy in the early 1960s), without such basic services as electricity; and among the lowest wages in Europe for workers in what little industry there was. Emigration became a social movement during the last decade of the fascist state. More than a million people decided to go to the older destinations of Brazil, Mozambique or Angola, or the newer ones of France and West Germany. Emigrant remittances constituted a vital source of government revenue by the 1970s (Cabral 1986; Reis and Nave 1986). But much of this was devoured by the costs of fighting the colonial wars, rather than in investment.

Small wonder, perhaps, that the adjective 'political' (*políticos*) was added to the title of *African Systems of Kinship and Marriage* in its Portuguese translation of 1975 – the year after the military coup. Some Portuguese students were quite understandably taken aback to find how central a place corporate descent groups occupied in British kinship theory. The next chapter will consider what, if any, were the points of contact between British and Portuguese ways of thinking about kinship, taking as its point of departure the students' use of the genealogical method as part of their second-year studies.

132

Notes

1 This point was made by one of the Greek conveners (Alexandra Bakalakis) of the workshop, 'The Anthropology of the Periphery – Peripheral Anthropology', at the first E.A.S.A. Conference in Coimbra, Portugal (31 August – September 1990). She compared the exotic artefacts that often decorate North American (and European) anthropologists' offices, with the classic anthropology texts (mostly by northern European and American authors) which are the counterparts in Greek anthropologists' offices. This reflects a quite different position occupied by the texts when anthropology is an import discipline, and fieldwork is carried out at home or close to it.

2 In Lisbon: Instituto Superior de Ciências Sociais e Políticas (I.S.C.S.P.); Universidade Nova de Lisboa (U.N.L.); Instituto Superior de Ciências do Trabalho e da Empresa (I.S.C.T.E.). Other institutions which include an Anthropology course within their degree curricula: Universidade de Coimbra; Museu de Antropologia de Coimbra; Universidade da Beira Interior; Universidade do Porto (Sociologia – Anthropologia); Universidade Católica (Teologia – Antropologia Filosófica); Universidade do Minho; Instituto Politécnica de Viana do Castelo (Antropologia Cultural); Escolas Superiores de Educação, in Braganca, Leiria and Setubal (Dossier Ensino, Associação Portuguesa de Antropologia, 1991). See also Fernandes Dias 1991, p. 12.

3 I obtained a teaching post at I.S.C.T.E. in October 1983, as *professora auxiliar*: Ferreira de Almeida *et al.* (1988) provide an interesting analysis of the social backgrounds of I.S.C.T.E. students and how they varied between the three *licenciaturas*.

4 See, for example, the Special Issue of *Sociologia Ruralis* (1986, XXVI, 1), 'Portuguese Perspectives/Perspectivas Portuguesas'.

5 I completed my Ph.D. in Cambridge in 1981, having done research on 'changing family and household organisation' among farmers in south-west England.

6 The other 'prime movers' were Robert Rowland, Joaquím Pais do Brito, José Carlos Gomes da Silva, Raúl Iturra and José Fialho.

7 For example, we never questioned the existence of annual examinations, although there was criticism of the lack of compassion for personal circumstances. The single bitter example of a mature student friend for whom there was no option but to sit her Final exams despite the deaths of her two brothers in a car accident shortly before, will suffice to make this point.

8 The architecture of I.S.C.T.E. produced bewilderment among outside visitors in the early 1980s since there was neither a reception desk

at the entrance nor other clear indications as to where rooms or persons might be found. It was very much an 'insider's' world. It is interesting, in this context, to note the imagery evoked by Vale de Almeida, now a lecturer at I.S.C.T.E., who refers to 'academic corridor politics' (1991a, p. 19).

9 Although, as we shall see in Chapter 5, bone was involved in the nineteenth-century English vision of conjugality: the wife became 'bone of her husband's bone'.

10 The ossal relics of saints are enshrined – only a post-modern Madonna would play with such symbols.

11 The origin of this metaphor belongs to the time of writing up my Ph.D. thesis in a room with such a mirror, designed for observing 'supervisions' (tutorials) in the Department of Social Anthropology in Cambridge.

12 See the papers from the seminar, 'Kinship and the New Reproductive Technologies – Anthropological Perspectives on Assisted Kinship', held at the University of Manchester, 19 September 1991 and published after this book had gone to press (Strathern 1992b).

13 *Cavaquismo* refers to the political movement associated with A. Cavaco Silva, who became Prime Minister of Portugal in 1986.

14 It might perhaps be argued that feminist theory occupied a similar conceptual space in 1970s British social anthropology. Concern with gender issues expressed cultural preoccupations and also turned over some of the orthodoxies (cf. Strathern 1988).

15 This was my second year of teaching at I.S.C.T.E., and the first in which I held full responsibility for the ASI course. I was much impressed by this combative attitude (cf. Bouquet 1985b).

16 As the *Sunday Times* team put it, 'A remarkable number of young Portuguese had become thoroughly radicalized by 1974 – not least by the ceaseless activities of the P.I.D.E./ D.G.S. [secret police forces] among students. And many had formed close links with the clandestine political parties of the left' (1975, p. 93). During the summer of 1974 there were purges (*saneamentos*) of university and, in some cases, school staff who had collaborated with the former regime, particularly those who had informed the secret police of the illegal political affiliations or activities of students or pupils. Classes were abandoned that summer as this process gathered momentum. Educational administration collapsed, and in both Lisbon and Coimbra universities, revolutionary students' committees were set up: 'parents were staggered to have previously dutiful children returning home from school and denouncing them as fascists' (*ibid*, p. 104).

17 Salazar contrasted the corporate state with the previous regime

in a radio broadcast of 1934: He referred to the 'permanent agitation, *coups d'état*, street fighting, anxiety, anarchy, inadequate public services, insecurity of life and property, discredit, economic ruin, general retrogression ... many revolutions, but yet no Revolution'. This he contrasted with the dictatorship, which 'established peace, assured order, purified the moral atmosphere, added dignity to political action, elevated public morality, confirmed the credit of the State, awoke national conscience, directed the progress of the nation's economy, raised the standard of living of the rural population, apportioned work, organised the nation's material and moral interests for the common good, and created a worldwide prestige'.

18 The Champalimaud group was such an empire. It began by monopolising the cement industry in the 1940s, later diversifying into tourism, insurance and ranching in Angola. Champalimaud also owned the Banco Pinto e Sotto Mayor, which had itself absorbed the steel firm Siderurgia in the 1950s.

CHAPTER FOUR

SWITCHING PERSPECTIVES

I. Exploring Portuguese kinship

Portuguese readings of British structural–functionalism brought a two-headed monster to light. First, reactions precipitated by these texts served to illuminate new areas for discussion which would have been invisible in the English setting. The obsession with descent, to take one example, and the way in which descent theory was cast, show up in the distinctive forms of Portuguese expression and understanding. Second, the meanings being attached to the English texts in this Portuguese setting, barely ten years after the April Revolution of 1974, diverged from those which existed in the British context.

This chapter will attempt to go beyond what could be inferred of a Portuguese view from the textual interplay discussed in the previous chapter. The fact that all the students studying social anthropology at the time under discussion had lived through the April Revolution is quite central both to the meaning of education itself, and to the subject they had chosen to study. The Revolution altered ideas about authority, hierarchy and structure, and provided them with material from close at hand, from their own lives, upon which they constantly drew in their discussions of anthropology. This built-in reflexivity was quite other than, for example, anthropology at home (Jackson 1987). Precisely what was the point of studying early-to-mid twentieth-century British anthropological thought amid all this? The assumption that these are classic texts that every anthropologist must study at some time or another in their career, misses the point. The only rationalisation that seemed to make any sense was that the alien character of this material might prove a useful foil against which to gain new perspectives on Portuguese society.

There are two main reasons why the genealogical method assumed such proportions under these circumstances. First, the method provides an understanding of the basic rationale underlying the theory. British kinship theories, terminology and diagrammatic representations do, as previous chapters have shown, require a thorough grasp of this method. Second, given the evident interest in studying aspects of Portuguese life, the method also holds out a promise for exploring Portuguese kinship. This chapter will concentrate on points of contact between English and Portuguese understandings of kinship by examining how far the genealogical method was, in fact, an 'enabling device' for this kind of exploration. The result will be to introduce 'kinship' material that does not occur 'naturally' in the English context, such as names; while other material, such as pedigrees, that *does* appear to translate, but does not do so fully.

Portuguese kinship is not uncharted territory

Portuguese kinship is not uncharted territory. Portuguese ethnologists, such as Jorge Dias and Ernesto Veiga de Oliveira, were already interested in the nature of the family as early as the 1950s (Dias 1953, 1961). Willems published an article on Portuguese family structure in the early sixties, based on research carried out in 1954. This account of aristocratic, bourgeois and peasant/proletarian family practices ranges back over the first half of the century and earlier (Willems 1962). Callier-Boisvert first attempted a systematic analysis of the Portuguese kinship system in 1968 (Callier-Boisvert 1968). Her paper covers such themes as 'filiation', spiritual kinship, the geographical distribution of family types, and the transmission of names and property. Cutileiro wrote of kin ties in the Alentejo, particularly emphasising differences between the propertied and the propertyless. While stressing the lack of institutionalised forms of mutual help based on kinship, he nevertheless regarded kinship as a medium for personal identification (Cutileiro [1971] 1977). After the 1974 Revolution, a new generation of foreign-trained Portuguese and foreign anthropologists made this topic their own. A sample of this work can briefly be mentioned. Rowland approached it from the perspective of historical demography and family systems (Rowland 1984).

O'Neill examined the different developmental cycles of land-owners' (*proprietários*), well-off and poor farmers' (*lavradores*) and female day labourers' (*jornaleiras*) domestic groups in Trás-os-Montes (O'Neill 1984; also 1987). Pina-Cabral considered the peasant world-view in the Upper Minho, and has subsequently contrasted this with Oporto bourgeois notions of *casa* and *família* (Pina-Cabral 1986, n.d.) Household composition has also interested historians (Arriscado Nunes 1986). This wave of interest during the 1970s was followed by the first generation of Portuguese-trained anthropology students, which shares in the general enthusiasm for the social sciences noted by do Sousa Santos (*op. cit.*).

Precisely because it is not uncharted anthropological territory, the subject matter can appear almost self-evident, and the ways of approaching it uncontentious. Yet the mechanics of generating information and problematics sometimes obscures assumptions – in the procedures as well as in the 'subject matter' to which they are applied. 'Exploration' in the present discussion refers to examining these assumptions through the friction points when Portuguese anthropology students tried to gain practical insight (in the conventional British sense!) into the kinship universe of an 'Ego', using the genealogical method. This strategy for exploring kinship differs profoundly from the approaches of those already mentioned insofar as it places an exogenous method in the hands of Portuguese anthropologists in the making, and then uses their difficulties to locate their sense of relatedness. Intellectual problems on the part of informants are usually glossed since the anthropologist controls the method. The process of translation remains firmly in his or her hands; informants merely provide the basic material. If, however, some of the methodological tricks are taken out of their bag and placed at the disposal of indigenous anthropologists, then part of the process of making anthropological knowledge is unveiled. I must add that it was never my intention to use the genealogies in this way: the present analysis post-dates the teaching.[1]

Pedigree and genealogy

The genealogical method rests, as Barnes has clearly shown, on a conceptual distinction between pedigree and genealogy (Barnes 1967; Barnard and Good 1984). Although Rivers uses the two terms almost interchangeably in his 1910 article, he also seems to have differentiated between them. The difference has been spelled out by later authors: pedigree refers to indigenous representations of kinship (whether oral or graphic), while genealogy connotes the systematic representation of that knowledge by the anthropologist. The genealogy is a scientific record made in standard format by the anthropologist, with random errors removed, evidence duly verified, and the testimonies of different informants combined and consolidated. The pedigree is the information provided by informants in a culturally specific fashion (Barnard and Good 1984, p. 21).

Explaining this distinction in Portuguese was not as straightforward as it might appear from an English-language textbook. A number of students asked what pedigree 'meant' in English. There seemed to be no Portuguese equivalent. The *Dicionário Escolar* gives *genealogia* and *linhagem* as synonyms, while Augé's *Os Domínios do Parentesco* 'explains': Pedigree (= line), *laço genealógico, linha* (Augé 1978, p. 80). That is, pedigree (= line), 'genealogical tie', 'line'. The problems with translating pedigree are considered at length in the final chapter. Here, I do no more than indicate the conceptual difficulties the term presented for Portuguese students. Although they could see the distinction between an indigenous representation of kinship and a formalised one, the semantic content of the English pedigree was obscure. Most found it necessary to use the italicised English term to refer to it in their essays.

The pedigree/genealogy contrast made room for Rivers's fundamental methodological precept: the transition from the realm of personal names known by informants, to the abstract system of relationships underlying those names which interested him as a scientist. The ways in which people remember, order and represent this information were subordinated to the formal system for extracting it. Although later British versions of the genealogical method place more emphasis on encouraging people to talk around the subject, and make use of their discourse for interpreting the data collected, the principle remains the same: the translation from 'local dialect' to standard, global idiom. The nuances of this standardisation are considered in the following chapter. The focus here is on charting dissonant senses, and using them as paths into the territory which we (as outsiders) call Portuguese kinship.

Genealogia portuguesa

Part of the Portuguese students' problems with the pedigree/genealogy distinction was their own notion of *genealogia*. A. de Mattos provides an excellent insight on popular understanding of genealogy, its associations with heraldry, nobility and so on, in his *Manual da Genealogia Portuguesa*, published in 1943. Lancastre e Tavora recently referred to this work as 'practically obligatory' for anyone wishing to study genealogy. It is, he notes, the only publication of its kind in Portugal, but should be read with some caution since it deals mainly with so-called noble genealogy and is deficient in research techniques (Lancastre e Tavora 1989, p. 58). De Mattos addresses a popular, if perhaps anachronistic, conception of genealogy, kinship and so on, while at the same time attempting to systematise. His hybrid discourse is interesting since, in the process of making prescriptions, his critiques of current practice provide evidence about it. The corporate State was based upon monopolies by certain wealthy families. But the hierarchical social order was much more generalised: privilege, or lack of it, was closely tied to birth and family membership. The de Mattos text therefore gives an idea of what some students found so distasteful about the apparently obsessive interest of British anthropology in kinship – at more or less the same time.

Genealogy had always been considered important and recorded in Portugal, according to de Mattos. He mentions the examples of João Camelo's *Livro Velho de Linhagens*, and the *Nobiliário* of the Conde D. Pedro, which together provide a panorama of the nation's nobility and aristocracy. The genealogy is also the historical basis for cults of the dead and ancestors which have, since time immemorial, inspired the 'most elevated human sentiments'. De Mattos invokes the most diverse concrete examples to substantiate this claim – rather like anthropologists inventorising indigenous representations of genealogical reckoning (e.g. Barnes 1967). De Mattos's examples range from a carving of the Tree of Jesse in the Chapel of St Francis's Convent in Guimarães (showing the an-

141

cestry of the Blessed Virgin Mary), through Spanish depictions of the earthly ancestry of Jesus Christ, to vaguer references to India, Greece and Rome. Barbarian esteem for noble birth, acquired by chivalrous deeds on the battlefield, is seen as a prelude to monarchy.[2] De Mattos stresses noble sentiments, such as those associated with cults of the dead, both to underline the outcome of past interest in genealogy and as a reason for continuing with it. Genealogical lore had become decadent during the eighteenth century and quite unfashionable after the French Revolution. By the fascist period, however, when de Mattos was writing, there was a revival of interest in the subject. The gulf between the 'reliable' genealogy of distant historical times, and this modern renaissance certainly made the contemporary genealogist's task more difficult.

De Mattos defines genealogy as a 'written record of the generations' or, more poetically, as the 'rosary of the generations'. The religiosity of this image of recording and remembering generational time is not random. Moral responsibility was involved in studying the generational evolution of lineages (*linhagens*). On the other hand, the order of the generations starting out from one individual was a 'biological' rather than a 'philosophical' matter. De Mattos distinguishes betweeen genealogies: 'historical' comprised (in descending order) royal, aristocratic, noble and notable; while 'popular' consisted in 'bourgeois' and 'popular'. Despite assertions to the contrary, de Mattos was mainly concerned with 'historical' genealogy. This corroborates Cutileiro's assertion, several decades later, that kin relations had absolutely no significance for agricultural labourers in the Alentejo (1977, p. 177).

De Mattos identifies generational time, which corresponds to a human life span, as the most important temporal unit for genealogical study. This concept of generation has both a biological sense, where it concerns the individual, and a philosophical one, when a plurality is involved. Kinship, *parentesco*, is the nexus, tie or bond of blood, and situation of each member, in relation to other members of the same family (1943, p. 47). The family is conceived as a 'trunk' descending from the ancestor who gave rise to it (*o antepassado que deu origem à família*), for the purposes of genealogical study. Many Portuguese genealogical representations follow the opposite logic: with the apical ancestor at the base of the figure, and the most recent living members at the top.

142

De Mattos is rather critical of a number of these, dismissing both their historical and their aesthetic value. For his purposes kinship should be recorded in lines (*linhas*) and measured in degrees (*graus*): there is a *linha recta* (direct line) and *linhas transversal* or *colateral* – (transversal or collateral lines).

The social value of genealogy

De Mattos specifies the social value of the genealogy as studying the generations across time. These generations constitute that unit of blood traditions which is the family. The family, in its turn, was the 'cell-model' of the State, the *grande família*. There was nothing more socially valuable than preserving and strengthening the family. Genealogy, as the study of the generations, therefore made an important social contribution.

The notion of the family as the State in miniature was one of the most objectionable for the post-1974 generation of Portuguese anthropologists. The revolt of children against their parents at the time of the Revolution (cf. note 16, Chapter 3) is consistent with this identification between fascist State and family. De Mattos saw genealogy as obliging people to think about the past, recollecting the names of those who had served their society and fatherland so loyally (*ibid*, p. 77). These reminders of past glories redound to living descendants. Honouring a name inherited by chance is a source of natural conscious pride, quite different from ridiculous vanity.[3] Understanding the right and proper dignity inherent to that name (*o brio inerente ao nome*) creates a responsible atmosphere. Refusal to recognise all this is tantamount to denial of the personality, and that is contrary to human intelligence (*ibid*, p. 78). Names serve to make people aware of their present responsibilities by reference to past celebrities. The transmittability of an illustrious name, besides relating to family traditions, 'feeds into' the State, contributing to its health and reputation.

It was therefore a matter of regret that not everyone of good family seemed to agree with this. The apparent egalitarianism of certain renowned families smacked of destructive, false modesty. The dead are, after all, part of the family and should never be forgotten. Only those without an honourable memory of their ancestors, or quite unable to remember them, could be forgiven for failing to tell their children about them.

Historically, genealogy supports the political status quo, with

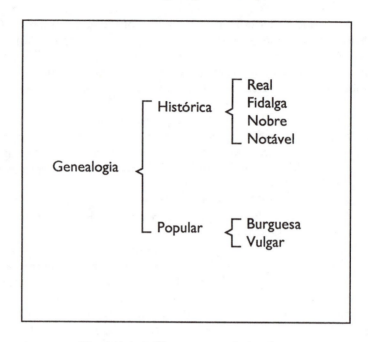

Figure 4.1 Different types of genealogy

the concentration of power and prestige in the hands of certain families. This was accomplished through alliances between those of the same genealogical 'value'. De Mattos's diagram (Figure 4.1) of the different types of genealogy, mentioned earlier, illustrates what he means by genealogical 'value'. De Mattos nevertheless saw the family as threatened by disintegration. He asserts that only the hierarchical discipline of recalling the generations, combined with Christian morality, was capable of providing a measure of cohesion. This is an interesting commentary on the perceived fragility of the family. All kinds of artifices were required to keep it together: genealogy, Christian morality, pride in forebears and so on. The family was no more conceived as a natural unit than the State. This is why the significance of ancestral knowledge was not restricted to the family, but a matter of public interest and social value. De Mattos defines the historical value of genealogy as that which affects the nation; the social value of genealogy is that which concerns intimate family life, and the moral patrimony of the family unit. The connection between the two might be understood through biography, which provides access to a specific epoch.

De Mattos believed that the process of recording genealogical information ought to take place in every Portuguese home (*em todos os lares Portugueses*). It would serve as the family identification papers. The memories bequeathed in this way to children by their grandparents would be a source of legitimate pride for them. Parents should be responsible for this. Given the illiteracy of an overwhelming number of ordinary people (*populares*), the suggestion scarcely seems to apply to them. The author does, however, provide the interesting example of Póvoa and Nazaré fishermen who painted their boats and other fishing tackle, tombstones, and even church doors, with private, family marks which also symbolised differentiation; and showed the personal situation within the genealogical trees from which they originated (*ibid*, p. 80). The accompanying diagram (Figure 4.2) shows that family marks or symbols could be used and inherited.Thus, although popular and bourgeois genealogies were not classified 'historical', de Mattos's own example suggests otherwise. At the end of his book he praises the genealogy as a 'rosary of the generations':

born in the misty depths of time, already diluted in human memory, it gets lost on the foggy horizons of the future. It originates in ignorance and amnesia, and in anxiety about the unknown. It is the only invisible but shining thread capable of mending the worn but rich brocade of our traditions. It is a discipline which orders Man, whether he likes it or not, reducing him, even if he considers himself liberal in outlook, to a simple link in an interminable succession, the immensity of which is beyond comprehension. It is the genealogy which can elevate us, but also plunges us into the depths of thought and emotion! In life, in love, in pain and in death, the genealogy is always the tablet upon which these sentiments are prepared and perfected! The ten Christian commandments include 'Honour thy Father and thy Mother'. Yet this prescription is only complete when our grandparents, the parents of our parents, are also included. And there we are again, enmeshed in the genealogy! Genealogical memories are the footprints of life which remain in the dust of time! (*ibid*, p. 131, my translation).

The genealogy brings 'interminable succession' and 'immensity beyond comprehension' into the orbit of mortal memory. The beads of the rosary which prompt religious devotion are like the names of ancestors which constitute the honour of a family and a

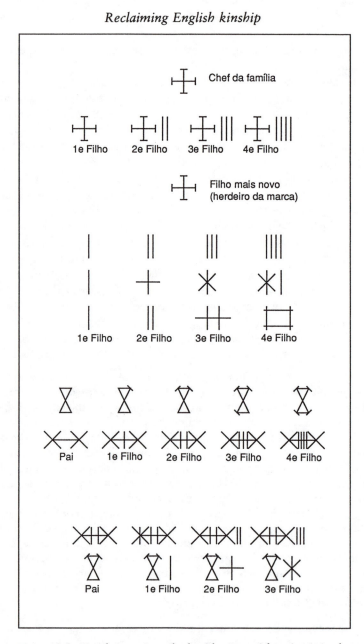

Figure 4.2 Tombstone inscribed with signs. After António dos Santos Graça

nation. Let us turn to the issue of Portuguese names in more detail.

Names. From concrete to abstract?

De Mattos was vexed by his compatriots' inconsistent ways of composing names. His concern to regulate and limit naming practices occupies an entire chapter of his manual, which is devoted to how naming practices might be regulated and restricted, indicating both the value attached to composing a name, and the different emphases expressed by the variety involved.

Names are the concrete means of access to an abstract system of relationships in Rivers's genealogical method. One of the most striking things about the genealogies collected by students was the evident reticence – both on the part of those interviewed and those doing the interviewing – about listing the full name, especially the *sobrenomes* and *apelidos* ('surnames' or family names: *apelido* is the name by which a person is 'called'). Callier-Boisvert notes, 'Portuguese names are rather long, and there is a tendency to abbreviate them in conversation, and to use only that of the mother's father which appears first' (Callier-Boisvert 1968, p. 92, my translation).

Conversation is a matter on which I shall have more to say. But would the length of name seriously inhibit recording it for scholarly purposes? I shall first consider family names, *sobrenome(s)* and/or *apelido(s)*, before going on to look at 'Christian' names.

The order of family names

The inconsistencies of Portuguese name formation confronted de Mattos with difficulties, as a genealogist. Contemporary anthropologists face similar problems when doing historical research. Brettell, for example, describes using parish registers in the Minho:

Any individual generally had two family names. However, there was no universal pattern to which of the four family names a child would be given. Nor was there necessarily any fixed order to the names. Thus, the offspring of José da Silva Rodrigues and Ana Castro Fernandes could have had any one of a dozen or more last names, including simply Rodrigues or Fernandes. Indeed there seems to have been some tendency for daughters in the family to receive their mother's names and sons to receive their father's names. Thus siblings could have different last names. But the fact that none of this is predictable makes record linkage difficult when there is no other clue to identification (as in the death

registers before 1860). Furthermore, individuals were frequently identified by nicknames, particularly nicknames that had to do with geographical sites in the parish, such as João Rodrigues dos Possos or Ana
Victoria de São João. Often this was necessary because there were
several adult men or women with virtually identical names. Women
were very frequently identified by nothing more than their given names,
such as Maria de Jesus of Outeiro (Brettell 1986, p. 276).

Variations in ordering the constituent elements of Portuguese
names are explained by de Mattos as a series of fashions or
practices which came into being at different historical moments,
but which failed to supplant one another entirely. This was why
he found it easier to reconstruct the reasons for the present chaos
than to specify some 'original' norm of name formation. Following
Leite de Vasconcellos, he identifies shortage of names as the reason
for invention and elaboration (Leite de Vasconcellos 1928). In the
beginning, there were simply patronyms. When these became insufficient for the population then first names (often that of a
maternal grandfather) were inserted before the patronym. The
famous example of the first Portuguese king's name illustrates this
principle (Figure 4.3). The shortage of names was also responsible,
according to this theory, for the transformation of some fathers'
names into *apelidos* (surnames) by altering the endings: Rodrigo

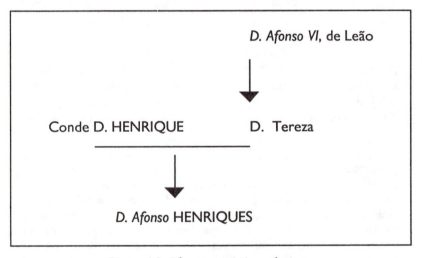

Figure 4.3 The transmission of names

would thus become Rodrigues, Henrique Henriques. Other introductions included the use of terminological designations – *neto* (grandson), *sobrinho* (nephew), *mano* (colloquial form of brother), *primo* (cousin), *[irmão] colaço* (foster brother), *furtado* (=hidden, ?illegitimate), and *parente* (kinsman) – *alcunhas* (nicknames),and placenames, all of which in de Mattos's view assisted in the process of human identification (cf. Lancastre e Tavora 1989, chs. 2 and 3).

In contrast to the dearth of *apelidos* was the need that arose at a given historical moment to maintain and transmit certain surnames (usually the maternal one) for inheritance purposes. The father's surname was then added to the maternal surname. And so a rule, based on custom, began to develop: the first surname (*o primeiro apelido*) to attach to the given ('Christian') name (*o nome próprio*), or to the name immediately following this baptismal name (*sobrenome*), is the paternal surname (*o apelido paterno*) (Mattos 1943, p. 65). This appears to mean:

First name(s) + Paternal surname + Maternal surname

(This is the opposite to Spanish practice.) During the nineteenth century, the order changed again, imitating the French (*sic*) pattern: the father's surname was transported to final position:

First name + Maternal *apelido* + Paternal *apelido*

The legacy of all this was chaos (*uma grande confusão*). The example provided by de Mattos is reminiscent of the difficulties encountered by anthropologists attempting record linkage forty years later.

António de CASTRO m. Maria de AZEVEDO
↓
José

Formerly their son would have been called:

José de Castro, or, José de Castro e Azevedo.

However, the new shortened version of that name, 'ploughing

away at it as if it were couchgrass' (*que está a lavrar como se fôra escalracho*) would be:

José de Azevedo.

Although the family de Castro would continue through José, it would be known as Azevedo. This was an inevitable consequence of using maternal *apelidos*, which could easily be avoided in de Mattos's view. If the name were formed according to French rules, it would be:

José de Azevedo e Castro, or, José de Castro (for short).

The problem with the first solution, according to de Mattos, was that although the name is well organised, the Castro family comes to be known as Azevedo. In the second case, the Castro family continues to be known as Castro, but since the name has lost its place it would not be transmitted to José's sons and grandsons. The male surname would disappear and, with it, the memory of a long sequence of generations, of the highest moral value for that family.

Another consequence of using maternal *apelidos*, especially in the final position, was that their shortened versions produced nominal variation between generations of the same family. Thus José de Campos's grandson might well be called António de Queiroz, while he himself was the grandson of Manuel de Sousa. De Mattos regarded this as an affront, and thought that it would be much better if everyone (i.e. the males) bore the same protective family name, receding back into the mists of time. What is of interest for present purposes is that this quite clearly was not the case.

Other sources of variation included the fact that not all siblings would use the same surname. Traditionally, the eldest son inherited the paternal surname, while the others took *apelidos transversais*: the second son, the maternal surname; the third son, that of a paternal uncle, and so on. De Mattos regarded this practice as appropriate to the past when secondary children created new families, but scarcely appropriate to the present in which it merely added to the havoc. De Mattos briefly mentions variation in women's *apelidos*, especially during the seventeenth, eighteenth and nineteenth centuries, when they frequently took their grand-mother's name, especially if she were also their godmother. This may coincide with the tendency identified by Brettell for girls to take their mother's surname (and boys their father's) in the nine-teenth-century Minho (*op. cit.*). Brettell suggests that this practice not only underscores the importance of mother–daughter ties in north-western Portugal, but also indicates a flexible inheritance system wherein the notion of preservation of patrimony is weak (Brettell 1986, p. 266). De Mattos, the genealogist, was clearly convinced of the need to establish the transmission of the paternal patronym.

De Mattos's argument was that the moral significance of the name was of much greater consequence than casual observation might suggest. There is nothing more nationalistic, he argued, than the constitution of a name, since it reveals tradition, which is the 'very substance of a nation's greatness'. If the procedures for composing a name were in 'chaos', this did not augur well for the moral health of the nation more generally. De Mattos's remedy consisted in trying to achieve a balance between the ethical rights of expression involved in naming, and the obvious (to him) need for restraint and order to avoid decadence. It is, however, the father who seems to dispose of this right. He is assumed to wish to rekindle the name of one of his ancestors in one of his children, alongside the *apelido* by which that child is known (*fazer reviver num filho, juntamente ao apelido de que use, um que fosse de qualquer seu antepassado*) (Mattos 1943, p. 69). The phrase *fazer reviver* translates as 'to make (or cause) to relive'. The notion of causing the name of a dead person to live again in a newly born one, is important for the sense of Portuguese relatedness being explored. The constitution of a name, precisely because of its variation and apparent confusion, seems to be a sensitive register of both knowledge and emotion. De Mattos recognised this in emotional terms, but was confounded by it in practical terms as a genealogist. Diversity thwarted the systematisation of genealogical knowledge, and is a most significant commentary on *genealogia portuguesa*.

The 'solution' proposed by de Mattos clearly expresses his dilemma. He suggests that a person's name ought to be con-stituted, obligatorily, by the given name (*nome próprio*) and the usual family name (*apelido*). This would mean, in effect, the given name (*nome próprio*) followed by the *sobrenome* (*apelido* imme-diately following the given name), followed by the *apelido* (usual family name). The first *apelido* or *apelidos*, and thus presumably the *sobrenome*, ought whenever possible to originate from the paternal line. The last *apelido* or *apelidos* should originate from the maternal line, although its (or their) use should not be obliga-tory. A name 'originating from' the paternal or maternal side need not imply the surname used by father or mother, since they often have badly formed names, but derived from the stock of names belonging to their respective families. A person's name ought to be limited to a maximum of six elements.

He also proposed that double-barrelled names should be re-tained, especially when already in use for three generations, or used by mother's father or father's father on becoming distin-guished. But where such names had only been created at marriage, then the paternal component alone should be transmitted. Finally, if father and son bore the same name (i.e. first name and patro-nym, as in Jorge Branco (father) and Jorge Branco (son)), they ought to be distinguishable from one another. In the nineteenth century this had been done by adding *velho* (the older) and *moço* (the younger) to their respective names. This changed during the nineteenth century to *sénior* and *júnior*; by the 1940s, *filho* was commonly added to the son's name, or the patronym was re-peated, as in Torres e Torres.

If one of the preoccupations of Portuguese naming seems to have been a dearth of names (not enough names to go round), then the plethora of 'solutions' people found provoked a second order of fears concerning disorder and moral decay. A substantial part of the problem, in de Mattos's view, originated with the inclusion of maternal *apelidos* in the name. He would have welcomed a patro-nymic solution such as the English one. The fact is that this was no more than the wishful thinking of a genealogist, caught in a dilemma of his own making. By appealing to 'tradition' embodied in name formation he was invoking the very diversity and incon-sistency he wished to eradicate. The problem was that Portuguese naming practices do not necessarily lend themselves either to the process of making a genealogy, or to historical record linkage (cf. Brettell 1986).

Pina-Cabral, also writing on the Minho, stresses the centrality of naming for the individual's insertion in the group (Pina-Cabral

1986, p. 132). Although the Civil Code stipulates rules for the transmission of surnames, these are of only secondary importance locally, according to this author. Residents of Paço and Couto distinguished between surnames which are written (*apelidos que se escrevem*) and surnames which are not written (*apelidos que não se escrevem*). 'They confront legal surnames with an informal and uncodified way of naming, which they definitely prefer in everyday usage. Indeed neighbours are often unsure of one another's legal surnames' (*ibid*).

This is one example of an anthropological way out of the problem: to establish an opposition between legal/formal/codified/written and informal/uncodified/unwritten/everyday (i.e. accessible specifically to the anthropologist by means of participant observation). However, it sidesteps the problem of meaning inherent in such proliferation, diversity and abbreviation. Naming, in Callier-Boisvert's formal analysis of the kinship system, is neatly translated into terms with which other anthropologists will feel at home, without transmitting any of the sense of chaos and dilemma found, for instance, in de Mattos:

The transmission (*filiation*) of both name and property shows a certain measure of bilateralism (*bilinearité*), whether in terms of the name or of property. The transmission (*filiation*) of the name is patrilineal at all levels, and bilineal from one generation to the next. It is a form of double descent (*filiation*) patrilineal with a bilateral inflection (Callier-Boisvert 1968, p. 93, my translation).

The French term *filiation* is certainly problematic for the English reader with a concept of descent at the back of his or her mind: how can a name descend? Names are 'transmitted' in the English jargon. Similarly, how can property 'descend'? It is inherited, according to the British anthropological idiom. But, as we have seen in the second part of Chapter 3, *filiation* is not 'the same thing' as descent. Caught between the paradoxes of descent and *filiation* it is easy to lose sight of what is actually at stake: the irregularities, complexities and nuances of the Portuguese name.

Cutileiro, writing of the Alentejo, denies that names, in themselves, constitute a means of personal identification. He does, however, assert that the origins of each person are clearly public property, and that part of the consideration they receive is derived from family predecessors. He insists that the use of kin ties as a means of personal identification is linked to economic level and subject to personal manipulations. *Latifundiários* (some unjustly) claim aristocratic ancestors. Workers, on the other hand, were often known by their first names followed by the name of the estate on which they worked until 1900. Where properties were inherited in the maternal line, maternal *apelidos* were better known than paternal ones.

Landless labourers in the Alentejo would thus present a problem for the genealogist. While the great landowners of that region were well aware of the significance of their kinship ties, rural workers were ignorant of them to the point of not knowing how old their brothers and sisters were,[4] in the same way that they did not know their second cousins with any certainty. Beyond these relatives, according to Cutileiro, they were almost totally ignorant of their genealogical tree (Cutileiro 1971, p. 133). But is almost total nescience of their respective genealogical tree the same thing as being unaware of what kinship ties represent? This is one of the central problems with a definition of kinship which is more or less equivalent to genealogical ties: people then appear to 'have', to 'use' or to 'confuse' them in varying degrees.

Teaching British kinship theory involved propagating an intrinsically 'British' method which, although intended to facilitate their studies, presented students with a series of problems. Their assumptions about kinship, learned in the Portuguese context, clashed with those that are built into the anthropological theory and method in question. Their difficulties illuminate those assumptions, and hence what Portuguese 'kinship' means. The stumbling-blocks encountered so far include the English notion of 'pedigree'; associations between *genealogia portuguesa* and the ideology of the *Estado Novo*; and Portuguese family names which do not lend themselves to that movement from concrete to abstract that is so fundamental to the genealogical method. The second part of this chapter pursues further the question of what is in a Portuguese name, and then goes on to consider what this says about the composition of the person.

II. Portuguese constructs: from *nomes* to *conversas*

The Portuguese understanding of the person is conditioned by notions of *simpatia* and *saudade* which, in their turn, affect demeanour in general and *conversa* in particular. The further these *un*familiar ideas about relatedness are pursued, the more difficult it becomes to compress them into a genealogical understanding of kinship.

Nomes próprios

Let us consider for the moment the formation of the *nome próprio* – variously referred to as the 'Christian', 'first' or 'given' name in English – which translates literally as 'own name'. This name was formerly chosen from the Catholic calendar by the godfather (*padrinho*). Otherwise, the father would invariably 'choose' the godfather's name as a way of honouring him, and repaying the enormous favour of 'taking on' this godchild (*O nome do padrinho para o homeagear, pois era a melhor maneira de pagar o alto favor que dele recebia* (De Mattos 1943, p. 97)). There is an echo here of the idea of a father making an ancestral patronym 'relive' in one of his children. The difference is that the *nome próprio* was taken either from the calendar of saints by the godfather, or 'borrowed' from the godfather himself by the father. The godparent might be a member of the family or someone external to it, with the upper hand in an asymmetrical relationship. The practice of the godparent choosing the *nome próprio* had sadly declined by the 1940s, according to de Mattos. Children were increasingly given names conjured out of pure parental fantasy, which would mean nothing at all to them. Sometimes the child would take a parental first name. But since naming the baptismal infant after the godparent was one of the strongest motives for the dedicated affection characteristic of the godparent–godchild tie, de Mattos feared that it would lose all sense.

He need not have worried. Cutileiro, writing on godparenthood in the Alentejo at the beginning of the 1970s, quotes the popular saying: *Quem não tem padrinhos morre mouro*. The literal translation, 'those without godparents die Moorish', has the sense of 'pagan' or 'heathen', but also 'drudge' or 'slave'. A child without godparents does not stand a chance in life. Cutileiro explains that godparents are really responsible for a child's entry into society, even though baptism seems to be about spiritual salvation (Cutileiro 1977, p. 275). Pina-Cabral, writing of the Minho in the eighties, also draws attention to the role of godparents in doing what the parents cannot do:

At the baptism, the child receives its name. Before it became common for parents to attend the baptism, the name of the child was chosen by the godparents who were expected to consult the parents before reaching a final decision. Nowadays the emphasis on the choice of name is on the parents, who nevertheless do feel obliged to consult the godparents. As it happens, it is frequent for a child to receive the name of its grandparents, whether or not they are still alive. This practice is consistent with the fact that it is very common for grandparents to be godparents (Pina-Cabral 1986, p. 118).

The religious tone of Portuguese first names is striking to a non-Catholic outsider. Combinations of Maria (Mary) and José (Joseph) are found in the names of both men and women: Maria José and Maria João (lit. Mary Joseph and Mary John) are popular women's first names. Since Maria is such a common name, women frequently use the masculine part of their names: so that 'João', and 'Zé' are often heard referring to females.[5] However, while 'José Maria' certainly exists as a man's name, this is shortened to 'Zé. Furthermore there is a quite distinctive male name, Mário, ending in 'o' and with the emphasis on the first syllable (as indicated by the accented 'a'), so that the interchangeability of José and Maria is not symmetrical between the sexes. The 'crossing' of first names on a gendered basis nonetheless constitutes an interesting parallel with the 'crossing' of family names. Maria may be combined with a reference to a moment in the Blessed Virgin's life: for example, Maria das Dores (Mary of the Agonies), Maria da Assunção (Maria of the Assumption), Maria da Conceição (Our Lady of the Conception, Portugal's patron saint) or Maria do Ceu (Mary of Heaven). These names may be shortened to 'Dores', 'Ção' or 'Ceu'. Maria can also be combined with other names, such as 'Maria Antónia' or 'Ana Maria'.

One of the genealogies collected by the students for their 'practical' contained some notable exceptions to this religious inspiration for names. It embodied instead a Republican spirit with, for example, Tolstoi and Lénin used as first names. These children were not, however, baptised – only registered. This case is probably the kind of exception that proves the rule.

Portuguese naming involves the selection and orchestration of specific ancestral names from the respective families of the child's mother and father, with some regard for reasonable length. It also involves relationships which may be designated intra- or extra-familial through godparenthood. Godparenthood, in certain parts of the country, involves horizontal ties between parents and god-parents who become *compadres* and *comadres*, as for example in the Alentejo.[6] Where these relationships involve social asymme-tries, those in the higher position may sometimes try to excuse themselves from assuming the relationship (Pina-Cabral 1986, pp. 118–19). There is also a notion of dilution in the Alentejo: if someone takes on too many godchildren, then what can be ex-pected will be spread thin (Cutileiro 1977, p. 278). Illegitimate children, or those whose mothers had been unsuccessful in finding godparents for them might, in the Minho, be given saints as godparents (Pina-Cabral *op. cit.*).

The complexity of Portuguese names reflects ideas about related-ness: they embody ways of specifying or emphasising already existing relations, or creating new ones. These ideas are particu-larly important for an understanding of Portuguese kinship. Kin-ship in itself seems unable to capture this sense of relatedness because it is profoundly embroiled in genealogical notions, which in turn appear to exclude certain portions of the population. This genealogical underpinning seems to be imported as, for example, when Cutileiro assumes (in the language typical of mid-century British social anthropology) that these are formal ties composed of reciprocal and exclusive rights and duties (Cutileiro 1977, p. 169).

Relatedness, on the other hand, is a concept which allows for different nuances. It does not presuppose that genealogical rela-tions are necessarily the most important. It includes other kinds of constructions, such as godparenthood, and the invocation of saints. It places the emphasis on configurations of relations already in existence before a child is born and through which it will experience the world.

If Portuguese names crystallise so much information about diverse relations, then this may be a reason for the reticence noted. A person may, of course, move away from that mesh of associ-ations which his or her name condenses. But even so, the name remains. De Mattos clearly indicated the issues of identity wrapped up in a name. He did so by connecting individual to national identity while making a plea for more consistent naming practices. Although his motivations were those of a thwarted genealogist, his unintended commentary is valuable for all that. *Genealogia portuguesa* only applied to a limited portion of the population, despite the suggestion that everybody ought to record their family tree. Portuguese names were one of the biggest stumbling blocks for the genealogist: that was why he called for regulation. He claimed that the diversity of naming practice resulted from successive changes of fashion in the ordering of the constituent elements of the name. This was why it was difficult to specify the 'original' tradition of Portuguese name formation. And yet it is to this unspecifiable 'tradition'[7] that he appeals to justify the call for standard order.

De Mattos's suggestion that identities are tied up in names may be worth examining from another angle. The next section will look first at naming and State officialdom. Then it will consider the ethos of Portuguese culture as portrayed by Jorge Dias. His analysis provides an image of the person in Portuguese culture. I shall try to see how his idea of the person might be connected with complex names, and what this tells us about a Portuguese sense of relatedness.

Names and identities: the State

The ethnographic analogy which resounded in my mind, while still in Portugal,[8] was the use of names among the Iatmul (and Chambri) peoples of the Middle Sepik River in Papua New Guinea (Bateson 1936; Gewertz 1983; Errington and Gewertz 1987). Bateson describes the totemic system as 'enormously elaborated into a series of personal names – spirits, birds, stars, animals, pots, adzes etc. etc. – of his or her clan – and one individual may have thirty or more names' (Bateson [1936] 1958, p. 127). Apart from a person's thirty or so names, the ancestral names memorised by erudite men might be as many as ten or twenty thousand. These were used in the competitive oratory (debating) which took place in Iatmul men's houses. Nominal proliferation and 'hoarding' opened up enormous possibilities for stealing or otherwise appropriating ancestral names, and hence power.

One of the esoteric systems into which contemporary Portuguese naming feeds is the State and its bureaucracy. It is compulsory to carry an identity card (*bilhete de identidade*) in Portugal; it is a means of identification frequently required in daily life. It lists a person's full name, along with other personal details, and includes a photograph and right forefinger print. Obtaining such a document is an elaborate procedure: forms must be completed, stamps and/or signatures are required from other institutions, such as the Town Hall (*Câmara Municipal*), on official stamped paper (*papel selado*) – which remained in use until 1989. The questions on an application for a first-time identity card (*pedido de bilhete de identidade*) sound uncomfortably close to those of the genealogical method. There are questions about where the person was born: parish, municipality and district (*freguesia, conselho, distrito*); when; where he or she is now resident; and profession. The space for the name (*nome*) anticipates a maximum of 167 letters for the applicant and each of his parents – which leaves enough room for a Iatmul name!

Official identity, symbolised by full name, bureaucratically re-corded, is sometimes distinguished by anthropologists from 'social' identity as if the two had little to do with one another. An over-emphasis on practice, which has been identified by Ortner as typical for certain authors during the 1980s (Ortner 1984), can seem to remove the importance of official practice from daily life. It is tempting indeed to polarise official and practical identities immanent in a Portuguese name: the official, almost abstract, name which appears on the *bilhete de identidade*, and the concrete name or names by which a person is known. But this reckons without the folk knowledge of names, or at least the connections between persons to which they can refer, which is part of daily life. This knowledge is certainly restricted to particular persons, such as those for whom it is impossible to mention someone in a conversation (*conversa*) without immediately 'situating' him or her in relation to half a dozen others, either by names or by way of kinship categories (see below).

The Portuguese name is both abstract and concrete. It is con-crete in the sense that there is a person bearing that name. It is abstract in the official sense, as on identity papers (*bilhete de identidade*). But does it embody abstract or concrete relationships? Do these relationships surface in *conversas* in concrete or abstract ways? Can we say that a relationship is an abstraction when it is simultaneously evoked by two conversing persons? There are un-doubtedly variations between class and age groups regarding knowledge of and interest in the connections expressed in names. However, the very elaboration of the naming system suggests an established concern for these matters. Portuguese relatedness is a matter of almost constant, concrete expression; more abstract, but not entirely so, is the system of names with which it articulates. This was beautifully expressed by one of those interviewed for the genealogy practical, in 1987, who said:

You know, this genealogy thing runs in the blood. We are a document which serves all other documents. My story and that of my family stretches back to childhood and it is composed of endless tales but also enormous silences which surround certain matters. (*Sabe, essa coisa da genealogia anda-nós no sangue. Somos um documento que serve todos os documentos, e a nossa história e da nossa família vem da infância, das longas histórias ou dos enormes silêncios que às vezes se seguiam a certos assuntos.*)

The notion of 'being' a document, expressed by this elderly man in the course of constructing his genealogy and life history, seems to underline the abstraction of official identity echoed in the genealogical method. 'A document serving all other documents' seems to flatten a person into a pile of papers. Yet, in the same breath, come personal and family 'stories' – and silences. The two extremes form part of personal consciousness and reality (cf. Bourdieu 1986, pp. 71–2).

The abstraction of official identity renders the person anonymous: an identifiable individual who is part of a bigger system. But 'persons' (*pessoas*) are also insistently concrete. This was the closest Portuguese analogy I could find for the contrast between the person and the statuses occupied and roles enacted that inheres to British kinship theory. In order to elaborate upon this analogy, it is necessary first to examine the Portuguese notion of the (concrete) person.

The person: the nation as a person

Nunca soubemos separar o sonho da realidade, ao contrário do inglês, que procede friamente, orientado pelo seu sentido prático (Dias 1971, p. 21).

We never knew how to separate dreams from reality, contrary to the English, who proceed coldly, oriented by their commonsense (my translation.)

Certain Portuguese writers have specified the characteristics of Portuguese culture as if it were a person: they personify it. This genre of national character writing is not, of course, restricted to Portugal (see, for example, Huizinga 1935). However the form and content it takes in Portuguese literature are quite distinctive. Some post-1974 social scientists object to this kind of writing on principle, and reject it as 'unscientific'. Yet the fact that the theme continues to engage writers even after 1974 suggests that it may be more difficult to exorcise from the scholarly imagination. Among those who have not rejected this way of depicting the nation are António Saraiva, with his *personalidade cultural portuguesa* (1981, Chapter 3), where he writes of 'contours of the Portuguese nation figure' (*as feições da figura da nação portuguesa*). *Estudos do carácter nacional português*, (Portuguese national character studies), was the title of a series to which Jorge Dias contributed two essays: '*Os elementos fundamentais da cultura portuguesa*' (The fundamental elements of Portuguese culture), and '*O carácter nacional português na presente conjuntura*' (The Portuguese national character under present conditions).

This personification of being Portuguese, as if of a nation in the form of a person, was also present in de Mattos: recognition of the social value of the genealogy (the equivalence between nation or *Patria* and family) was seen as an affirmation of personality (*a personalidade*) and human intelligence (Mattos 1943, p. 78).

Although there is no established scientific method for attempting to characterise a nation's individuality, and plenty of risks, Saraiva still felt it was worthwhile trying to do so (1981, pp. 81ff). Taking a cue from these authors, I shall examine the personal nature of these Portuguese ideas. These aspects will be connected back to the foregoing section on names and what they represent, as well as building forward to the section on *conversas* and relatedness.

National character

One of Jorge Dias's first published attempts at distilling the Portuguese character was for a South African university audience, in English (Dias 1964). Later, in 1971, he reformulated and expanded some of his ideas in Portuguese. 'To describe the traditional national character in a phrase', he writes, 'we can say that the Portuguese is a mixture of dreamer and man of action, or better still, an active dreamer, who has a certain practical and realistic basis' (1964, pp. 100–1). This paragraph is translated almost word for word in the later Portuguese publication. He continues in the same vein: conduct is not rooted in cold will, but feeds upon the imagination and dreams, since the Portuguese is more of an idealist, emotive and imaginative, than a reflective man. He shares with the Spaniard a noble revulsion for stinginess, pure utilitarianism and comfort, but harbours a paradoxical taste for ostentatious affluence and luxury. Unlike the Spaniard, however, he lacks any strong abstract ideal, or pronounced mystical tendencies. The Portuguese is, above all, profoundly human, sensible, loving and generous, without being weak. He dislikes inflicting pain and avoids conflicts, but if his pride is wounded he can become violent and cruel. His religiosity has a similarly peculiar human basis. It lacks the abstract, mystical or tragic nature of the Spanish, although it encompasses a strong belief in miracles and the miraculous.

Dias singles out the Portuguese capacity for adapting to their surroundings without losing their character. He portrays this character as strongly individualist, but with a great sense of human solidarity. Portuguese sobriety contrasts with the exuberant spontaneity of the other Latin peoples. They have little sense of humour, inhibited as they are by their sense of irony, and fear of being made a fool of in front of others who might not share their views. These contradictory factors contribute to that complex mentality and paradoxical temperament which is closely associated with *saudades* (Dias *op. cit.*).

Saudades

There is a parallel between the problem of translating the English notion pedigree in Portuguese, and that of putting Portuguese *saudades* into English, *pace* Michaëlis's rendering as 'the joy of grief' (Michaëlis de Vasconcellos 1922, p. 10). Brettell, writing in the context of emigration with return, translates the term as 'nostalgia or yearning for the homeland, and particularly for the village where one was born and the family one has left behind. *Saudade* embodies a Januslike approach to life – a simultaneous looking to both the past and the future' (Brettell 1986, p. 263). It was still more complicated for Dias: a strange sentiment of anxiety which seems to result from the combination of three distinct mental types: the lyrical dreamer, most closely related to the Celtic temperament; the Germanic Faustian type, and Oriental or fatalist type. Sometimes *saudades* will show their religious or amorously based poetic side, tending either to dissolve into Nature, or in a rather static repetition of images and sentiments. Sometimes it is the permanent preoccupation with distances, with other worlds, and other lives (Dias 1971). This can lead to active involvement in great undertakings. However, in times of decadence and disgrace, *saudade* can degenerate into morbid revelry in past glories, as is so magnificently expressed in the urban song form, *fado* (Costa and Guerreiro 1984).

Saraiva draws attention to the contradictory duplicity of the sentiment of *saudade*: the pain of absence whilst savouring the memory in the present. He characterises it as being in two times and two places simultaneously, which may also denote a refusal to choose: neither recognising that the past is indeed a bygone, nor fully assuming the present. It can work both as an accelerator and a brake on action, if such a mechanical image can convey the qualitative subtlety of the sentiment. It is, anyway, a complex, variegated emotion, bitter-sweet, not particularly propitious to action; and it must have contributed much to the disoriented and paradoxical impression the Portuguese personality has made on many foreigners (Saraiva 1981, p. 88).

Dias argues, and Saraiva seems to concur, that these characteristics furnish some of the enduring elements of Portuguese culture: the expansive and dynamic temperament; permanent restlessness and activity; the idealism of this activity, almost never preconceived on the basis of cold and calculated interest. Michaëlis de Vasconcellos would certainly have disagreed: she argued that *saudades* were a twentieth-century construction (1922, pp. 66-67).

Appearances

The Portuguese are reported to scorn avarice and be indifferent to the comfort so valued by northern and central European peoples (Dias 1971), expressed for example in the concepts of *gemütlichheit* (German), *gezelligheid* (Dutch), and cosiness (English). The Portuguese love of ostentation, pomp and luxury is a quite different, but equally significant theme. Such luxury does not result from comfort, indeed it seems almost the opposite: a mere product of the imagination rather than the senses. Dias reports that Portuguese beds were the most costly in Europe in 1971, and that the streets were filled with expensive cars. Yet there were few centrally heated houses, and still fewer with living rooms. These same houses might have salons and even ballrooms full of Indian and Chinese porcelain. More modest persons, whose houses were completely lacking in the most basic comforts, walked the streets elegantly and luxuriously attired. The least distinguished, uneducated clerk cut more of a figure in the street than a well-heeled, well-connected German or Swiss intellectual. Similarly a servant, who scarcely earned enough to eat, dressed impeccably in the latest fashion.

Such was the importance attached to appearance that a middle-class man would never think of removing his jacket and tie, even in the countryside in summer. (Perhaps especially there, bearing in mind Santos's (1990) remarks about the landed bourgeoisie.) Although these habits were already beginning to change in the early 1970s due, according to Dias, to the combined influences of sport and the cinema, attention to appearance continues. One of Rentes de Carvalho's hints to the Dutch holidaymakers in Portugal is that clothing is a delicate issue (*gevoelig punt*). He warns against making an exhibition of oneself: better keep your shorts for the beach.[9] Women are warned against deep décolletés and clothes which scarcely cover them. These may be mistaken for an insult (*belediging*) or, worse still, an invitation even in cosmopolitan Lisbon. It is easy to imagine that such dress would be quite unacceptable in the provinces. And don't get all togged up in exotic clothes: Carnival is in February, and Portugal is not Hawaii. Local taste is serious, all of which invites a certain modesty (Rentes de Carvalho 1989, p. 10).

Simpatia

There is no contradiction between addiction to appearances and the value attached to *simpatia*, indeed there is a direct connection between the two in the Portuguese ethos of person. The *Dicionário da Lingua Portuguesa* defines *simpatia* as:

an affinity formerly thought to exist between certain bodies; the act of participating in the affective states, the joys and sorrows of others; compassion; agreement or fusion of the emotions; communion; natural attraction of one person for another, or for a thing; inclination; the beginning of love.

outrora, afinidade que se supunha existir entre certos corpos; facto de

164

participar nos estados afectivos dos outros, nos seus desgostos ou alegrias; compaixão; acordo ou fusão dos sentimentos; comunhão; atracção natural de uma pessoa por outra, ou por alguma coisa; inclinação; começo de amor.
(Lat. *sympathia,* do gr. *sympátheia*).

The substantive *simpatia,* then, involves a capacity to share the joys and sorrows of others: a kind of permeability of the self which takes into account the affective condition of those with whom one is in contact. The adjective, *simpático,* concerns that which inspires *simpatia*: it is frequently applied to persons – as a way of saying how nice they are. This *simpatia* is not separate from the person (a role), it is part and parcel of their being. It is, in a sense, an imaginative projection of the personality – to feel what others are feeling. In this respect it resembles Dias's portrayal of the Portuguese concern for appearances: this, he says, is a mere product of the imagination and not of the senses. But even as a product of the imagination, appearance makes a concrete contribution to a person's *simpatia.* This comes across in Rentes de Carvalho's advice to Dutch tourists: you will be better received if you take care to dress in a manner which expresses respect for the host population. Metropolitan and provincial Portuguese alike could be shocked by or gravely misunderstand the careless informality of northern European attire for a sunny southern holiday, even in 1989.

This appeal for respect through dress is echoed in what Rentes de Carvalho says about the language. Portuguese, he says, is a difficult language and it is better to be polite and smiling than to attempt phrase-book parrotology. Polite and smiling (*hoffelijk en glimlach*) is, of course, a mimed expression of *simpatia*; this is the quality which should be transmitted first, even before language, to ensure a good reception (Rentes de Carvalho 1989, p. 14).

The motif of the nation as a person, and the person as a complex combination of *saudades,* concern for appearance, which is in turn connected with *simpatia,* gives a glimpse of the Portuguese ethos. This ethos can only be grasped as a textual construct, produced by or for reference to a reality external to Portugal. The attempt by Portuguese authors to distil the essential ingredients of 'being Portuguese', provides a number of clues. These will be pressed into service to examine the methodological difficulties encountered by Portuguese anthropology students in 'applying' the genealogical method. My suggestion is that the Portuguese notion of person, roughly sketched on the basis of these secondary sources, may have been one of the most significant obstacles – as the section on *conversas* will show.

Before considering the *conversa*, however, a formal aspect of the genealogical method which presented difficulties must be mentioned.

The order of possession

The distinctiveness of a Portuguese sense of abstraction, already discerned in naming, is echoed in the logical ordering of 'possession' by which relationships are expressed. However 'abstract' the British notational system may seem, it is concretely tied to the possessional logic of the English language. The Portuguese translation of Augé's introduction to kinship vocabulary in *Les Domaines de la Parenté*, gives the following account. Firstly there is a list of terms which express relations within the elementary family; these, we are told, are generally English in origin and with universal validity (*Os termos pelos quais se exprimem as relações no interior da família elementar são geralmente de origem inglesa e têm uma aplicação universal*):

M	Mother	(*Mãe*)
F	Father	(*Pai*)
Z (or S)	Sister	(*Irmã*)
B	Brother	(*Irmão*)
D (or d)	Daughter	(*Filha*)
S (or s)	Son	(*Filho*)
W	Wife	(*Esposa*)
H	Husband	(*Marido*)

More distant relatives, the text continues, are designated by composite forms of these abbreviations. For example, the patrilateral cross cousin (female) would be indicated by FZD (father's sister's daughter); while MFBss refers to the mother's father's brother's son's son (*Os parentes mais afastados são designados por compostos destas abreviaturas. Exemplos: a prima cruzada patrilateral será indicada por* FZD (father's sister's daughter, *ou seja, a filha da irmã do pai*); *a sigla MFBSS lê-se* mother's father's brother's son's son, *o que equivale a filho do filho do irmão do pai da mãe* (Augé 1978, p. 62)).

But are the English notational terms universally applicable?

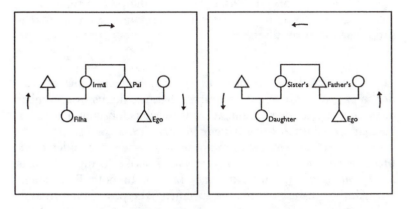

Figure 4.4 Opposing logical directions of the English and Portuguese possesives

Portuguese anthropology students found the reverse order of the English possessive (to that in Portuguese) something of an obstacle. Their own genitive sequence, as in *filha da irmã do pai*, takes the opposite direction to father's sister's daughter (Figure 4.4). Although this may look trivial, it is clear that the logical tendencies are opposite in each case. The Portuguese order starts from the most distant component and works back through a series of interconnecting relationships towards 'Ego'.[10] The English system works from Ego to the most distant element: father's sister's daughter. It could be said that this construction diffuses the relationship: it fades into the distance. The Portuguese (and other Romance languages) construction, on the other hand, draws the connecting elements in towards Ego, focusing rather than diluting them. The Portuguese habit of speaking of 'we' (*nós*), rather than 'I', appears to support this.

The question at this stage is whether students were engaged in a 'scientific' exercise, or in some kind of mental gymnastics. This is not to dismiss the value of mental gymnastics in clarifying the pathways of connectedness. The genealogical method has the virtue of illuminating the Portuguese (or any other) order *vis-à-vis* the English. The point is that the argument cuts both ways. If the

English order reveals the Portuguese, then the Portuguese order must also reveal the English. This proposition is not, of course, contemplated either by the original or subsequent reworkings of the method. My concern here is less with the precise significance those logical directions in either case. The point I wish to emphasise is the two-way flow.

Personalising relationships

The Portuguese language provides some further examples of relationships which are drawn 'inwards'. Saraiva discusses a number of these as Portuguese grammatical inventions, arguing that it is a language with little formal rigour (Saraiva 1981, p. 72).

Portuguese dispenses with the possessive when it is understood. More usual than *Falei com o meu pai* (I spoke to my father), is *Falei com o pai* (I spoke to (the) father). In both French and Spanish this possessive must be specified. The possessive pronoun is omitted in Portuguese where the context or situation make it redundant. Saraiva comments, 'In this case, and probably in others, there is no boundary between the matter under discussion [lit. the extralinguistic situation] and the discourse. Other languages make this distinction for reasons of mere grammatical etiquette, which insists that the discourse should be complete and that there should be a strict separation between the discourse and the matter which is external to the language' (*ibid*, my translation).

Saraiva's illustration is an interesting one. It concerns a kinship category: the relationship between the speaker and his father is so obvious that it is unnecessary to specify it linguistically. (This observation will be important for the next section on *conversas*.)

On the other hand, Saraiva argues that Portuguese accepts constructions which are grammatically redundant and apparently logically incorrect, as a form of compensation. The definite article before the possessive pronoun: *o meu chapeu* (lit. the my hat) is such a case. The possessive 'my' determines and defines the hat, so that the definite article is not required: it ought to be *meu chapeu*. In a similar vein, verb endings and noun number frequently do not agree. It is the sense and not the form which is important: words are influenced by what is thought and not automatically determined by what has just been said. Words are constantly deflected from their grammatical orbit by some factor which is not present in the discourse. Saraiva cites the lucid illustration of Camões who applied the adjective *apressada* (feminine ending, 'hurried') to the masculine noun *o planeta*, since the planet he had in mind was *a Lua* – the Moon (*ibid*, p. 73, my translation). The most notorious hybrid form is the inflected or personal infinitive, for which there is no equivalent in any other Indo-European language. The personal infinitive manages to be both noun and verb at the same time, by adding personal endings to the infinitive form. For example, *saber* – to know, *saberes* (infinitive + *tu* ending) – you + to know. The meaning is difficult to translate: although it is, of course, possible to specify when it is used (Willis [1965] 1971, pp. 337–41). Saraiva compares the personal infinitive to a mermaid: having the upper torso of a woman, and that of a fish below the waist. We can imagine such a creature but it does not really exist. Yet it is a useful combination of absolute and relative: it allows the infinitive, a form of the verb which performs some of the functions of a noun (*uma forma nominal*), to be 'personalised'. Saraiva compares it to taking a short-cut outside traffic regulations in order to arrive (more quickly) at a destination. Anyone who has travelled in a Lisbon taxi attempting to beat the rush-hour traffic will understand what this means!

The personalising aspect is the most interesting point for present purposes. It harps back upon the theme of a specific Portuguese sense of relatedness. In the following section I shall try to explain why I think this sense of relatedness is at odds with the genealogical method, and what this implies for the project of 'exploring Portuguese kinship'.

Conversas

One of the most striking images of life in Portugal is that of the conversation: *a conversa*. It is impressive, to an English eye and ear at least, for the intensity with which participants engage in it. Another feature is its protractedness: those involved are often late for other appointments due to their immersion in a *conversa*. Lastly, the pervasiveness of the *conversa* should be mentioned: it can take place under a range of circumstances: on public transport, in a corridor, in the street, in a café or *em casa* – at home, or rather, in the house.[11]

In producing this image of ubiquitous, interminable and assiduous Portuguese loquacity, there is a mute contrast with sparse elliptical conversational insipidity, functioning somehow as a standard against which a Portuguese *conversa* necessarily gains in vibrancy. The standard is implicitly English, concerning styles, times and places for talking and, the unspoken opposite, which is silence. English silences are undoubtedly different from the Whalsayan silence so effectively employed by Cohen to introduce the British social anthropological tradition and the Other:

> In Whalsay, Shetland, where I have conducted research during the last fourteen years, conversation among men, whether in public or private, is often punctuated by lengthy silences. The men may whistle softly and tunelessly through their teeth, or occasionally sigh 'aye, Man!', but it is essentially silence (Cohen 1990b, p. 203).

But Cohen prefers to contrast Whalsay with Plouhinec volubility and Valloire reticence, leaving English ellipsis to our imaginations. British ethnographers have generally avoided gross national comparisons. Although writing about 'their people' involved a hidden comparison, they have been characteristically reticent about their 'own society' (cf. Chapters 2 and 3). Outside ethnography, however, such contrasts make for particularly effective – sometimes notorious – literature. Rentes de Carvalho, for example, writing of the Netherlands, where he has lived since the 1950s, provides a series of *gestalt* images of Portugal.[12]

This practice ought, in my view, to be elevated to a central methodological and theoretical precept: 'observations' on other ways of doing things are rooted in the observer's position. This means that any observation of mine about the conversing Portuguese only becomes 'objective' if its 'other side' – English reticence – is also incorporated into the analysis.

What strikes the (English) outsider about the *conversa* – apart from its ubiquity, interminableness and intensity – is the frequency with which kin categories appear to frame, punctuate or anchor the matter under discussion, irrespective of what that might be. I am not suggesting that 'kinship is a topic of conversation'. We need to return to Saraiva's comments about the lack of boundary between discourse and extralinguistic topics of conversation, discussed in the previous section. Kinship categories seem to saturate discourse without being external to it: they are not a 'topic', they are part and parcel of what is being said. '*A mãe* [mother – 'my' is understood] said this', '*o tio* [uncle] did that'; '*a cunhada*' [sister-in-law], 'o sogro' [father-in-law] ... form constant reference points in a conversa. They are what might (in English) be termed the hum of conversation: scarcely perceptible, and yet an essential part of the fabric of converse.

Kinship categories as conversational parameters represent an important insight on the Portuguese sense of relatedness. The students' difficulties with the genealogical method certainly involved a clash between a distinctive form of conversing, and an imported methodology for 'collecting kinship data'. But the premises of talking and the premises of collecting information in a methodical way are what are really at issue. These premises engender two disparate images of relatedness: one Portuguese and the other English. Let us first examine the explicit Portuguese image.

The formality of the Portuguese social milieu, which often strikes visitors from non-Latin countries, involves a lot of activity accompanied by standard verbal formulae (cf. Kröll 1984, pp. 29ff). Kissing (beijinhos), hugging (abraços), and hand-shaking (apertos de mão) are an integral part of greeting, both formal and informal, so that the verbal phrases already mentioned (such as 'Como está(s)?') would be bald and impolite without the non-verbal engagement which goes with them. Similarly, it is considered simply good manners (bem educado) routinely to ask for permission before performing quite ordinary movements. 'Dá licença?' or 'Com (sua) licença', when entering or leaving a room, before ending a telephone conversation, getting up from or sitting down in a chair, is the stock accompanying phrase. This phrase often elicits the response, 'Faz favor!' ('if you please').

This stream of courtesies (delicadeza), verbal and non-verbal, shows the person making constant reference to an other or others in the course of his or her actions. These verbal and non-verbal forms of consideration for others deserve to be seen in relation to saudades. For this notion includes remorse at having failed to esteem, enjoy and give effusive recognition to other people's company (cf. Michaëlis de Vasconcellos 1922, p. 76). It is not simply a matter of oiling and smoothing interactions between people. There is a more extensive sense of relatedness, which the attention given to initiating and concluding conversas embodies and expresses. Rentes de Carvalho has written of the saudade of saudade: feeling in the present the saudade that should only be felt in the

171

future (Rentes de Carvalho [1972] 1989, pp. 187–8).

It is important to stress that this is not 'formal' or 'official' behaviour. It is a way of showing esteem by drawing the other into the magnetic field of the self: constructing a verbal bridge between the performative self and the other. There is no separation, such as the English might make, between the person and these conventions. The Portuguese person is that which he or she visibly expresses or withholds. There does not seem to be an essential 'self' which retires 'home' to recover from all that role-playing in the world 'outside'. These contrasting pairs of notions, self/role(s), home/outside world, private/public do not work (if they work at all) in identical ways for English and Portuguese. Let me try to explain why they do not work in the same way by returning to the point about English reticence or silence.

The verbal expressions in Portuguese, *calar a caixa* meaning *deixar de falar*, to stop talking (*lit.* 'shut the box'), and *fazer caixinha* (to keep a secret), are interesting in this connection. *Caixinha* is the diminutive of *caixa*, which means receptacle or box for transporting something – in this case, the voice, or speech. If one doesn't talk, one is *calado*: silent, discrete, quiet, exaggerated. *Calado* comes from the verb *calar* – to be silent, to hide, to keep quiet. Speaking is normal; silence is suspect, or it is directed to specific ends. *Simpatia* and *carinho*, the positive values, are expressed verbally and non-verbally, such that the persons involved are drawn into the affective states of the others, whether these be happy or sad. *Carinho* is the expression or demonstration of *simpatia*: the opposite is *chato*: that which is flat, smooth, even, indistinguishable (*que não tem relevo*; *liso, plano, baixo, rasteiro*).

The attention to verbal and non-verbal details such as these is likely to be connected with the importance attached to personal appearance, as discussed by Jorge Dias (1971). Care of the body and its clothing is not dismissed as superficial and unimportant to the essential person, it is an expression of being a person. This daily routine is interspersed by visits to the hairdresser, where manicure, pedicure and depilation are also available, for what seems to be large numbers of the population. That care of the self can sometimes be extended to others, as with the removal of a stray hair from the shoulder of a fellow conversant, which is regarded as an expression of *carinho* or *mimo* (attention) rather than an impertinent invasion of personal space. The English analyst might be inclined to interpret as 'social control' this kind of attention to every detail of personal appearance, bodily movements and courtesies in face-to-face interaction. But for those enacting these forms, their absence would affront and offend.

This can be seen outside the circle of *simpatia* and *carinho* as, for example, sometimes happens in urban streets. 'The street is a jungle' (*a rua é uma selva*), one colleague remarked to me. It was the absence of those pleasantries demarcating civilised life to which he referred. Male innuendo towards women in the street has been a particularly irritating facet of metropolitan life in Portugal as recently as the 1980s. There are simply places where a woman should not 'be' or 'go' unaccompanied (cf. Willems 1962). While such undesired attention is usually only verbal, this is a big 'only' since it reflects the negative side of the value attached to utterance, where it is combined with an ethic of machismo.

The problem of names led, inexorably, to the nature of the person; the nature of the person leads to the nature of relatedness. It is already possible to appreciate some of the students' difficulties with the British genealogical method. Let us briefly recapitulate them. Firstly, the initial distinction between pedigree and genealogy connotes alien concepts of the abstract and the concrete. Collecting and listing names was a concrete means to an abstract end in Rivers's view of relationships, and that which carried over into much of the theorising which followed until the 1950s or so. The full name is both an abstraction but also a source of potential knowledge and a basis for conversation, to many Portuguese. It is possible to extrapolate the person from the name, and its referent. The abstract person-as-document serves as a source for the many official papers generated during a lifetime, linking them with their kin. 'Blood' assumes a curiously bureaucratic colouring from this perspective. This abstraction is opposed to the tender, caring and attentive person engaging in *conversas* and other typically human interchange. Person, in this sense, pays great attention to details of appearance, to gesture, and to referencing others, who may be either present (in which case they will receive *carinhos*, be asked for leave (*licença*) and the like); or absent, as signalled by the parameters of kinship or some other matrix of relatedness: *o meu vizinho* (my neighbour) or *o meu colega* (my colleague) are used in the same way.

The relatedness which pervades speech refers, therefore, not to

173

an abstract system of relationships but to a state of knowledge. Saraiva discusses the third person singular form, *o senhor* or *a senhora*, which is the oblique way of getting around the problem of how to address someone who falls outside the range of the speaker's intimacy (Saraiva 1981, p. 90). But even this way of constructing a third person, as it were, where the person one is addressing is not known, can be modified extensively. *Senhora doutora*, for example, is a current way of addressing a female academic. Names can also be used to soften the impersonality of this form: *a Mary*, for example, both keeps the distance judged necessary while at the same time personalising the indirectness. Knowing in itself can already constitute an expression of *carinho* and *simpatia*. The expression, '*Sabe*' (*lit.* 'You know'), is constantly used in conversation; so too are *olhe* (look) and *ouve* (listen) – all verbal cues for catching someone's attention. '*Sabes uma coisa?*' ('Do you know what?') That was how the man who made the metaphor about the genealogy being a document serving all other documents began. He said, '*Sabe, essa coisa da genealogia...*' Knowing the connection between yourself and other people, or simply between a person (or persons) under discussion and others, who may be people one has never met: knowing such details as the kind of car they drive, their profession and number of children, all this bespeaks an intense interest in others. Some find this a salutary and healthy concern. It can, of course, degenerate into gossip (*bisbilhotice*) or slander (*má-língua*); but there is no necessary implication, at least as long as there is trust (*confiança*) between the parties.

Some might call this small-minded. Certain students felt, perhaps understandably, awkward that such trivial (to them) details should apparently occupy so much of people's mental space, time and energy. Some clearly felt that kinship, as it was identified with the old regime, ought to be replaced by more equitable kinds of relationships, both as a result of the 1974 Revolution and, more generally, as part of social evolution. A number of those who were interviewed by the students in the course of the genealogical practical were clearly trying to shake off the yoke of this specific sense of relatedness. Others acknowledged that despite predictions about individuals' life-chances in modern societies, the privileges and handicaps inherent in being born into this or that particular family continue to exercise a perplexing degree of influence.

Beyond the ideological positions involved, some were critical of the genealogical project on theoretical grounds. How could one, they asked, possibly generalise about 'Portuguese kinship' or 'kinship in our societies' on the basis of a single genealogy? (This was not, of course, the intention: the aim had been both to give practical insight into British kinship thinking and provide a tool with which to explore Portuguese kinship.) Apart from the problem of quantification, there was also scepticism about the terms in which the analysis was being made. How could one move from 'individual' to 'system' in this way? How could one avoid confusing 'subjective' and 'objective' structural parameters? They felt sociologically offended by the exercise.[13] The kind of subjectivity involved may also have been culturally offensive. The isolable individual from whom it is possible to extract information out-of-context, or rather out-of-*conversa*, goes against the grain of Portuguese relatedness. Favret-Saada makes the point that you cannot talk about witchcraft in Normandy without practising or countering it (Favret-Saada 1977). Segalen observed that talking family swiftly turned into power relations in her Brittany research (Segalen 1985). Kinship is no more neutral as a topic of conversation than witchcraft. In what does the passage from the *conversa* to the genealogy consist?

Some students successfully circumvented the problem by using genealogical information as the means of orienting the reader through the relations under discussion. One successful example of this approach was the analysis of four representations of a famous ancestor by generationally and otherwise distinct members of a bourgeois metropolitan family. This ancestor was a poet who died young and without issue. The significance of relationships claimed or repudiated was undiminished by the fact that they were not by direct descent. The facility with which kinship was handled in this instance was closely connected with the form chosen by the student concerned: the ancestor was used as a talking point, eliciting distinctive positions from the four persons interviewed. Furthermore, the 'author' of the genealogy was also a member of the family concerned; his informants were father, aunt, sister and cousin to him. The genealogy he constructed was more concerned with pathways of significance within a family, than with tracing the 'extent' of genealogical knowledge and the like.

Relationship or connection of some kind between the inter-

175

viewer and the interviewed – whether in terms of what we call 'kinship', various kinds of domestic relationship (housekeeper, maid), friendship, or professional association – emerged as having enormous importance for the successful completion of a genealogy. This corroborates the intimate connection between knowledge about relatedness embodied in a *conversa*, and the conventions of a *conversa*. The two appear to be difficult to sunder. A relationship of mutual trust (*confiança*) is a *sine qua non* for such purposes. Cambridge students 'practised' field techniques, including the compilation of genealogies, on Elmdon residents in the 1960s.[14] Marilyn Strathern recalls how Elmdon people suggested they might 'look in the library' for the information they were seeking: 'The barrier of privacy demarcates the area over which a person has control precisely because, like anything else he produces, information may be alienated – that is, no longer measured in reference to the producer but commoditised' (Strathern 1984, p. 181). The unease experienced by Lisbon students about collecting a genealogy in the mid-1980s had less to do with the invasion of privacy, than with the total lack of sense of 'collecting' such 'information'. '*Não tem a ver comigo*' (*lit.* 'it has nothing to see [= 'do' in English] with me'; the use of the verb *ver* gives a visual nuance to the connectedness being invoked here. This visual aspect is consistent with the nature of the *conversa*: the expression of concern for other people, and in the same spirit, concern for one's own appearance is set against the pain of unbearable absence. The project of collecting as 'information' an integral part of *conversa* – relatedness – using an imported method was senseless. The genealogical method is neither wholly 'official', in the spirit of the *bilhete de identidade*, although it seems concerned with the same sort of area of 'information'. Nor is it simply a series of *conversas*: the process of recording as information what is built into speech as knowledge, subverts any pretensions to *confiança*. It is a hybrid.

What can appear as the 'pragmatic' solution of taking mothers, grandmothers, sisters, colleagues and maids as informants, goes to the heart of the sense of relatedness I am trying to capture: the people between whom speech is appropriate or with whom the conditions exist for it to become so.

In conclusion

The genealogical method used by Portuguese anthropology students mostly on their fellow countrymen and –women had the virtue of demonstrating that what might be glossed as 'context' in British terms, or 'just talk', is in fact central to the Portuguese sense of kinship. Kinship is not simply knowledge of those to whom one 'is related': it pervades conversation, relating the conversants through shared categories whether or not they happen to 'be kin'.

This chapter has traced this sense of kinship in the *simpatia* of the *conversa*, where persons participating in one another's joys and sorrows frequently do so by almost non-stop invocation of categories of relationship. Some people find it important to locate each person mentioned by connecting him or her to others in various ways. This apparently positional sense of self (cf. Errington and Gewertz 1987) is belied by the fact that the speaker expresses 'personality' when speaking. Interest in and knowledge about others is a way of demonstrating *simpatia*, although of course there is always the risk of degenerating into *bisbilhotice* or *má-língua*. This risk, however, only serves to accentuate the field of values involved, like *saudades* felt in advance of absence (cf. Rentes de Carvalho *op. cit.*). Most sinister are those who shut up, say nothing, give nothing away. These are the real marginals, the kinless. But this is not the same as the 'subjective', achieving self evoked by Errington and Gewertz. Dias's portrayal of the Portuguese national character, although verging at times on caricature, provides many insights into what is more a notion of being than a notion of self (*per se*).

What has all this got to do with kinship as an analytical category? If one starts from the assumption that information ('raw data') can be formally collected and transcribed into comparable 'kinship systems', then it is of course possible to proceed as Callier-Boisvert did, to certain observations concerning the 'Portuguese kinship system'. But if the very terms by and in which the material is collected run counter to the form taken by the knowledge in question, then the process of translation becomes much more problematic. The aesthetics of interrelationship as a form of Portuguese knowledge are concerned not with cold facts of connection, whether biologically based, socially reinterpreted or idiomatically expressed. They are instead concerned with states of being which

177

more or less correspond to discursive or expressive states. It is difficult to conceive of Portuguese kinship as an abstract entity, because it is already partially abstract at the level of naming which, in the original terms of the British method, was conceived as 'concrete'. The concreteness of expression, verbal and non-verbal, ties up with a notion of the person as an essentially speaking person, necessarily related to others. The silent person, *calado, maldisposto* or *chato* – secretive, off-colour or simply unpleasant – already verges on the impersonal. Interrelationship is not the problem. That is taken for granted, although it can certainly be subverted in any number of ways. The main problems arise when there is no form of interrelationship, interaction or communication.

Portuguese converse (*conversa*), and of course the persons (*as pessoas*) who engage in it, has been the medium for exploring both the sense and the expression of relatedness, which is called 'kinship' in English. This analysis relies upon a contrast between Portuguese and English.[15] The students' use of the genealogical method served as a way of structuring this exploration. It does, however, carry with it a further set of implications within the two-way perspective which is being built. The next chapter considers the collision points from the 'other side'. I reiterate the point that the genealogical method has been made to stand for this other side of Portuguese kinship: English kinship.

The perspective which has been pieced together here raises novel questions. Firstly, by putting the method at the disposal of second-year anthropology students, and then by taking the problems and inconsistencies they expressed seriously. The Portuguese sense of relatedness flies in the face of that which underpins the genealogical method: the passage from concrete names to abstract relationships. The very terms of the method are at odds with the kind of knowledge embodied in the *conversa*. The contents of names, and the idea of relatedness, the order of possession, the nature of persons – all lead in opposite directions from the assumptions which inform the method itself, and much of the anthropology which came to rely upon it implicitly as a 'tool of the trade'. The point is not whether a genealogy can be compiled in Portugal – or anywhere else for that matter. The overwhelming majority of the students completed the task they had been set. It is rather the process of making knowledge, rather than what passes for knowledge in its translated form, which is at stake here. Collecting

genealogies with the aim of constructing or reproducing a model
of 'Portuguese kinship' runs counter to the Portuguese sense of
that area of knowledge and discourse. By reformulating 'kinship'
as 'relatedness', one can examine how this is built into the *conversa*. The approach only 'works', however, if one or more sets of
implicit contrasts are made explicit. These contrasts are not
achieved by 'comparison' (placing different exhibits side by side),
but by tendering significant particles of one's own approach for
scrutiny. Our own implicit meanings may, paradoxically, only be
grasped in the course of being actively confounded. This finding
is not, of course, limited to the Portuguese material. It must,
however, provide serious grounds for reconsidering the 'knowledge' which is conventionally charted by the genealogical method
of British anthropological inquiry, and the territory which lies on
the other side of the looking-glass.

Notes

1 The similarities between extraneous material artefacts and extraneous textual ones only struck me later, when documenting a Melanesian collection (Bouquet and Freitas Branco 1988).

2 See L. Krus (1985) on the creative use of mythological genealogy by medieval knights, especially younger disinherited sons, who sought renown through chivalry. Alliance with the goat-footed woman, *a dama pé de cabra*, was one of the motifs of legends concerning the ennoblement of secondary heirs. See also T. Braga, *Novos Contos Portugueses* ([1914–15] 1987).

3 Among the vanities about which he is particularly scathing is the use of name particles by those with pretensions to nobility. *De*, for example, is correctly applied in names of geographical origin; exactly the same applies to *do*, *dos*, *da* and *das*. The linking particle, *e* (and) is correctly used to emphasise the connection between surnames: for example, António de Almeida Machado Loureiro e Noranha. In this case, one of the surnames is geographical in origin, while the other symbolises a particular genealogical branch. The Portuguese *de*, then, is unlike the French *de*, the Dutch *van* or the German *von* – all of which are indices of nobility. (Cf. Lancastre e Tavora 1989, p. 8.)

4 There is a discrepancy between this passage in the Portuguese version of 1977, and the English version of 1971. In English the labourers are 'often ignorant of the ages of their fathers' or mothers' siblings', in Portuguese of their (own) brothers' and sisters' ages (*ignoram muitas vezes as idades dos irmãos e irmãs*, 1977, p. 176).

5 Saraiva emphasises the prevalence of the Cult of the Virgin in Portugal, reflected in the name Maria. He argues that Maria even becomes a kind of designative particle of the female sex, allowing any name to be feminised: for example, Maria João (instead of Joana) or Maria Manuel (instead of Manuela). The Virgin acts as an intermediary, facilitating contact with the paternal God. She is the divinity effectively in charge. It would not take much for the God of Portugal to be a woman, which would effectively reduce conflicts and oppositions between the sacred and the profane (Saraiva 1981, p. 92).

6 This relationship can exist officially while, however, having little social significance (cf. O'Neill 1984, p. 361, for Trás-os-Montes).

7 This was a refraction of the *Estado Novo* in a series of areas; cf. Vale de Almeida 1991b.

8 Apart from beginning work on the Portuguese collection from former German New Guinea in the autumn of 1986, I also taught an Option course on New Guinea ethnography at I.S.C.T.E. during the

same academic year. The material in which one is immersed does, of course, influence what one sees about one! (I only became aware of the extensive French literature on naming after leaving Portugal.) It may seem strange to some that I do not refer to such 'Mediterranean' literature on names and naming as Vernier's on Greece (in Medick and Sabean 1984). Part of Vernier's discussion concerns the sacred duty of *anastassi* – bringing ancestors back to life – by systematically using the ancestral Christian name of the male and female lines (Vernier 1984, p. 40). The analysis is, however, mainly concerned with 'fulfilling one's obligations, honouring them [i.e. a father or a mother] and honouring oneself, reproducing the symbolic capital of the allied lines and hence one's own, in short, reproducing the conditions of one's own value' (*ibid*, p. 43). Furthermore, it concerns Christian names only, and not family names. But more important still, my analysis does not belong to the 'Mediterranean studies' genre. The emphasis on approach here makes it, perhaps, especially fitting that Bateson's pioneering work should be discussed.

9 The beach behaviour and dress of 'English' (*Ingleses*) was scathingly commented on in 1990 Portugal by the Portuguese. Every detail is noted: tan, clothes, posture, hair, gait (O'Neill, pers. comm.).

10 'Ego' does not, of course, have to be the speaker. It is a notional Ego relative to whom the relationship specified has more distant or closer components.

11 The literal translation of *em casa* is 'in the house' and is, I think, preferable to 'at home', since *casa* lacks the connotations of home (cf. Johnson 1986). A house is not a home; nor could 'home' conceivably be extended to the café in the way that *casa* is in terms of sociability. One example will illustrate this point. It is common for hundreds or even thousands of people to have their breakfast (*tomar o pequeno almoço*) in a nearby café, often standing at the *balcão* (the counter) to sip their *bica* (an espresso coffee) and eat a small sponge cake (*um bolo*), sandwich (*uma sande*) or croissant. Nothing is considered more normal or mundane than going for a coffee in the local café after lunch or dinner at home. Many people eat lunch and even dinner in one of the thousands of restaurants found everywhere. Hence, if a large part of 'home' revolves around commensality in the home, it is easy to see why *casa* may be devoid of this homeliness. Different modes of sociability are at issue (cf. Pradhan 1990).

12 Rentes de Carvalho enjoys considerable popularity among the Dutch, perhaps because of the novelty of a Portuguese writing about the Netherlands in Dutch, perhaps due to his wry portrayal of them. Take this description of the Dutch family:

In the restricted family group (*gezin*), selfishness seems to be the most apparent force at work. This is expressed not only in rough manners, but also in a kind of short-circuiting in the communication between family members, in a lack of tenderness and affection, as if these were feelings for which one ought to be ashamed. Combined with this is a tolerance which might at first sight be taken as respect for another's freedom, but could as well be interpreted as supreme indifference between the parents, between parents and children, and *vice versa* (Rentes de Carvalho [1972] 1989, p. 30, my translation).

For Rentes de Carvalho the norms are clear – in a series of unexpressed oppositions:

selfishness	concern for others
rough manners	good manners
short-circuited communication	communication
lack of tenderness and affection	tenderness and affection
ashamed of feelings	feelings normal
laisser-aller	concern for others

The first column, which explicitly summarises the negative characteristics of the Dutch, contrasts with the second, where implicit, positively valued (Portuguese) characteristics are deduced.

Similarly, the Dutch writer, Gerrit Komrij, who lives in a Portuguese village in Trás-os-Montes, uses it as a setting for his novel *Over de Bergen*. The Portuguese hero of the novel is unmistakably 'Dutch', however, in his obsession with the house and insentience to Portuguese sensibilities, especially concerning 'relatedness'. His portrait of a Portuguese birthday meal is an excellent example of Dutch squeamishness about commensality *'thuis* (at home), when this includes those outside the *gezin* or, on ceremonial occasions perhaps, the *familie* (Komrij 1990). *Warm eten* (hot meals) are too intimate to be shared; *gezelligheid* with non-family, and sometimes even family, should restrict itself to coffee and sweetmeats or cocktails and *hors d'œuvres* (cf. Pradhan 1990).

13 Portuguese sociologists, as distinct from anthropologists, have only rather recently become interested in kinship. See, for example, O'Neill's otherwise favourable review of Madureiro Pinto's work on Penafiel (O'Neill 1988).

14 See Audrey Richards's 'Foreword' to Marilyn Strathern's *Kinship at the Core*. She writes, 'I have lived in a number of small African villages, making quite a close study of one, and I had often wondered whether it would be possible to do the same sort of work in an English village of roughly the same size ... In 1962 I had the opportunity to do

182

this, when Edmund Leach and I, both members of the Department of Social Anthropology at Cambridge University, decided to give some of our students a little experience in interviewing and the handling of notes before they started out to do fieldwork themselves. We felt that the collection of genealogies and family histories would be a practical way of giving them this opportunity' (Richards 1981, p. xi).

15 Although this technique, as the Rentes de Carvalho (Portuguese–Dutch contrast) example illustrates, is not exclusive to this combination.

CHAPTER FIVE

DISCLOSING ENGLISH KINSHIP

Quando há povos que registam a genealogia de cavalos e cães, * *como um garante, à margem da biologia, da selecção das suas raças APU-RADAS, é muito, ou, sequer, de estranhar, que do mesmo modo se proceda no que respeita com a espécie humana?*
**O conhecido pedigree (Mattos 1943).*

When there are peoples who record the genealogies of horses and dogs,* as a guarantee alongside biology, of the selection of their purified races, is it any wonder that they apply the same procedure to human beings?
*The known *pedigree*.

The need for reflection on an anthropological commonplace

It is still an anthropological commonplace that 'references to kinship networks are employed as an orientation and identification device by non-Western peoples everywhere', and since the procedure requires nothing more than the recognition of the biological facts of birth and death and the social facts of paternity and maternity, '[o]ne really can collect a genealogy from any people ... and expand that genealogy as far as the informant's memory will carry him' (Schneider 1968, pp. 13–14). Hence the universality of the kin-based network as a context for individual identification and placement is taken for granted. Claims made for the versatility of the method are premised on this postulate (Hackenberg 1973, p. 297). Leaving aside the fact that Schneider has completely revolutionised his thinking on kinship (Schneider 1984), the assumption is generally intact. Barnard and Good's assertion that every ethnographer, whether kinship specialist or not, is expected to come home from the field with a description of 'the kinship

185

system', bears this out for British social anthropology (Barnard and Good 1984, p. 1).

Collecting genealogies is considered indispensable to making an adequate description of the kinship system. Yet kinship is almost invariably regarded as 'more important in the society which the anthropologist studies, than the one from which he or she originates' (*ibid*, p. 2). Urban, industrial, Western societies are portrayed as having other kinds of institutions to regulate their economic and political affairs, so that 'kinship tends ... to be much less evident in the public domain: kinship relationships become above all domestic relationships' (*ibid*, p. 34). Questions about a person's relatives are regarded with suspicion, unless they are already well known to the respondent. Barnard and Good nonetheless still urge anthropologists to collect genealogies, even under these inauspicious circumstances, and although their dimensions may be fairly restricted. 'As usual genealogical knowledge may be considerable if advantages are to be gained thereby, or interests safe-guarded' (*ibid*).

The methodological imperative (to collect genealogies) despite the theoretical expectation that the kin relationships they represent are less important in 'own' society than in others, is one of the paradoxical positions already noted in Firth and his colleagues' work on middle-class kinship in north London (cf. Chapter 3). Firth and his colleagues began systematically to obtain genealogies for their study in north London 'as soon as possible and, if it could be managed, before kin were discussed at all' (Firth *et al.* 1970 p. 33). Why this insistence on the collection of genealogies? The issues discussed in previous chapters suggest that far from being a standard procedure, the genealogical method is a problematic part of the machinery for generating a particular kind of anthropological knowledge.

Although crucial to British studies of kinship, few anthropologists have reflected on *how* the genealogical method constructed knowledge and how this in turn was connected with their 'own' indigenous ideas about kinship.[1] Perhaps such 'introspection' went against the British 'grain' in former times, which was why it took a French anthropologist to pose the relevant question (Bourdieu [1972] 1977, p. 207; cf. Chapter 2).

Portuguese students' queries showed up assumptions hidden in the method. The notions of 'pedigree', 'descent', 'the concrete vs.

the abstract', the genealogical 'Ego', personalising the animal world, and the 'Englishness' of the method, were all called into question in Portuguese. Genealogical diagrams were an endless source of mirth, irreverently referred to as *bonecos* (dollies) – a revealing Portuguese commentary on the stick-like figures and their supposed 'relationships'. While these concepts and figures may have background status for the English-speaking anthropologist, such 'background' is a corpus of implicit theory for non-English speakers. What kind of people and mode of thinking produced this theory?

The present chapter considers how one might proceed with 'disclosing' the implicit theory that I have argued is lodged in the Riversian genealogical method. First, the overlap between pedigree and genealogy is examined, with the suggestion that (folk) connotations which anthropologists and genealogists prefer to shelve ought, in fact, to constitute points of departure for exploration. Two aspects of pedigree are considered particularly important: first, the emphasis on the *written* (and graphic) record, as the guarantee alongside biology of control over procreation; second, the folk analogy between human and animal breeding contained in pedigree helped perhaps to shape the 'descent bias' of the genealogical method. How could one document the osmosis between folk and scientific ideas concerning animal and human relationships? I propose to take a collection of children's classics (Beatrix Potter's *Peter Rabbit* stories) as a kind of miniature ethnography for the early-twentieth-century English middle-class literary 'voice' in which the anthropological ideas we have been examining were expressed.

Theoretical ideas in the social sciences are usually explained in terms of other sets of theoretical ideas. The linkage between popular and scientific theories is less frequently attempted, although Strathern and Wolfram have set important precedents for the study of class and the law respectively, in relation to English kinship (Strathern 1981, 1982a, 1982b, 1984; Wolfram 1987). My own contribution will be to examine how connotations of *pedigree* embedded in the genealogical method might be connected with English ideas about animality, personhood and distinction. My suggestion is that we can construct an ethnography of early-twentieth-century middle-class English kinship by establishing relationships between what are usually seen as two quite unconnected 'worlds'.

The 'trace' of pedigree in genealogy

The handful of anthropologists who *have* studied English kinship empirically have been keen to establish the difference between 'scientific' and popular understandings of genealogy. Anthropologists working 'abroad'[2] would consult genealogical experts as a matter of course. It is therefore interesting that anthropologists who have worked 'at home' have little to say about professional genealogists, or seem mainly concerned to emphasise the difference in anthropological uses of the instrument. Firth and his colleagues mention that a few of their middle-class English informants were expecting a 'genealogist's field day' (Firth *et al.* 1970, p. 50). As if to set the record straight, they underline their divergences with professional genealogists by denying interest in 'family origins as such', playing down any suggestion of concern with the descendants of famous persons, and by emphasising the importance of 'imaginary' as against 'factual' ties (*ibid*, p. 33).

The distinction between 'fact' and 'recognition', with anthropologists interested in the latter, blurs the specificity of beliefs about the factual basis of kinship ties. This blurring effectively insulates an area of knowledge from scrutiny. The device ensures impunity for certain assumptions hidden in the genealogical method, with effects reaching well beyond it. 'Conjectural' history was banned in structural–functionalist anthropology, with two important results. The first and better-known of these was to deny the history of non-literate peoples. The second, equally potent, was to make Western understanding(s) of history sacrosanct. Firth *et al.* (*op. cit.*) distinguish 'historical accuracy' from 'imaginary links', without questioning the sense of that 'historical accuracy'. It seems to be an unchanging sphere where professional genealogists, *inter alia*, are deemed to be competent. Anthropologists present themselves as good at sifting social reality from imaginary beliefs.

Genealogists, like anthropologists, seem keen to make their own distinctions: Wagner, for example, dissociates the genealogy (as a schematic record), from the snobbishness attaching to pedigree. This affectation he attributes to distinctions originally made in the animal world. Animal eminence nonetheless 'fed on the fact that noble families must know their pedigrees', so that the two were mutually reinforcing in a way that makes it difficult to give priority to either (Wagner 1975, p. 1). If genealogists had difficulties in disentangling genealogy from pedigree, what of analogous distinctions sought by anthropologists? The pedigree/genealogy alternation within British social anthropology depends upon suppressing or 'drastically translating' the pedigree (indigenous representation) in favour of a genealogical ('scientific') rendering. When the 'pedigree' originates from another culture and language, the act of translation may seem inevitable. The same logic cannot apply to the English case. The connotations of English pedigree – snobbishness, animal breeding, 'breeding' in the noble sense – were intrinsic to the original rationale for recording genealogies. Disclosing the English kinship content of the genealogical method thus implies taking seriously the 'trace'[3] of pedigree from which certain genealogists and anthropologists seem eager to distance themselves. These connotations include the control of procreation through keeping written records that enable the careful channelling of 'blood', as a key to nobility. These ideas form the obverse of nineteenth-century discourses which emphasise the *negative* stereotyping of the animal (cf. Corbey 1991).

Pedigree, in this sense, seems to be about the other side of uncontrolled animality and I propose to use it as a point of departure for an empirical exploration of English kinship ideas. After all, the study of English kinship need not be exhausted by information on how kinspersons interact with one another or the use to which connections are put in everyday life (Strathern 1982a, p. 89). Indeed, we risk draining relationships of the very current of sociality which binds interactions into a process, if we attempt to break them down into constituent interactions (Ingold 1990, p. 222). I shall try instead to establish some connections between what would conventionally be seen as quite disparate kinds of evidence in order to grasp the mode of understanding embodied in the genealogical method. This I shall sometimes refer to as *pedigree thinking*. Let us begin with some etymological clues to the term *pedigree*.

Pedigree as a written record, and the connotations of animal breeding

The *Oxford English Dictionary* (*O.E.D.*) explains *pedigree* as a record or representation, and includes references to animal as well as human ancestry or descent. Apart from the crane's foot (*pé de grue*) shape of the pedigree, the *O.E.D.* mentions *bee* and *horse* pedigrees as examples from the natural world.[4] Bees and horses occupy quite specific positions in English taxonomy. Leach has described the bee as an exception to the class of insects and reptiles, usually regarded as enemies of mankind and liable for extermination, since they are credited with superhuman powers of intelligence and organisation (Leach [1964] 1972, p. 51). Thomas refers to the beehive as the 'most impressive monarchical community' (Thomas 1983, p. 62). Horses, like dogs, are regarded in a very special light by the English: 'both are regarded as supernatural creatures surrounded by feelings that are ambiguously those of awe and horror' (Leach *op.cit.*, p. 45). The dictionary definition of pedigree evokes the hierarchical order of the hive, with its Queen, drones and workers, and the Thoroughbred horses so enthusiastically bred by the Queen and aristocracy.[5] Regard for the hierarchical orders of bees (which are domesticated, not exterminated), and horses (which are bred, not eaten), may lend themselves to analogy with an English view of 'class society'.

Russell, in a work on heredity and animal breeding in early modern England, describes how 'detailed parentage of an individual animal suggested for mating is analysed' (Russell 1986, pp. 18–19). 'Parentage' and 'parentage over several generations' *look* as though they refer to parent–offspring ties through time. Pedigree *seems* to concern the possession of notable ancestors whose qualities are transmitted between parents and children. However, the transference of these distinctive qualities is *supported by* 'detailed parentage': 'Detailed parentage ... is analysed'. It is thus the *record* – the knowledge – that counts; the pedigree is, as de Mattos put it, a 'guarantee alongside biology'. Controlled rather than random matings are being guaranteed. It is the control exercised over a process so closely identified with nature which transforms breeding into a skill. The skills of recording and analysing pedigrees seem to have been metaphysically bolstered by the human owner's own 'breeding'.[6] In other words the nobility, who seem to exercise control over their marriages (and hence the intermingling of blood in their offspring), are distinguished from the common ranks where chance appears to govern the convergence of partners. 'Breeding' emphasises the behavioural outcome of controlled procreation: being well-bred implies having 'natural' good manners and gentility.

Pedigree analysis may have been erroneous in animal breeding, and the beliefs about transmittable qualities may not have been corroborated by the results of such crosses. Pedigree was, nonetheless, firmly entrenched in other beliefs about the transmission of exceptional human qualities from noble ancestors.[7] Russell suggests that parallels between the human obsession with title, hereditary position and social caste, on the one hand, and animal pedigrees on the other, are too obvious to need emphasis (Russell 1986, pp. 18–19). Obvious though they may be, the implications seem to have escaped the attention of most anthropologists concerned with English kinship. The many more who have used genealogies to collect and organise ethnographic materials from further afield, were probably oblivious to the analogue.

The connotations of pedigree appear to have formed part of English literary/bourgeois background knowledge: although not directly applicable to themselves, still part of what they *knew*. These references could be invoked, ignored or dispensed with when this was considered appropriate as, presumably, for 'scientific' purposes. In the case of the genealogical method, the 'recording' side of pedigree was elaborated while the cultural connotations were quietly shelved. The fact that an outside observer, such as de Mattos (above), draws attention to the connections between the written record and animal breeding, helps (the 'inside' ethnographer) problematise the hidden reference to animal pedigrees. These connotations can be quite obscure for anthropologists unversed in English or English culture. They tend to be assumed perhaps because of the 'institutionally defined power relations' between the English language and mode of life *vis-à-vis* those it represents (Asad 1986, p. 157). When these assumptions, which are embodied in anthropological texts, become pedagogical materials for non-English-speaking anthropologists, then the territory 'behind' recording genealogical knowledge (for example) becomes urgently required ethnography.

Anthropological pedigree and the task of 'scribe'
De Mattos was so impressed by the recording of animal pedigrees that he used it to further his own argument about the significance of human genealogy in 1940s Portugal. English animal and human pedigrees fed upon one another, and this was how the term acquired overtones of superiority. Although the practice of keeping Thoroughbred pedigrees may well have been 'imported' from Arabia in the seventeenth century, it was assimilated to English thinking to promote a 'pure' native Oriental type (Russell *op. cit.*).

These 'Thoroughbred' pedigrees were the pride of their owners –
a metonymic celebration of their own 'breeding'.

The social anthropological genealogy consists in recording recognised blood and marriage connections between people in the
population studied. The historical *raison d'être* for English pedigree
is completely discarded. Yet, the anthropological discrimination
between pedigree and genealogy echoes the genealogist's differentiation between the record and the uses to which it was put in
selective breeding. That was how Wagner could claim that genealogy
contains none of the 'overtones of superiority' which pedigree came
to acquire. He explains his interchangeable use of the two terms
as a matter of style: avoiding the repetition of genealogy too often.
The anthropological use made of the pedigree/genealogy alternation
suggests other, more profound reasons. Where the anthropologist
performed the task of 'scribe', transforming oral 'pedigrees' into
standard genealogies, it was easy enough to suppress the implicit
content (the 'pedigree') of genealogy, by switching the term onto
the other indigenous representation. The same logical procedure
cannot be applied to English kinship because the genealogical
method is so suffused with pedigree thinking that it is almost
impossible to disentangle the two. This may help to account for
the perception of English middle-class kinship as a nonentity.

The original sense of pedigree is not, of course, *directly* translated
into genealogical terms. The notion of reckoning descent through
either the male line or the female line, as a criterion for group
membership, is an outgrowth of the basic notion of selective
breeding. This is quite explicit with animals, but camouflaged as
'descent reckoning' when applied by anthropologists to human
groups. The abstract idea of reckoning descent is retained; the
underlying value attached to controlled mating and heredity is
apparently discarded, although it is in a sense basic to the very
existence of a 'system of relationships'. The vertical 'hereditary
principle' is central to this concept of kinship. The system works
'sympathetically' in the animal world. The aristocrat's 'breeding'
is somehow metaphorised in the performance of his bloodstock,
particularly racehorses.

These now historical ideas are part of British anthropologists'
'common knowledge' and not, perhaps, taken very seriously. They
should certainly not interfere with the 'scientific' use to which the
genealogy is put; they can simply be set aside. There is, however,

a striking similarity to Löfgren's argument that the Linnaean approach to the natural world can be seen as a (Swedish) folk taxonomy, while recognising that it is the foundation of modern scientific taxonomies. Löfgren connects the new emphasis on science with learning as a source of symbolic capital for the aspiring bourgeoisie (Löfgren 1985, pp. 194–5). The lack of an explicit indigenous ethnography for British kinship theory, means taking the terms of that theory on trust. Non-English-speaking anthropologists may be puzzled (as Portuguese anthropology students were) by the connotations of animal breeding in pedigree. They may not find the comparison between human 'breeding' and animal breeding self-evident. The topic *can* open up a series of questions about English beliefs concerning animals. Portuguese students, for example, observed the bizarre, to their way of thinking, lavishing of affection on pets by the English. The implicit contrast for them, of course, lay in the singular absence of equivalent endearments bestowed on fellow human beings. If the Portuguese 'personalise' through the *conversa*, is it not equally true that the English 'personalise' the animal world? But are the persons identical in each case?

The *conversa* offered a way of understanding a Portuguese sense of relatedness. May it also be the case that 'personalised' English animals reflect an English sense of relatedness? Löfgren has discussed 'thinking with animals' as part of historical processes of class formation and conflict, cultural hegemony and resistance in Sweden (*op. cit.*) Did British kinship theories also involve 'thinking with animals', in a specifically English fashion? We need an account of English middle-class intellectual thinking with animals contemporary with the genealogical method. If we accept 'ethnography' as Malinowski's invention, at least as far as British social anthropology is concerned, then we are dealing with ethnographic prehistory. There are, however, alternatives which are tied up with the very nature of English middle-class intellectual culture. Children's stories are a promising source of such an ethnography, given middle-class emphasis on the 'internalisation' of moral values (cf. Gorer 1955, p. 229), and the 'obsession' with education (Firth *et al.* 1970, p. 345).

Margaret Lane suggests that Beatrix Potter's emotional response to certain things in childhood are by now part of our own vision (Lane 1985, p. 119). The imprint of the *Tales* on the English literary middle-class world-view parallels that of the genealogical method on British social anthropology. The intersection between them lies, I suggest, in the way of accommodating the 'other' worlds of primitive man and natural history respectively. Rivers's method was apparently projected 'outwards' onto others (for an adult audience), while Potter's fiction seemingly turned 'inwards' upon the imagination (for children). But they share an underlying notion of pedigree flowing, like sand in an old-fashioned egg-timer, from one container to the other so that it may be illuminating to discuss their respective works alongside each other.

Rivers's desire to 'uncover the protopathic elements in humanity – to see beneath the epicritic veneer to "the dog beneath the skin"' (Langham 1981, p. 75), associates the genealogical with the animal level in the same vivid imagery that is encountered in Potter. The importance of descent in Rivers's theorising is matched by Potter's belief in heredity (Lane 1985, p. 28). In later life she became a sheep farmer in the Lake District, and held that 'strongly marked personality can influence descendants for generations. In the same way that we farmers know that certain sires – bulls, stallions, rams – have been prepotent in forming breeds of shorthorns, thoroughbreds and the numerous varieties of sheep ... the most remarkable old character among my ancestors was old Abraham Crompton' (*ibid*, p. 24).

The *Tales* of Beatrix Potter belong to approximately the same era as the genealogical method. Their respective authors were roughly contemporaries – although Potter survived Rivers by more than twenty years. Both came from southern, middle-class backgrounds. Whereas Rivers was able (albeit with some difficulty) to make a scientific career, Potter failed to gain entry into the male-dominated circles of natural history, and turned her talents to 'imaginative truth' (*ibid*, p. 116). The apparently unrelated audiences and discourses enhance the connections to be established. How unrelated were the audiences in fact?

'Children's' stories?
Leach's thought-provoking essay, 'Animal categories and verbal abuse', concerns the nature of taboo: the fuzzy penumbral area between concepts where obscenity – inhibited expression – originates. His analysis has been criticised for failing to specify class and other complexities (Howe 1981; Löfgren 1985). More pertinent for present purposes is Leach's point that language does more than

provide us with a classification of things, it actually moulds our environment; it places each individual at the centre of a social space which is ordered in a logical and reassuring way. Children perceive the social and physical environment as a continuum. They are taught in due course to impose a discriminatory grid which separates things, each of which is labelled with a name (Leach [1964] 1972, p. 48).

One way that some English children learn to impose these discriminations upon the world is through stories specially written for them. Such stories are obviously not limited to children since they are initially chosen and read aloud by adults.[8] Here I take issue with the 'childishness' both Lane and Lurie attach to Potter's characters. Lane suggests that the imaginative identification of an animal species with a particular character is 'of course, an easy and natural step in a child's mind' (Lane 1985, p. 127). Lurie likewise emphasises that there is something attractive to children about animals – they seem to feel comfortable with and akin to them: 'after all, it is not so long since they too were inarticulate, instinctive small creatures, with simple animal needs and pleasures' (Lurie 1990, pp. 95–6). This perspective ignores the fundamental complicity between parents and children in what Giddens calls the 'unfolding of childhood' (Giddens 1989, Chapter 3), or Ingold refers to as the 'unfolding of social relationships' (Ingold 1990, p. 222).

Adults 'return' with children (and with fresh insight) to 'children's stories' which are an integral part of English literature. As literature they perform one of the 'bridging' operations between generations, but also between 'individuals' who might otherwise be deemed to share very little on an interactional or indeed a 'structural' basis. English middle-class kinship is a good illustration. Firth and his colleagues, for example, state that kinship is not a structural feature of modern British society. Obligations and responsibilities have to be assessed in the light of personal judgement, not formal rule (Firth *et al.* 1969, pp. 452–3). Yet personal judgement depends on the terms in which one has been taught to discriminate. These, as Leach suggests, are not random, but are already structured into the linguistic categories learned as a child.

The classifications and categories which transect the world may not, in themselves, tell us very much about the ways in which they are related in practice. Beatrix Potter's stories do just that. Part of

195

the significance of this alternative ethnography is the fact that anthropologists too were once children. We need to return to the kinds of literature they grew up on in order to document the 'origins' of their middle-class literary 'voice', *qua* folk idiom. Children's literature is in this sense as much a part of our anthropological vision as the scientific literature usually invoked. The methodological step that led 'backwards' from the 'world' of mid-twentieth-century British kinship theorists, to Rivers's genealogical template, and thence to 'pedigree', is mirrored in the procedure now being followed. The next step is from the notion of 'pedigree', thus identified, into a 'world' of English animal-persons.

The world of Peter Rabbit

The 'world' of Peter Rabbit is simultaneously fantastic and familiar. The settings are mainly although not exclusively rural:[9] Scotland, Wales, the Lake District and Devon provide visual backgrounds for the stories. These were favourite holiday destinations for the Potter family as, indeed, they were for other middle-class, urban English families of the period. It is a partially named world, at times very precise: Gloucester (Westgate Street, College Court, College Green), Cat Bells (a hill by Derwent Water); at times more emblematic: Owl Island, Little Town Farm, Bull Banks, Pettitoes Farm, Market Town, Over-the-Hills, Piggery Porcombe, Stymouth. This partial naming has the effect of familiarising concepts such as 'hill', 'wood', field', 'farm', 'farmyard', 'house', 'garden', 'village', 'lane', 'lake', 'pond', 'hedge' and 'bank', which are left unspecified. The carefully observed settings and characters make the imaginative ingredients credible and convincing: it seems perfectly normal that rabbits speak English, foxes dress like gentlemen, and mice have manners. The final story, *The Tale of Little Pig Robinson* (1930), even sketches an 'other' world: the tropical island of the Bong Tree, made startling by a kettle boiling cosily beneath a bread-fruit tree improbably loaded with 'iced cakes and muffins'.

We think of the animals populating this otherwise unmistakably English landscape as native British species[10] – excepting Alderman Tortoise and the grey squirrels, chipmunks and brown bear in *The Tale of Timmy Tiptoes* (1911). The repertoire includes fox, badger, squirrel, owl, hedgehog, rabbits, mice, rats, cats, dogs, ducks, hens, pigs, frog and toad. Human beings appear in many of the

196

stories but, although powerful, never really dominate them. The rats are evicted from Tabitha Twitchet's and move in on Farmer Potatoes's barn (*The Tale of Samuel Whiskers*). Lucie recovers her pocket-handkins and pinny from Mrs. Tiggy-Winkle. Peter Rabbit and his cousin Benjamin plague Mr. and Mrs. McGregor (*The Tales of Peter Rabbit, Benjamin Bunny* and *The Flopsy Bunnies*). It could be said that animals and humans are on the same level – all are *persons*. Some of the animal-persons were modelled on human characters: Old Brown, a feudalistic male owl, was based on an old lady who lived on an island in Derwent Water. Mrs. Tiggy-Winkle was a hybrid of Kitty McDonald (a Scottish washer-woman) and Beatrix's own pet hedgehog named Mrs. Tiggy-Winkle. Mr. John Dormouse (*The Tale of Ginger and Pickles*) was based on the Sawrey shopkeeper (Mr. John Taylor) who stayed in bed for several years.

Although certain species tend to be associated with particular zones ('wild' animals with wood or hill; 'domestic' animals with farmyard, garden or house interior), they are constantly breaching boundaries. Indeed, most of the *Tales* involve physical dislocation 'out of bounds': for example, from wood to garden (*Peter Rabbit*); from farmyard to hill/wood (*Jemima Puddle Duck, Mrs. Tiggy-Winkle*); from garden to lane (*Tom Kitten*); from living room, via chimney, to attic (*Samuel Whiskers*). The striking fact that all the main figures are animal-*persons*, with names (such as 'Mr. Tod' or 'Mrs. Thomasina Tittlemouse'), well-rounded characters, and able to command perfect English complicates, but does not con-tradict, Leach's point about learning to classify 'remote' and 'homely' areas in the environment.

All the species are equally 'at home' on their respective terri-tories – irrespective of our own preferences for 'nicer' or 'nastier' persons amongst them. Even Mr. Tod's 'shocking place' (Bull Banks) – 'something between a cave, a prison and a tumble-down pig-stye' – has a remarkably well-appointed kitchen: 'There was an immense empty pie-dish of blue willow-pattern, and a large carving knife and fork, and a chopper. At the other end of the table was a partly unfolded tablecloth, a plate, a tumbler, a knife and fork, salt-cellar, mustard and a chair – in short, preparations for one person's supper' (1912). This kind of domestic detail not only makes the unpleasant people convincing, it is the very basis for transforming animals into 'persons'.

197

Potter sometimes refers to animal species as *races*, as in her dedication to *The Tale of Samuel Whiskers*: 'In remembrance of Sammy, the intelligent pink-eyed representative of a persecuted but irrepressible race'. Different species certainly interact: badger–fox–rabbit (*The Tale of Mr. Tod*, 1912), human–fox–duck–dog (*The Tale of Jemima Puddle Duck*, 1908); rabbit–mouse–cat–human (*The Tale of Benjamin Bunny*, 1904); cat–dog (*The Pie and the Patty-Pan*, 1905); cat–rat–dog (*The Tale of Samuel Whiskers*, 1908). Inter-species friendships are always somewhat ambiguous, often running aground on commensality. The classic case is Ribby (a cat)'s invitation to a dog (Duchess) for afternoon tea (*The Pie and the Patty-Pan*). Ribby wants to treat Duchess to mouse pie – just the dish that Duchess most dreads. Duchess goes to enormous lengths to try to keep up appearances. She breaks into Ribby's house in her absence and tries to substitute her own veal and ham pie for Ribby's mouse and bacon. Her deception is uncovered during tea, and the story ends with Ribby vowing to invite her Cousin Tabitha Twitchet next time she wants to give a tea-party! It was Ribby's vanity which made her want to invite Duchess, 'a most genteel and elegant little dog; infinitely superior company to cousin Tabitha Twitchet'; and it was her downfall. Cousin Tabitha (who kept the village shop) was disdainful about Ribby's pretensions: 'A little *dog* indeed! Just as if there were no CATS in Sawrey! And a *pie* for afternoon tea! The very idea!' It was the quest for refinement, gentility and breeding that led Ribby to imagine Duchess to be better company than another cat (especially her own cousin). In principle there seems to be nothing against this: both speak (and write) English and seem to (want to) observe the same code of good manners. The unmentionable point is that the dog cannot bring herself to eat mouse. That is species-defined. It refers to a source of fundamental inequality between persons: a phylogenetic difference that ought to keep cats and dogs apart.

If commensality is already difficult, intermarriage between the species is quite out of the question. There certainly are conjugal relationships within species: for example, mice (Hunca Munca and Tom Thumb), rats (Samuel Whiskers and Anna Maria), and rabbits (Peter Rabbit and his cousin Flopsy), but scarcely alliances. Some persons even seem able to dispense with one (especially the male) conjugal partner: there is no mention of Tabitha Twitchet's spouse (she appears in *The Pie and the Patty-Pan* (1905), *The Tale*

198

of Tom Kitten (1907), and *The Tale of Samuel Whiskers* (1908)).
Who is the father of Tom Kitten, Moppet and Mittens? Likewise,
all we know of Peter Rabbit's father is that he was put in a pie
by Mrs. McGregor (*The Tale of Peter Rabbit* (1902)). We only
'see' old Mrs. Rabbit going out shopping, or ministering camomile
tea. Who was Benjamin Bunny's mother? Only old Mr. Bouncer
survives to rescue his son and nephew from the McGregor garden
(*The Tale of Benjamin Bunny* (1904)), and later to neglect the
offspring of a cousin marriage between Benjamin and (Peter's
sister) Flopsy (*The Tale of Mr. Tod*). Pigling Bland, like Little Pig
Robinson, appears to have neither 'mother' nor 'father': pigs
apparently have 'aunts'. Aunt Pettitoes, an otherwise 'worthy
person', is admonished because her family is not well brought up.
She sends her son [*sic*] Pigling Bland to market because she cannot
support 'eight of a family'. Robinson's Aunts Dorcas and Porcas
send their nephew to market because they themselves are too fat
to squeeze over the stiles. The term 'Aunt' is sometimes used by
an illegitimate child to refer to its natural mother where that
relationship is not recognised (as in rural Devon). The lack of
control over procreation is terminologically deflected.

Reproduction seems almost 'given' for some of the species, as if
they were self-perpetuating. Offspring suddenly 'appear', as they
literally can do in illustrations: for example, in Hunca Munca's
cradle, stolen from the doll's house of Jane and Lucinda (*The Tale
of Two Bad Mice*), or rocked and cuddled by Goody Tiptoes at
the end of *The Tale of Timmy Tiptoes*. There is something of a
'descent bias' in Potter's view of inter-species relations – just as
there is pervading the entire genealogical method. Phylogenetic
differences between the species seem to become differences of
descent among a single species of 'persons', who appear to be on
more or less civilised terms. Yet these persons remain fundamentally divided on the score of procreation – in sharp contradiction
to the 'generous' interpretation of evolution. It is not that we are
given the details of descent – instead the outcome of descent must
be read from the conduct of these persons.

Domestic animals, whose breeding is firmly controlled by
human beings (such as cows, horses and especially sheep), figure
only marginally in the *Tales*. Horses draw waggons in *The Tale
of Johnny Town-Mouse*, and *Pigling Bland*; and there is a shop-
keeping sheep, named Fleecy Flock, in *The Tale of Little Pig*

Robinson. It is also true that pigs are the main characters in two tales (*The Tale of Pigling Bland* (1913), and *The Tale of Little Pig Robinson* (1930)). However, *natural* history seems to have excluded (for the younger Beatrix Potter at least) the larger domestic animals. Most of the characters in the *Tales* belong to species whose reproductive behaviour *seems* exactly opposite to the control inherent to pedigree. So what has pedigree thinking to do with them? The problem is analogous to that of the middle-class anthropologist's 'vicarious' (or simply offhand) borrowing of pedigree in order to formulate 'primitive' kinship.[11]

Potter's self-imposed tasks of 'scribe' and 'artist', drawing upon natural history to formulate 'imaginative truth', borrows a notion of breeding that can be traced back to pedigree. The wilderness of wild animals' procreation is transmuted into a civilised world, according to certain written and graphic conventions, whereby the species interact *as characters* through the medium of the English language and an English code of manners. While mating behaviour was absolutely off the agenda, 'breeding' (demeanour as the outcome of that behaviour) was not. For example, Johnny Town-Mouse and his friends have long tails, and they noticed the insignificance of Timmy Willie's tail when he came crashing into the middle of their dinner party; 'but they were too well-bred to make personal remarks'. The Johnny Town-Mouse example demonstrates that being 'well-bred' is not a question of a pre-ordained hierarchy among species: after all, other mice characters (Hunca Munca and Tom Thumb in *The Tale of Two Bad Mice* (1904)) have been identified as 'proletarian' (Rahn 1984). Like the popular English notion of 'class', being well-bred refers to a mixture of *savoir-faire* and phenotypic characteristics. Part of what seems to have been involved was being 'above' mentioning or appearing remotely concerned with the very features which matter most (like length of tail to a mouse).

There are certain similarities with the terms of Rivers's genealogical method applied to the 'primitive' sphere. Pedigree used the (implicit) idea of distinction (based upon the ability to control reproduction among certain domestic species and the nobility, that involved keeping records) to effect radical transformations: wild animals became 'persons', and primitive peoples acquired 'society', thanks to the literary efforts of those in a position and with an interest in mediation. The 'wild' and the 'primitive' could be transformed into civilised symbolic capital by those able dominate them intellectually.

Personalising the animal world

Potter's personalisation of the animal world illuminates the anthropological *person* fundamental to British kinship theory. La Fontaine, for example, identifies Radcliffe-Brown's sharp distinction between individual and person as the source of many contributions from British anthropologists (La Fontaine 1985, p. 125). Potter's characters may also assist in understanding the indigenous background to the theoretical concepts of 'individual' and 'role' that became central to the development of British kinship theory.[12] This theoretical distinction draws, I argue, upon 'local' ideas as much as scientific ones.

Potter's characters do not have 'roles' because they literally embody them. The interrelationships between persons in the *Tales* gloss irreducible differences between (and even within) the species. Mr. Jeremy Fisher, a frog in a tattered mackintosh, can never 'be' Sir Isaac Newton (in his black and gold waistcoat), or Mr. Alderman Ptolemy Tortoise (with a salad in a string bag). They may sit down to a dinner of roasted grasshopper together as friends; but they will always be three very distinctive individuals. If a 'person' is a duck, a fox, a kitten or a rabbit, we have a fair idea what to expect of them. Their personalities, names and clothing turn them into 'characters', 'dressing up' their essential identities – like a mask.

If masks can 'depersonalise' humans, then by the same token clothes are part of what serves to 'personalise' animal characters. As Ingold has put it, 'We see ourselves as animals plus' (Ingold 1990, p. 210). We discover the animal underneath when the disguise is removed. Clothing is to animals what masks are to men. It is the shawl and poke bonnet which transform a farmyard duck into Jemima Puddle-Duck, with a will of her own. The source of her discontent, incidentally, was thwarted motherhood: she wanted to be able to hatch her own eggs rather than entrust them to a hen for sitting. This is a hidden reference to the importance of procreation as a motive for the plots. Wearing clothes and bearing a unique name completes the transformation of animals into 'persons', or 'characters', able to represent what are seen as irreducible class differences among English people. At the same time, these characters hold something in reserve: underneath it all they are still animals.

Animal plus

Mason has argued that all discussion of 'body language', in which he includes clothing, is at one and the same time a discourse on self and a discourse on the other, involving a process of 'negative self-definition', by which the self is defined in terms of what it is not, namely the other (Mason 1990, pp. 90–1). Potter's animal-persons are self and other: they have names, speak English, wear clothing of the period, and are set in unmistakably 'English' landscapes. But they are still animals. One device for showing this is the loss of clothing. Let us consider some examples.

Peter Rabbit's blue jacket and shoes end up on Mr. McGregor's scarecrow after his wilful sortie into the garden, against the express wishes of his mother. This transgression, like that of his father before him (who ended up in a pie), is punished by reducing Peter to a small, sick rabbit running for his life back to the burrow. Tom Kitten and his sisters Moppet and Mittens relinquish their best clothing to the Puddle-Ducks while out of the garden – against their mother's orders. There is no solution but to banish them upstairs during the tea-party for which they had been so carefully groomed; there they revert to kittenish behaviour. In another story, Tom Kitten climbs the chimney to avoid being shut up in a cupboard by his mother on baking day. Lost in the flues, he falls unexpectedly into a space beneath the attic floor onto Samuel Whiskers's bed. Anna Maria, the old woman rat, is summoned: 'His coat was pulled off and he was rolled into a bundle'. The rats prepare to make him into a roly-poly pudding, using his mother's butter and dough stolen from downstairs. There is some poetic justice in the rats' decision to cook and eat Tom Kitten, given that Tabitha Twitchet and her family had eaten seven young rats for dinner the previous Saturday. Except, of course, that the cats are the rightful occupants of the house, while the rats 'infest' it as vermin. All are nonetheless 'persons'. Mr. Jeremy Fisher loses his galoshes and part of his mackintosh on an ill-starred fishing trip. Had he *not* been wearing the mackintosh he would have been digested by the trout which snapped him up. Fortunately, the trout so disliked the taste of the raincoat that it spat him out again, enabling a bedraggled Jeremy Fisher to swim ashore – a simple frog.

In other cases, the disclosure of the animal beneath the clothing is less an event within the story than an artistic image skilfully sprung upon the character portrayed. Jemima Puddle-Duck meets an elegantly dressed foxy gentleman who offers her the use of his woodshed to make her nest. Jemima lays her eggs and comes to visit them. 'The foxy gentleman used to turn them over and count them when she was not there.' The accompanying illustration shows a fox, without clothing, pawing the eggs with hungry eyes: 'pure fox at last' (Lane 1985, p. 118). Jemima almost ends her days as roast duck, but is saved by the farm collie. She loses that set of eggs, but later is allowed to sit on another. She is shown as a mother duck with her ducklings, and without any further embellishments, at the end of the story.

The state of clothing and the propriety of where it is worn is another way of establishing the character of the person and the role enacted. One of the 'disagreeable' people in *The Tale of Mr. Tod* is a badger: 'Tommy Brock's clothes were very dirty; and as he slept in the daytime, he always went to bed in his boots'. Only someone with as 'lamentable want of discretion for his years' as old Mr. Bouncer would entertain such an unsavoury type. The result is that Tommy Brock steals the rabbit babies who were in the charge of their grandfather, and prepares to make rabbit pie of them.

Naughtiness, ingenuity and cunning can all be expressed in the wearing, loss, recovery and laundry of clothing. It mediates spatial and social boundaries: as, for example, between farm and wood, garden and wood. In more extreme cases, part of the body can be lost. Squirrel Nutkin breaks his tail in two while escaping from Old Brown whom he has systematically insulted. Mrs. Tiggy-Winkle takes in washing and does ironing for many of the characters known from other stories. But she too is ultimately revealed as 'nothing but a HEDGEHOG!'

Lane contends, 'even the clothes in which her animals are so unerringly dressed contribute something, by however improbable a route, to our imaginative understanding of their characters' (1985, p. 117). Yet if that clothing serves as a disguise for the essential 'person', then many of the plots reveal the 'person' as an animal underneath it all. Different animal species 'personify' different characters. 'Personification' is represented by such additives as clothing, demeanour, and bearing a name. Jemima Puddle-

Duck, with her double-barrelled surname, maternal ambitions, poke bonnet and shawl, is a simpleton. What else could she be but a silly duck? The elegant, sandy-whiskered gentleman reading a newspaper among the foxgloves, who struck Jemima as 'mighty civil and handsome', is a cynical murderer – a fox. Mrs. Tabitha Twitchet is the image of an anxious Victorian parent: dressing up her kittens for visitors (*The Tale of Tom Kitten*), and stuffing them into a cupboard on baking day (*The Tale of Samuel Whiskers*). But when she cannot find Tom Kitten she becomes 'more and more distracted, and mew[s] dreadfully'.

Clothing helps to disguise the essential individual, just as its removal exposes the person for what he or she really is. Underneath the person is an animal: cat, pig, owl, toad, mouse and so on. Lane seems to assume that we are dealing with an animal world. 'Displayed in the trappings of their human counterparts, they reveal their own true natures by oblique methods, and we ever after know more about them for having observed their behaviour in significant disguise' (*ibid*). It seems, however, equally reasonable to read a *human* world from this animal-persons' microcosm. Apart from the fact that Beatrix Potter modelled some of her characters on (human) persons known to her, English pedigree suggests this kind of overlap.

There is then a disjuncture between the 'disguise' and the true animal nature underneath. This 'English' conception of the person seems to be composed of an 'inner', animal part that is 'given'; to which an 'outer' human part is added. Procreation belongs to the inner reality; while appearance, manners and so on go to compose the social person constructed on top of that, who must perform the roles assigned by 'society'. This is both a dramatic and an idiosyncratic notion of composing the person – as can be illustrated by a simple contrast with certain Portuguese ideas discussed in the previous chapter. The animals in *Contos Tradicionais do Povo Português* (Traditional Portuguese Folktales) certainly speak, but they are not 'dressed up' as persons in this English sense (cf. Braga [1914–15] 1987). Personal appearance seems, in the world of Peter Rabbit, to be about disguising an animal self, rather than expressing the very substance of relatedness, as it could do among the urban Portuguese. Portuguese surprise at the possibility of an English businessman dressed in a pin-striped suit, nonchalantly accompanied by his punk son, highlights this point. Such differences in dress are, from an English perspective, cancelled out by the invisible bond of parentage they share. The attention given to appearance in certain Portuguese circles, by contrast, is merged with ideas about being *simpático*: the self is not a hermetically sealed, bounded entity. Portuguese personhood is discovered through sympathy, empathy, and in the exchange of courtesies: greeting, conversing and taking one's leave. These are not seen as irksome formalities, stultifying some 'self' within. There seems to be much less of a disjunction between 'self' and 'person' (in the English senses of these terms) – if indeed they make any sense at all in the Portuguese setting.

Clothing, to middle-class English thinking, is part of putting on a role. The moral discomfort provoked by cosmetics in our culture (cf. Strathern 1979), is perhaps a logical outcome of the separation between self and roles. Where this separation is either less acute, or the terms themselves are different, then the attitude to clothing and cosmetics is likely to vary accordingly. Statements such as Leach's, that 'everyone is always and everywhere, more or less consciously, playing a role' (Leach 1989–90, p. 49), look increasingly problematic as generalisations – and as premises for theoretical concepts used for the analysis of others.

I should stress that I have dwelt upon the question of appearance not merely to build a 'comparison' with the Portuguese, but to stress a local vision of the world built into the background of a theory.

Concrete and abstract persons

The genealogical method moves from the (concrete) level of named individuals to an (abstract) system of relationships. There is an interesting mirror image of this move in the English 'persons' depicted in the *Tales*, and their 'materialisation' out of that context. Beatrix Potter's original images of animal-persons have generated further sets of artefacts. Dozens of commercial products featuring Peter Rabbit and the other characters have been produced over the past eighty years: lampshades, bookends, tea-cosies, china figures and crockery, jigsaw puzzles and face flannels. Within a few years of *The Tale of Peter Rabbit*'s publication (1902), Potter tried to find an English manufacturer for dolls (Lane 1985, p. 103). German-made dolls, however, undercut the native product[13] – something which drove Potter to anti-Free

Trade campaigning before the 1909 General Election. Wallpapers, colouring books, games, pocket handkerchiefs, a bookshelf and slippers followed. A version of the *Tales of Beatrix Potter* was filmed in 1971. As Taylor has put it, 'Peter Rabbit continues to give pleasure in hundreds of guises' (Taylor 1983, p. 80).

The characters have thus been unleashed from the confines of middle-class children's literature to roam twentieth century mass-consumption products.[14] The *Tales* generated artefacts which, although they seem to take on a life of their own, can always be traced back to an 'original' design. In this respect they resemble the genealogical method. Genealogical diagrams, or *bonecos* (dollies) as the Portuguese students called them, adorn hundreds of different monographs. The 'kinship system' more generally became fundamental to descriptive monographs.

It is as individuals that the animal-persons appear to be removable from the context of their stories, materialising (quite literally) as dolls, puppets and other images. In this unitary form, they take on 'concrete' lives of their own. Their interrelated existences on the page (in the stories) become abstractions. Here we may have the rubric for a middle-class English cultural idea: each (social) 'person' is essentially different from every other in terms of the raw animal material from which they are made. 'Kinship', or relatedness, refers to an underlying animal identity. While in one sense this notion of kinship is deemed obvious, it seems to become an individually focused abstraction, subordinate in public discourse to the idea of the concrete, role-playing person.

Beatrix Potter's animal-persons started life in personal letters to young friends. Over the course of almost a century they have been repeatedly removed, recontextualised and concretised as images which stand for intrinsic difference, for separate individuals. The details of their stories, however important, are combined with extraordinary images of animal species, dressed and behaving like 'English' characters. The *Tales* provide contexts and relationships in which persons make sense. Insofar as any character becomes independent of the Tale, it also becomes fictive. But that is exactly what can be done with images.

It is worth pointing out that this structure of recontextualisation is already present in the *Tales*. Potter placed characters or lines from much older nursery rhymes in her stories: the owl and the pussy-cat in *Little Pig Robinson*, the six little mice who sat down to spin and 'hey diddle dinkety poppety pet' in *The Tailor of Gloucester*; 'Tom, Tom the piper's son' in *The Tale of Pigling Bland*; and references to 'Miss Muffet' and 'Ladybird, Ladybird' in *The Tale of Mrs. Tittlemouse*. So perhaps it is not surprising that some of her characters have themselves entered new trajectories. Their distinctiveness, a strange combination of species-specificity and shared culture, makes them ready candidates for detachment.

Certain anthropological views of English middle-class kinship also emphasise the separation of the person (as an 'individual' or a 'character') from the relationships in which he or she is enmeshed. Firth *et al.* regard English kinship responsibilities as *personal* judgements, rather than structural conditions (cf. Firth *et al.* 1969, pp. 423–5). Yet if we consider one of the ways in which 'personal judgement' is formed – through children's stories – then the 'personal' begins to look very much more 'structural' (to stick with Firth's terminology). We are asked to take characters like Mrs. Tabitha, Jemima Puddle-Duck, and Mrs. Tiggy-Winkle as if they *were* essential persons. But in the same breath the veil is drawn aside and the persons are shown to be various animal species 'plus' English names, dress, language and manners belonging to the turn-of-the-century English bourgeoisie. The 'roles' of anxious parent, simpleton and industrious washer-woman are not intrinsic, but come about through interaction with other species: that is how their cat-ness, duck-ness and hedgehog-ness are disclosed. Left to themselves, we suppose, they could 'be themselves'. This perhaps explains the popularity of the detached, singular characters out of context. Except, of course, there is a context awaiting them – or rather a 'home'.

The role aspect looks invariable but seems to be simultaneously detachable from the essential Tabitha Twitchet, Jemima Puddle-Duck or Mrs. Tiggy-Winkle. Although 'only dolls', the composition of these beings is modelled on how the individual is deemed separate from his or her roles. The timing of Beatrix Potter's characters' escape (or release, depending on perspective) from the page was more or less simultaneous with the diffusion of her books. Is it the ability to retain the universe of relationships between the characters concerned, as an abstract mental construct, which permits any one of them to go it alone? Or is it the concrete singularity of each 'character' which makes him or her individually so appealing? These are two sides of the same coin – in Potter's view of kinship, as in middle-class English kinship more generally.

The species are not always presented as individuals; many belong to families, or even dynasties. Implicit notions of descent and heredity also enable individuals to hive off on their own; these are parameters which keep the anarchy of total individualism at bay. This is the fundamental 'animal' level of kinship which keeps species different. Relationships may be inevitable between these different species, but the intrinsic properties derived through heredity from the immediate parents and grandparents and, by implication, backwards *ad infinitum*,[15] are what give the individual his or her finite, self-contained quality.

It may seem an extraordinary leap from the genealogical method of British social anthropological inquiry to *The Tales* of Beatrix Potter, and back again. The point is that there are analogous concerns in both, although we are not accustomed to dealing with them together. Let us recapitulate. What we have are two English middle-class intellectualisations of the worlds of natural history and primitive man, transforming them into civilised symbolic capital. How did they do this? Animals are transmuted into 'persons' whose 'breeding' closely resembles that held responsible for the 'origins' of the English person. Primitive 'pedigrees' are translated into genealogies, paving the way for kinship to become the centrepiece of British social anthropology during the first half of the twentieth century.

While British anthropologists appeared mainly concerned with 'other cultures' or 'other societies', the terms of their interest were fashioned from within. The assumption seems to be that we are all, theoretically at least, 'social persons'. That permits the borrowing of 'pedigree' from another social stratum to translate primitive relatedness into our own terms. The problem is that social persons are deemed to be as unalike as one animal species to another underneath it all – at precisely the animal level of procreation that is the foundation of kinship. The *Tales* help to illuminate the contradiction: different animals have common ground between them as 'social' persons. Their existence as 'social persons' does nothing to alter their 'individualist' tendencies: some characters have fatal flaws which seem to be a matter of heredity: Peter Rabbit's attraction to the same garden where his father met his end as rabbit pie.

Few would dispute that the hand of Beatrix Potter drew as much

208

on her rather stifling, middle-class upbringing as on the 'natural history' she so carefully observed in composing her animal-persons: their names, speech and demeanour derive from an early-twentieth-century *English* perspective on variety. Yet the same proposition applied to early-twentieth-century British social anthropologists would be much less easily admitted. It is easier to keep track of Potter's position *vis-à-vis* her explicitly fictional characters than is the case with the 'scientific' texts on kinship under discussion. She even 'appears' in several *Tales* making quite explicit judgements on 'animal' behaviour: 'Aunt Pettitoes, Aunt Pettitoes! You are a worthy person, but your family is not well brought up' (*The Tale of Pigling Bland*). 'When I was going to the post late in the afternoon – I looked up the lane from the corner, and I saw Mr. Samuel Whiskers and his wife on the run, with big bundles on a little wheelbarrow, which looked very like mine ... I am sure I never gave her leave to borrow my wheelbarrow!' (*The Tale of Samuel Whiskers*). 'It is said that the effect of eating too much lettuce is "soporific". *I* have never felt sleepy after eating lettuces; but then *I* am not a rabbit. They certainly had a very soporific effect upon the Flopsy Bunnies!' (*The Tale of the Flopsy Bunnies*).

Kinship as an anthropological common denominator that allowed each 'society' to be analysed separately and then 'compared', fitted into an English middle-class way of intellectualising the world. The genealogy is a construction, just as Potter's animal-persons are: it translates ideas about other beings into terms that are not quite 'own', but are nonetheless 'known' and, moreover, authoritative. The fact that kinship is presented as a fundamental common denominator, and yet one that somehow failed to apply to the 'writers', was obscured by the very act of writing. Giddens synthesises the situation as follows: 'In most Western societies, kinship connections are for all practical purposes confined to a limited number of close relatives ... In many other cultures, however, especially small-scale ones, kinship relations are of overwhelming importance in most spheres of life' (Giddens 1989, p. 384). Writing establishes a new position of authority – it represents knowledge that is beyond the scope of what is being written about.

Let me illustrate what I mean. Leach has suggested that the disjuncture between individual and social person is a condition common to humanity (Leach 1989–90, pp. 53–4). But does this way of conceptualising the person apply wholesale to the English, let alone western Europe or the entire world? If cultural systems are neither static nor coherent, why should we expect to find a universal masking process? Could it be that the individual/social person dichotomy (like Potter's animal-person) is a specific construction of a quite specific fraction of the English-speaking world?

The theatricality of English life struck one Portuguese colleague: the endless scandals and exposés of public figures; detective fiction and spy thrillers; the ghosts, spooks and spirits haunting all manner of places; the worlds of Agatha Christie and Alfred Hitchcock. This dramatic side to English life depends upon a separation between the individual as a 'private person', 'at home', and the social personae thrust upon him or her in the performance of 'public' roles. This cultural division is more than echoed in the domestic versus public domains which became central to Fortes' version of descent theory. The developmental cycle of domestic groups seemed to offer a way of analysing relations clustered around productive and reproductive resources, over time (Fortes 1958; Goody 1958). Yet it too was based upon an implicit idea of domesticity which seems uncomfortably close to 'home' (cf. Strathern 1988; La Fontaine 1990).

A discussion of the English personification of animals, exemplified in Beatrix Potter's *Tales*, has brought us to the problematic division between 'self' and 'social person'. This division was intrinsic to British structural–functionalist kinship theory as it developed mainly through the analysis of 'other cultures'. 'In societies of simple technology most statuses are ascribed ... a person's place in society, his rights and duties, his claim to property, largely depend on his genealogical relationships to other members' (Mair [1965] 1972, p. 9). 'For every status there is an appropriate role. People are expected to behave as if they loved their wives and respected their headmasters, whatever their actual sentiments may be ... the social anthropologist is concerned with the way the roles are defined by society and what happens when they are not properly performed ... Social control comprises the whole range of social pressures directed to make people play their roles in accordance with these expectations' (*ibid*, p. 11).

Could it be that this theoretical model of the power of kinship and descent in 'societies of simple technology' was inspired by the English notion of descent (which was in turn inspired by a specific notion of pedigree), which generated a separation between the 'self' (as a 'descendent') and the always somewhat contrived 'social person'? We need to look more closely at the 'biological' composition of the person *qua* 'individual'.

The origins of the English individual

It is my contention that the 'individual' discerned in Potter's animal-persons is modelled on an early-twentieth century-English middle-class understanding of the 'person'. That understanding helps to elucidate the internal source of British anthropological interest in kinship: English middle-class kinship thinking. This perception calls into question various assertions about English kinship, from the 'individual' as its supposed 'pivot', through 'Ego-focused' (as distinct from ancestor-focused) descent (Macfarlane 1977, pp. 145–6), to the married couple as the 'centre-piece' of the system (Wolfram 1987).

The detachment of Beatrix Potter figures from the *Tales*, and their translation into other media, does not impare the original literary 'world' from which they were taken. The persons-in-context are, if anything, *secluded* from these imageries run riot. These persons, and their interrelationships, are present in the minds of those who have read them. This internalisation, in the sense of being well-read or well-versed in what stands *behind* the 'individual', seems to be a feature of a certain kind of 'kinship thinking'. The 'individual' is a deceptive construct in that, far from signifying something that stands by and for itself, it stands effectively for a 'world' – to those 'in the know'. That world, as we have seen, is composed of persons conceived as separate animal species 'related' synchronically through a shared 'culture', and diachronically through shared biogenetic material. Each character thus stands for the terms on which the world of natural history was 'personified'. These terms have been identified as 'pedigree thinking', in that they borrow ideas about the origins, composition and interrelationships of 'persons' that correspond with assumptions buried in the genealogical method.

I will try to develop this point by considering the English notion of consanguinity. Firth and his colleagues, elaborating on the English notion of a relative by blood, write of 'a peculiar, almost mystical quality ... sometimes attributed to consanguinity' (Firth *et al.* 1969, p. 94). Elsewhere they write that the notion of unilineal descent as an integrative principle is replaced (in English kinship) by that of consanguinity. The concept of 'blood relationship' also conditions the significance of the affinal principle, thought to rest on marital alliance between individuals, rather than a transactional alliance between groups (*ibid*, p. 459). How does this marital alliance between individuals affect children?

Wolfram records that heredity was, until about 1900, thought to take place through the transmission of blood rather than genes.[16] The wife, on the other hand, became a part of her husband – 'bone of his bone' (Wolfram 1987, p. 120) – through marriage, according to nineteenth-century doctrine. Was this a reference to the creation of Eve by God from Adam's rib? Did marriage thus restore the rib to its rightful place – the wife completing the being to whom she herself owed her physical origin? Husband and wife are nowadays sometimes referred to as 'one blood' and 'one flesh', shifting the emphasis away from the single (rather solid) notion of bone, onto two other fundamental body substances. The association between the married couple and bone has acquired a derogatory ring during the second half of the twentieth century as, for example, with the name of the feminist journal *Spare Rib*. While it is undoubtedly the case that bones *can* play a part in English kinship notions, just as *sangue* (blood) may form part of Portuguese *carne* (flesh – see Chapter 3), it is the distinctive emphasis which matters. The notion of the wife being absorbed into her husband's bone would seem to weight the other notion: heredity passing through the blood. Would that blood then be primarily the husband's, or both husband's and wife's? The English idea of a confluence of blood from two distinctive sources resulting in 'normal' offspring, suggests the latter.

Wolfram draws attention to the contrast between this idea of a healthy union, and a popular belief that incest can result in 'idiot' or deformed children (Wolfram 1987, p. 138). The 'improvement' of certain breeds of farm animals through close in-breeding of selected stock provoked moral disquiet about interfering with Nature. At the same time, inconsistently in Wolfram's view (*ibid*, p. 146), offspring are deemed to result from the excellence or otherwise of the original stock. Proximity might therefore be an advantage under certain circumstances, while 'new blood' could help 'in-bred' decadence in other cases. 'New blood' and 'in-breeding' are opposed, albeit in different ways, to random matings.

Perhaps this was what the genealogist, Wagner, had in mind when he referred to 'the slow but steady infusion of new blood from below into the upper classes which has been occurring since time immemorial' (Wagner 1975, p. 115). This, he believed, produced an 'amalgamation of contrasted elements of stiffness and movement; a structure or skeleton of permanent hierarchical form supporting an organism of slowly changing and ever mingling and recombining substance' (*ibid*, p. 92). The physiological imagery is interesting. 'Bone' refers to the hierarchical skeleton of social class, upon which is built a much more fluid organism of 'flesh' and 'blood'. Wagner was particularly impressed by the frequency of 'hidden links and bridges' between the social classes thanks to 'matrimonial cross-connecting' between the 'great' and the 'humble' (*ibid*, p. 88).

While Wolfram has characterised the husband–wife relationship as the 'centre-piece of the English kinship system' – two persons become 'as one', as distinct from two groups becoming allied – Strathern has emphasised that marriage and name-sharing do not obliterate the different birth origins of the married couple (1982, p. 86). Each partner remains a separate source of identity for their children. Her inference is that notions of 'close' and 'distant' relatives rest on some concept of biogenetic substance; through marriage to outsiders the amount is 'diluted' in succeeding generations (*ibid*, p. 81).

The transmission of biogenetic substance is not a straightforward matter in popular belief. An infant may be identified on first sight as having a 'Smith' nose, or a 'Jones' temperament, as if these were detachable parts passed on intact to the new bearer. These transmittable parts sometimes seem to be passed on personally: 'he's got John's nose and Mary's eyes'. Others seem to represent collective 'family' traits, as with the 'Smith nose'. English speculation on the physical and incorporeal 'origins' of the individual emphasises innate qualities expressed in the body or temperament. This is reminiscent of the seventeenth-century horse-breeders, who believed that the sire was responsible for the innate courage and personality of the horse, while the mare contributed to physical structure. The search for resemblances that depends upon an abstract notion of substances descending to the 'object of observation' (La Fontaine 1985, p. 126), comes very close to 'descent' as it is embodied in Beatrix Potter's animal-persons. The concrete relationships in which the infant is 'enfolded' (Ingold 1990, p. 222) simply by virtue of its birth are far less important when it comes to identifying a human being.

The contrast between English attention to personal 'origins', and Portuguese concern with composing a person's name, although in neither case exclusive, document significant distinctions among western Europeans, in beliefs about the constitution of the person (cf. Hollis 1985, p. 232). Strathern has noted that surnames tend to be treated as rather trivial or adventitious phenomena in accounts of English kinship: 'they are, we suppose, a residue of male bias, a reflection of the manner in which property or office may be passed down' (1982a, p. 94). She suggests that we might take account of the way that, contrary to network, the surname symbolises 'the flat designation of non-optional elements in a person's status' (*ibid*).

Portuguese names string together both father's and mother's family names. The definition is not preordained; there is room to invoke multiple origins. The ambiguity of the English (sur)naming system, in which a name may be shared by birth or by contract, does not exist. Marriage (in Portugal) is not an occasion for substituting the husband's surname for his wife's 'maiden name'. Instead she adds her husband's name to the ones she already enjoys. A married English woman's surname symbolises the hidden dimension of the two parental identities transmitted to children. Like the hereditary substances which are deemed responsible for noses, eyesight and intelligence, the mother's surname and origins must be sought out. There is no customary public formulation of these 'inner' realities. This basic source of differentiation, between the parents who are otherwise identified as 'one flesh and one blood', establishes a blueprint for further variations on the theme, 'the same, but different'. The unity of husband and wife, symbolising the notion of consanguinity, supposed by Firth, Hubert and Forge to have replaced unilineal descent as an integrative principle, begins to look much less unified.[17]

Beatrix Potter's characters share a common territory and culture (language, demeanour and so on), but are nonetheless irrevocably divided by latent evolutionary history. Their 'breeding' (or lack of it) shows up in their adventures – stories narrated by Potter. These accounts of the outcome of an unspeakable (because uncontrolled) breeding history, resemble the genealogical 'charter' within British ethnography. Pedigree thinking, borrowed from the highest social echelon of the local order, aestheticising as 'persons' those who might otherwise never have qualified as such.

The British genealogical Ego: a sense of impasse with the early-twentieth-century middle-class English 'self'

Firth and his colleagues argue that the social anthropologist's use of 'Ego' differs from that of a psychologist or psychoanalyst. The anthropologist is not concerned with problems of Ego's conscious-ness, relation to the self, etc. Instead, 'Ego' is the central point of a genealogical construction: the reference point for identifying the genealogical relationships expressed on the diagram. 'Ego' is also the major informant for the genealogy. Even if the information was obtained from several people, one of them must still be labelled as 'Ego' for discussing the kin relations involved (Firth *et al.* 1969, p. 33).

The genealogical Ego, like the 'social person', seems to be at a remove from the self. The 'personal focus' of the genealogy may not even exist, according to Firth and his colleagues! It is purely an organising device from which to map the genealogical construc-tion. Kinship is assumed to be such a basic system of linkages between people that in fact Ego is a position rather than a person. The genealogy is indeed used by anthropologists 'to establish the boundaries of society', relating living persons to the original founders (La Fontaine 1985, p. 137).

What does this aside on the genealogical Ego tell us about the English middle-class person and view of kinship? There is a para-dox involved. Kinship is assumed to be a basic system of linkages between people, yet it is handled as if it were an abstract system. This abstraction is heralded by one of those anthropological La-tinisms: 'Ego'. It seems as though a portion of reality must be suspended when kinship is being analysed. This Ego bolsters the static, map-like effect of the graphic genealogy which prompted Bourdieu's call for a social history of the implement. 'Ego' and a 'system of relationships' may be abstractions well-suited to a submerged notion of kinship, descending into and focusing upon the individual. Translated into a methodological procedure, how-ever, their specificity makes for a dubious way of exploring other notions of relatedness. The internal differences among what is sometimes lumped together as 'European' (or 'Western') kinship, make the 'exportation' of these notions as an implicit component of British kinship theory even more questionable.

Why should the genealogical 'Ego' be an abstract construction? Although it has become standard practice to combine genealogies with life histories, this does not alter the basic quality of the genealogical Ego (cf. Bourdieu 1986). Firth, Hubert and Forge indicate that 'the problems of the consciousness of the "Ego", its relation to the self, etc.' fall beyond the anthropologist's sphere of competence. Yet, the genealogical 'Ego' does, of course, set up a distinction and thereby generates a theoretical problem: what is it (or was it) about that English 'self' which makes (or made) it unsuitable as 'the central point ... the point of reference' for the genealogy (Firth *et al.* 1969, p 33)?

A sense of impasse with this English self and his or her roles is very well expressed by Leach: 'if all the world's a stage; if we are always social persons rather than individual selves, where is the true self? Does it exist? Can we ever know it? Can we ever dare to show it to others?' (Leach 1989–90, p. 50). Discomfort with the naked individual accentuates the sense of artificiality of the social person (cf. Newman 1987, p. 140). Leach seems to suggest that there might be a true self buried underneath all the roles and masks; but without the various camouflages by which it is known it would be barely identifiable. Indeed, he goes much further than this:

I am suggesting that Goffman's observation that we engage in a role-playing masquerade in 'everyday life' as well as in formal public situations needs to be very greatly extended. The play-acting is not just part of a communication system between actors who are all present on the stage at the same time. It also includes off-stage ancestors like the ghost in Hamlet who have to be invented and equipped with the appropriate set of masks in order to justify the multiple roles of the living self (1989–90, p. 52).

One interpretation might be that this 'self' is too remote from the social reality of role-playing to anchor a genealogy to it. The plurality of roles make it seemingly impossible to establish a single centre. Yet, we are told, the self as an individual is the pivot of the English kinship system. One way round the complexities of this self and its relationships with its own social personae, is by reinventing it as 'Ego'. The implications, however, are not so simple. For if the self becomes an abstraction (Ego), so too do the relationships which radiate from it.

The process of moving from the concrete level of named individuals to the abstract level of social relationships was central to Rivers's conception of the genealogical method. The singularity of the named, individual self depends upon biogenetic substances inherited from Leach's off-stage ancestors. It is this 'background' which accounts for the existence of the person as an individual 'subject'. Yet it is this very concreteness which must be sloughed off in a 'scientific' account. The abstraction of the written record makes it appear objective. This abstraction derives, however, from ambivalent attitudes about the very centre of the genealogy: the 'self' of the informant. Both the self, and the genealogical 'Ego', are entirely missing from descent theory, which concerns corporate groups and their perpetuity.

A specifically English notion – the 'self'– became intrinsic to the genealogical method, despite the attempt to overcome it with 'Ego'. It is, by extension, also implicit in descent theory. Radcliffe-Brown's sharp distinction between individual and person (1940, pp. 193–4), was made from a 'theoretical stance which ignores both awareness of self and the collective representations' (La Fontaine 1985, p. 125). That ignorance of the self and collective representations led to a remarkable ethnographic gap, which was based on the assumption that all individual human beings share the same motivations (cf. Leach *op. cit.*). While Leach's insights provide fascinating evidence for an English way of looking at the world, it is highly questionable whether his assertions can be generalised throughout the English-speaking world, or even within western Europe. Could we, for example, extrapolate from that English 'self' (and all that goes with it in terms of British anthropological theory), to Portuguese or French 'selves'? Would the notion even make sense in those settings?

Off the anthropological record

This chapter was inspired by Portuguese students' questions about a number of English terms, symbolising concepts and conceptual sequences, encountered in British anthropological kinship theories. The aim had been to try to elucidate those theories in a practical way by means of the genealogical method. However, the implicit theoretical content of the method in turn instigated a search for ethnography that might elucidate certain English concepts.

The notion of pedigree was queried by Portuguese students, unfamiliar with the overlapping of human and animal worlds in bloodstock breeding, and in the 'breeding' of nobility, which are background knowledge for at least some English. Thus the superimposition of pedigree and genealogy has been considered, together with reasons for recording pedigrees. These popular notions of distinction were apparently discarded when the genealogy was harnessed for 'scientific' ends. Considering, however, the concept of descent implicit in pedigree, the 'descent bias' pervading the entire genealogical method (Barnard and Good 1984, p. 28), and the way descent theory became the dominant paradigm for British social anthropologists by mid-century, pedigree associations (however vague or misplaced) seem to have hung on with remarkable tenacity.

The need to draw upon native competence to render such ideas intelligible to non-English anthropology students underlines the significance of 'background knowledge'. This explains the attempt to elicit some ethnographic clues from Beatrix Potter's *Tales* to demonstrate how pedigree thinking stretched far beyond those with a 'pedigree'. However imprecise the connotations, the notion of pedigree seems to have struck a chord of recognition across the literary spectrum, from children's literature to anthropological methodology. Beatrix Potter's characters, like Rivers's method, generated – and continue to generate – artefacts of English kinship thinking late into the twentieth century.

The broader notion of pedigree, or pedigree thinking, contains in fact a popular theory of personhood. Beatrix Potter's animal-persons are composed in a strikingly similar manner to the mid-twentieth-century anthropological 'person' as a role-enacting 'individual'. Rivers borrowed and translated the English (aristocratic) idiom of pedigree into the 'genealogical method'. It became a means of producing the obvious kinship artefact, the illustrative genealogy. It also became an implicit part of organising fieldwork and written ethnography, despite being overshadowed by more explicit ideals, such as participant observation.

The animal-persons in Beatrix Potter's Peter Rabbit stories provide 'ethnographic' material for analysing both the composition of the English person, and an underlying concept of kinship. Essential differences between individuals are expressed in terms of species specificity. Individuals (animals) are able to interact through their perfect command of the English language, their manners (or lack of them), possession of a name, the wearing of clothing and suchlike, all of which transforms them into 'persons'. The tension and the theatre of the stories lies in the extent to which this essential animality is revealed or concealed through the plots and their associated images. Phylogenetic history is recapitulated in every individual character, while the 'social' person emerges through inter-species relationships. There are a few direct references to this historical depth through off-stage ancestors: Mr. Tod, grandson of old Vixen Tod; Ribby's Great Aunt Squintina. It is understood, 'given', as an evolutionary fact. We tend to gloss over the depth of that descent – as can be seen from the successful detachment of the literary characters from their original context to embellish a wide range of artefacts as images – cut-out figures. 'Possession' of these objects revolves around identification with the 'persons' depicted on them which refer, however vaguely, to an original 'world' – more or less pleasing and congenial (cf. Carrier 1990, p. 703).

The sense of aesthetics which presumably motivates people to buy artefacts with Beatrix Potter 'persons' on them may also resonate in another set of kinship artefacts. Mid-twentieth-century British kinship theories were engendered by the scientific appropriation of a folk way of thinking about relatedness: the pedigree. Both 'authors', of middle-class origin, drew upon notions apparently more 'pertinent' to the social stratum above them to depict the lesser-known worlds of natural history and primitive man. The imprint of those notions upon the respective literary artefacts generated (the 'imaginary' world of Peter Rabbit, and the 'scientific' world of British structural–functionalist kinship theory) suggests their recombined readings might reasonably be placed on the late-twentieth-century anthropological agenda. That English middle-class kinship thinking has proved so recalcitrant to anthropological study should not be interpreted as evidence of its relative *un*importance. The present study suggests, on the contrary, that pedigree thinking was *so* important to English middle-class intellectuals that it was absorbed into the processes of making knowledge about other peoples. English pedigree became caught up in intellectual brokerage on an international scale. An ethnography of the people who produced this sort of knowledge can be constructed by turning to their other literary artefacts. Children's literature would seem to be a particularly promising source, given the value attached to education and the internalisation of moral values by the early-twentieth-century English middle class. The artefacts of pedigree thinking considered in the present study have long outlived their authors in both cases. Their worlds, where English was spoken and understood as they spoke and understood it, have disappeared and yet persisted. Although translated and reproduced, both the stories and the theories refer back to quite specific origins. The intersection of personal, imaginary and scientific worlds has remained largely off the anthropological record. While the difficulties of doing justice to the task are evident, that should not dissuade the attempt.

Notes

1 'Own' indigenous ideas here assumes that anthropologists *use* a middle-class, literary 'voice', whatever their class origins. The British/English distinction picks up on the ambivalence of claiming 'British' nationality or citizenship, and claiming in the same breath to be 'English'.

2 'Abroad' can include Wales, Scotland and especially Ireland. See, for example, R. Fox on the Tory Islanders who, interestingly, were 'very ill at ease with the standard genealogical method': they much preferred to start from a known ancestor and work downwards (Fox 1978, p. 31). 'The order in which the various segments of groups would be taken was more or less agreed on by the various narrators, who, incidentally, were all older men who styled themselves quite consciously 'sloinnteoiri' – genealogists' (*ibid*, p. 33).

3 I borrow the concept of 'trace' from Susan Sontag, who refers to the photograph as a 'trace' in the sense of 'something directly stencilled off the real, like a footprint or a death mask'([1973] 1977 p. 154).

4 *O.E.D.* definition of pedigree: 'The table of genealogy drawn up in some tabular form; an ancestral line for animals, such as bees or horses; a sense of origin or succession; descent in the abstract sense, especially ancient or distinguished descent; "birth"; a race or line; a family; a line of successions; loosely, a long series, a list or a string of people'.

5 Cf. Löfgren on the use of folk knowledge as raw material for scientific discourse. New scientific taxonomies of plants and animals reflected cultural ideas of hierarchy. The Linnaean system of eighteenth-

century Sweden, for example, reflects a feudal rather than a capitalist conception of society (Löfgren 1985, p. 193).

6 Thoroughbred racehorses were an aristocratic obsession by the late seventeenth century. The superior status of an owner was symbolised by the strength, speed and courage of his horse. 'A noble family's stud books and pedigrees were maintained with a precision which would have done credit to the College of Arms' (Russell 1986, pp. 18-19). The identification between aristocrat and racehorse provided the underlying rationale for that precision. The pedigrees of all modern Thoroughbred horses include one of the three legendary ancestral Arab/Turk horses imported in the late seventeenth and eighteenth centuries. Byerley Turk, Darley Arabian and Godolphin Arab are likened by Thomas to 'a kind of equine Adam, Noah or William the Conqueror' (Thomas 1983, p. 59).

7 'There was also a firm belief in the persistence of nobility or family superiority in those descended from distinguished or successful historical figures. In all human societies where an aristocracy has evolved, the original members of the ruling class usually owed their position to some superior skill, power, good luck or criminal activity. Besides the creation of legal systems to bolster their entitlement to privilege in perpetuity, they have frequently attempted to justify their continuing privilege by arguing that the superior power of the ancestor or ancestors is hereditary, so that membership of an aristocratic family of itself entitles its members to privilege and power in its turn' (Russell 1986 pp.18-19).

8 As Giddens has pointed out, 'The unfolding of childhood is not time elapsing just for the child: it is time elapsing for its parental figures and for all other members of society; the socialisation involved is not simply that of the child, but of the parents and of others with whom the child is in contact, and whose conduct is influenced by the child just as the latter's is by theirs in the continuity of interaction' (Giddens [1979] 1982, p. 130).

9 Beatrix Potter's own favourite, *The Tailor of Gloucester* (1903), has an urban setting. She allows herself the observation, at the end of *The Tale of Johnny Town-Mouse* (1918), 'One place suits one person, another place suits another person. For my part I prefer to live in the country, like Timmy Willie.'

10 This is obviously loosely phrased. As Wallace pointed out more than a century ago, 'Britain is separated from the Continent by a very shallow sea, and only in a very few cases have our animals and plants begun to show a difference from the corresponding continental species' (Wallace 1869, I, p. 16).

11 It is of course very striking that Darwin borrowed the notions of pedigree and genealogy to formulate his evolutionary theory of the origin of species, and to explain the descent of man (Darwin 1859, 1871). Darwin's understanding of natural selection was based upon the operation of selection among domesticated animals.

12 See, for example, Giddens ([1979] 1982, pp. 115ff.) on the various problems associated with role theory.

13 See the sardonic reference to the Policeman in Ginger and Pickles: 'Bite him, Pickles! bite him!', spluttered Ginger behind a sugar barrel, 'he's only a German doll!' ([1909] 1989, p. 217).

14 The characters have, in the process, come to stand for a certain 'Englishness' at home, but more especially overseas. Rupert Bear, Winnie the Pooh or the 'Famous Five', are arguably equally 'English'. However, they do not deal with familiar British species as persons, and miss the imaginative 'empiricism' of Potter's characters. It is also important to remember that Beatrix Potter became a major benefactor of the National Trust, donating 4000 acres together with a substantial sum to buy more land in the Lake District (Gaze 1988, p. 107).

15 This applies even to such 'lonely' figures as Mr. Tod. We learn, for instance, that he was in the very worst of bad tempers having broken a china plate, the last of the dinner service which had belonged to his grandmother, old Vixen Tod. The heirloom reminds him of his descent, which perhaps meant all the more to him for being such a solitary character?

Farmer Potatoes was driven nearly distracted by rats, 'all descended from Mr. and Mrs. Samuel Whiskers', who moved in on him after eviction from Mrs. Tabitha Twitchet's, 'children and grandchildren and great great grandchildren. There is no end to them!'

Ribby (a cat), trying to persuade her guest Duchess (a dog), that there is no patty-pan in the pie she is consuming for afternoon tea, invokes her Great Aunt Squintina (who died of a thimble in a Christmas plum pudding) to emphasise her assertion that she never puts any article of metal in *her* puddings or pies.

16 Wolfram, citing Dobzhansky, elaborates further on the underlying ideas of consanguinity:

> Parental 'bloods' were supposed to mix in the progeny so that the heredity of a child was a solution, or an alloy, of equal parts of the parental heredities. The heredity of a person was thought to be an alloy in which the heredity of each of its four grandparents were represented by one quarter, of each of eight great grandparents by one eighth, etc. (Dobzhansky 1955, cit. by Wolfram 1987, p. 13).

17 Although this contrasts, as might be expected, with working-

class conjugality as, for example, depicted by Young and Willmott (1957). They also underline the centrality of 'Mum' rather than 'Dad' to the family. Freeman, conforming to a pattern identified in earlier chapters, of historicising all his observations about the kindred, focuses mainly on the Iban. While he qualifies the notion of consanguinity, he draws upon 'evidence from a number of societies' (i.e. not contemporary England!) to suggest 'that what is basic is the fact that relations between kindred are governed by a special morality arising from the recognition of common descent' (Freeman [1961] 1968, p. 264). Considering such a morality based on the recognition of common descent in England, was simply not on the agenda.

CONCLUSION

It is of course open to any of us to use the terminology of description and analysis that most suits his taste and convenience. But this can impede rational discussion. For, as Alice retorted to Humpty Dumpty, 'The question is ... whether you *can* make words mean so many different things' (Fortes 1969, p. 280).

The reality of studying social anthropology, several generations on from the handful who originally addressed one another in their publications, is that the texts have long since been detached from the context in which they made sense almost automatically. The need for commentaries on the 'background' to the classic British texts somewhat resembles contemporary interest in the *European* histories of exotic artefacts. These texts are, of course, a specific kind of artefact: the valued constructions of men and women bound to a greater or lesser degree by the conventions of what may be termed 'middle-class, English, intellectual' discourse. One of the key constructions of this discourse was the apparent obviation of self – not so much the 'I' that had 'been there', bringing the testimony of the field to the written ethnography, as that which permitted, supported and fostered the I-form in its tautologous individualism. Personal background refers of course to more than a single person. It stands for the way in which people learn to discriminate and to think: it is the folk counterpart to what is conventionally covered by scientific or intellectual background.

Pinning down a scientific mode of understanding kinship to a quite specific *folk* conceptualisation is of practical, theoretical and political significance. There is little choice about coming to terms with the legacy of twentieth-century anthropology for those cur-

225

rently involved in the field. That legacy is most obvious in what have become the pedagogical 'classics'. We have to find ways 'back' into their distant circles of meaning. Attempting to find solutions to that seemingly practical problem discloses issues of a theoretical order. Switching perspectives is not a matter of trying on different positions and seeing which fits best. The very act of shuffling established orders of priority within anthropology is political in the widest sense of the term.

One way into the circle of meaning with which this book has been concerned was through a form of literature roughly contemporaneous with the formulation of the genealogical method. The method became more than one of the 'tools of the trade' in British social anthropological practice during the 1930s, '40s, '50s and even beyond. Despite its explicitly methodological place in the British repertoire, late-twentieth-century transpositions of the kind discussed in this book bring out an implicit theoretical content. That tacit theory revolves around the English notion of *pedigree*. Pedigree thinking cannot be explored within the confines of British anthropological discourse. Instead we have to venture into other, essentially middle-class, *fin-de-siècle* English writing which, like the genealogical method, has long outlived the specific moment of its production. The World of Peter Rabbit has spread far and wide beyond the confines of the original texts. The ideas of control and distinction that are built into pedigree are also discernible in Potter's animal-persons narratives. The genealogical premise of relatedness has thus been widely diffused – in the classics of British social anthropology, certainly, but also in the bedtime stories that contribute to sustaining inter-generational conceptual frameworks.

The incorporation of pedigree into anthropological methodology for assimilating knowledge about others is a peculiarly fascinating manoeuvre by early-twentieth-century English middle-class intellectuals. Borrowing pedigree was perhaps a simultaneous assertion of being 'above' this kind of ranking system, while recognising the power of its connotations when harnessed to intellectual objectives they defined.

My account of teaching these texts in Portuguese is one of what I imagine are many similar stories among late-twentieth-century anthropologists. The point is not so much how English class intervenes in the process of making knowledge, especially for later generations of anthropologists who do not share the same 'background'. It is more a question of how to reach a position from which the complexities in which we are embroiled become visible, let alone intelligible. It is increasingly clear that no account of another 'society' is complete without a complementary account of that which the author treats as 'background'. Translation is a *two*-way process: for if we render (our) exotic familiar, we also need a way of estranging ourselves from what is (to us) familiar, so that others may be able to perceive our assumptions. Would-be ethnographers of Britain face a unique challenge due to the hegemony of the English language in academic anthropology. This tends to banish the Englishness of that language into obscurity. Translating 'British' anthropological ideas, originally phrased in English, into Portuguese, had the salutary effect of disclosing several hidden assumptions.

The refusal of some British anthropologists to indulge in what they dismiss as 'introspection', 'narcissism' and 'expiation', is intrinsic to the arrogance of those whose language predominates within anthropology. Their refusal is tantamount to a denial of the reality of studying anthropology several generations on from its inception. While the use of language may well be a matter of taste and convenience, recognising this should promote a more responsible and reflective attitude among those who command such languages as English within the field of anthropology. The classical texts of British social anthropology have now joined the more generalised flow of exotic artefacts around the globe. Like all exotic artefacts, they acquire meanings beyond the 'antique value' of first editions. These accretions clamour for attention in the field of anthropological pedagogy. They also open up the possibility of writing new kinds of ethnography.

BIBLIOGRAPHY

ALMEIDA COSTA, J. & A. SAMPAIO E MELO 1983. *Dicionário da Lingua Portuguesa*, Oporto: Porto Editora Lda.

ARENSBERG, C. & S. KIMBALL 1940. *Family and Community in Ireland*, London: Peter Smith.

ARRISCADO NUNES, J. 1986. 'On household composition in North Western Portugal. Some critical remarks and a case study'. *Sociologia Ruralis*, XXVI, 1, pp. 48-69.

ASSOCIAÇÃO PORTUGUESA DE ANTROPOLOGIA (A.P.A.) 1991. Dossier 'Ensino'. Lisbon.

AUGÉ, M. 1978. *Os Domínios do Parentesco. (Filiação, Aliança Matrimonial, Residência)*, Lisbon: Edições 70. Portuguese translation of *Les Domaines de la Parenté*, 1975, Paris: Maspero.

ASAD, T. 1986. 'The concept of cultural translation in British social anthropology', in CLIFFORD & MARCUS (eds), pp. 141-64.

BANKES, G. 1991. 'Fieldwork projects in undergraduate anthropology', *Anthropology Today*, 7, 3, June, p. 21.

BARNARD, A. & A. GOOD 1984. *Research Practices in the Study of Kinship*, London: Academic Press.

BARNES, J.A. 1954. 'Class and committees in a Norwegian parish', *Human Relations*, 7, pp. 39-58.

BARNES, J.A. 1962. 'African models in the New Guinea Highlands', *Man*, 62, pp. 5-9.

BARNES, J.A. 1967. 'Genealogies', in A.L. EPSTEIN (ed), *The Craft of Social Anthropology*, London: Social Sciences Paperbacks in association with Tavistock Publications, pp. 101-127.

BARNES, J.A. 1968. 'Networks and political process', in M.J. SWARTZ (ed), *Local-Level Politics. Social and Cultural Perspectives*, Chicago: Aldine, pp. 107-130.

BARNES, J.A. 1980. 'Kinship studies: some impressions of the current state of play', *Man* (n.s.) 15, 2, pp. 293-303.

BATESON, G. [1936] 1958. *Naven. A Survey of the Problems Suggested by a Composite Picture of a New Guinea Tribe Drawn from Three Points of View*, Stanford, Calif.: Stanford U.P.

BELMONT, N. 1974. *Arnold van Gennep, le créateur de l'ethnographie française*, Paris: Payot.

BERTAUX, D. (ed) 1981. *Biography and Society. The Life History Approach in the Social Sciences*, London: Sage.

BODIGUEL, M. & P. LOWE (eds) 1990. *Campagne française, Campagne Britannique. Histoires, images, usages au crible des sciences sociales*, Paris: Éditions L'Harmattan. (Translated into English as LOWE & BODIGUEL.)

BOHANNAN, P & J. MIDDLETON (eds) 1968. *Kinship and Social Organization*, New York: The Natural History Press.

BOUQUET, M. 1984. 'The differential integration of the rural family'. *Sociologia Ruralis*, 24, 1, pp. 65-78.

BOUQUET, M.R. 1985a. *Family, Servants and Visitors. The farm household in nineteenth and twentieth century Devon*, Norwich: Geo Books.

BOUQUET, M.R. 1985b. 'Home thoughts from abroad', *The Times Higher Education Supplement* (19.4.85), p. 12.

BOUQUET, M.R. 1985c. 'Still green about the English village', *The Times Higher Education Supplement* (20.12.85), p. 13.

BOUQUET, M.R. 1986a. "You cannot be a Brahmin in the English countryside'. The partitioning of status, and its representation within the farm family in Devon', in COHEN (ed), pp. 22–39.

BOUQUET, M.R. 1986b. 'Posfácio', FOX in pp. 327–338.

BOUQUET, M.R. 1987. 'Bed, breakfast and an evening meal: commensality in nineteenth and twentieth century Hartland', in M.R. BOUQUET & D.M. WINTER (eds), *Who From Their Labours Rest? Conflict and practice in rural tourism*, Aldershot: Gower, pp. 93–104

BOUQUET, M.R. 1989. 'Trialectics of the genealogical method of British social anthropological inquiry', in M. SEGALEN (dir.) with C. MICHELAT and M. COADOU, *Actes du Colloque, Anthropologie Sociale et Ethnologie de la France* (Paris: 19, 20, 21 November 1987), Louvain: Editions Peeters, pp. 125–142.

BOUQUET, M.R. 1990. 'On labelling. The ethics and aesthetics of amnesia', *Trabalhos de Antropologia e Etnologia*, Homenagem a Ernesto Veiga de Oliveira, XXX, 1–4, (Oporto: Sociedade Portuguesa de Antropologia e Etnologia), pp. 31–43.

BOUQUET, M.R. 1991. 'On two-way translation' (Comment), *Man* (n.s.) 26, 1, pp. 162–163.

BOUQUET, M.R. forthcoming 'All modern conveniences: properties of home comfort in English farmhouse accommodation', in T. SELWYN (ed), *Chasing Myths. The Anthropology of Tourism*, Cambridge: C.U.P.

BOUQUET, M.R. & H.J. DE HAAN 1987. 'Kinship as an analytical category in rural sociology: an introduction', *Sociologia Ruralis*, XXVII, 4, pp. 243–262. Special Issue: 'Analysing Kinship', M.R. BOUQUET & H.J. DE HAAN (eds).

BOUQUET M.R. & J. FREITAS BRANCO. 1988. *Melanesian Artefacts, Postmodernist Reflections/Artefactos melanésios, reflecções pósmodernistas*, Lisbon: I.I.C.T./Museu de Etnologia. Exhibition catalogue.

BOURDIEU, P. 1969. 'Intellectual field and creative project', *Social Science Information*, 8, 2, pp. 89–119.

BOURDIEU, P. 1977. *Outline of a Theory of Practice*, Cambridge: Cambridge University Press. Translation: Richard Nice (*Esquisse d'une Théorie de la Pratique, Précédé de Trois Études d'Ethnologie Kabyle*, Geneva: Librairie Droz, 1972).

BOURDIEU, P. 1980. *Le Sens pratique*, Paris: Editions de Minuit.

BOURDIEU, P. 1986. 'L'illusion biographique', *Actes de Recherche en Sciences Sociales*, No. 62/63, June, pp. 69–72.

BRADLEY, T. & P. LOWE (eds) 1984. *Locality and Rurality. Economy and Society in Rural Regions*, Norwich: Geo Books.

BRAGA, T. [1914–15] 1987. *Contos Tradicionais do Povo Português*, 2 vols. Lisbon: Publicações Dom Quixote.

BRETTELL, C. 1986. *Men who Migrate, Women who Wait. Population and History in a Portuguese Parish*, Princeton, N.J: Princeton U.P.

BRITISH ASSOCIATION FOR THE ADVANCEMENT OF SCIENCE: A Committee of Section H. 1929. *Notes and Queries on Anthropology*, (Fifth Edition). London: Royal Anthropological Institute.

BROMBERGER, C. 1982. 'Pour une analyse anthropologique des noms de personnes', *Langages*, 66, pp. 103–124.

CABRAL, M.V. 1986. 'État et paysannerie. Politiques agricoles et strategies paysannes au Portugal depuis la seconde guerre mondiale', *Sociologia Ruralis*, Vol. XXVI, 1, pp. 6–19. (Special Issue: Portuguese Perspectives/Perspectivas Portuguesas.)

CALLIER-BOISVERT, C. 1968. 'Remarques sur le système de parenté et sur la famille au Portugal', *L'Homme*, VIII, 2, pp. 87–103.

CAMPBELL, J. 1964. *Honour, Family and Patronage*, Oxford: Clarendon Press.

CAPLAN, P. 1988. 'Engendering knowledge. The politics of ethnography' (Part 1, and Part 2), *Anthropology Today*, 4, No. 5, Oct, pp. 8–12; No. 6, Dec, pp. 14–17.

CARRIER, J. 1990. 'The symbolism of possession in commodity advertising', *Man* (n.s.), *25*, 4, pp. 693–706.

CARRITHERS, M., S. COLLINS & S. LUKES (eds) 1985. *The Category of the Person*, Cambridge: C.U.P.

CHIVA, I. 1987a. 'Entre livre et musée. Emergence d'une ethnologie de la France', in CHIVA & JEGGLE (eds): 9–33.

CHIVA, I. 1987b. 'Le musée-laboratoire, service public de recherche', *Ethnologie Française* (Hommage de la Société d'Ethnologie Française à Georges Henri Rivière), 17 (1), pp. 61–63.

CHIVA, I. & U. JEGGLE (eds), 1987. *Ethnologies en Miroir. La France et les pays de langue allemande*, Paris: Éditions de la Maison des Sciences de l'Homme.

CLIFFORD, J. 1986. 'Introduction: Partial truths', in CLIFFORD & MARCUS (eds), pp. 1–26.

CLIFFORD, J. 1988. 'On ethnographic authority', in *The Predicament of Culture. Twentieth Century Ethnography, Literature, and Art*, Cambridge, Mass.: Harvard U.P. pp. 21–54.

CLIFFORD, J & G. E. MARCUS 1986. *Writing Culture. The Poetics and Politics of Ethnography*, Berkeley: University of California Press.

CODRINGTON, R.H. [1891] 1972. *The Melanesians. Studies in their Anthropology and Folklore*, New York: Dover Publications Inc.

COHEN, A.P. (ed) 1982. *Belonging. Identity and Social Organisation in British Rural Cultures*, Manchester: Manchester U.P.

COHEN, A.P. (ed) 1986. *Symbolising Boundaries. Identity and Diversity in British Cultures*, Manchester: Manchester U.P.

COHEN, A.P. 1990a. 'Travaux récents en anthropologie rurale de la Grande Bretagne', in BODIGUEL & LOWE (eds), pp. 293–305.

COHEN, A.P. 1990b. 'The British anthropological tradition, otherness and rural studies', in LOWE & BODIGUEL (eds), pp. 203–221.

COLSON, E. 1986. 'Obituary. Lucy Mair', *Anthropology Today*, 2, 4, Aug, pp. 22–24.

CORBEY, R. 1991. 'Freud's phylogenetic narrative', in R. CORBEY & J. LEERSSEN (eds), *Alterity, Identity, Image*, Amsterdam: Rodopi.

CRESSWELL, R. & M. GODELIER (eds) 1976. *Outils d'enquête et d'analyse anthropologiques*, Paris: Maspero.

CUISENIER, J. & M. SEGALEN 1986. *Ethnologie de la France*, Paris: P.U.F.

CUTILEIRO, J. 1977. *Ricos e Pobres no Alentejo. (Uma Sociedade Rural Portuguesa)*, Lisbon: Livraria Sá da Costa Editora. Translation of *A Portuguese Rural Society*, 1971 Oxford: O.U.P.

DARWIN, C. [1859] 1972. *On the Origin of Species*, A Facsimile of the First Edition, New York: Atheneum.

DARWIN, C. 1871. *The Descent of Man and Selection in Relation to*

Sex, London: John Murray.

DAVIS, J. 1977. *People of the Mediterranean*, London: Routledge & Kegan Paul.

DE SOUSA SANTOS, B., 1990. *O Estado e a Sociedade em Portugal*, Oporto: Edições Afrontamento.

DIAS, J. [1948] 1981. *Vilarinho da Furna: Uma Aldeia Communitária*, Oporto: Instituto para a Alta Cultura; Centro de Estudos de Etnologia Peninsular (Lisbon: Imprensa Nacional da Moeda).

DIAS, J. [1953] 1981. *Rio de Onor: Comunitarismo Agro-pastoril*, Lisbon: Editorial Presença.

DIAS, J. 1961. *Ensaios Etnológicos*, Lisbon: Junta de Investigações do Ultramar, IX

DIAS, J. 1964. *Portuguese Contribution to Cultural Anthropology*, Johannesburg: Witwatersrand U.P.

DIAS, J. 1971. 'Os elementos fundamentais da cultura portuguesa', and 'O carácter nacional portugais na presente conjunctura', *Estudos do carácter nacional português*, Lisbon: Junta de Investigações do Ultramar; Centro de Estudos de Antropologia Cultural. Estudos de Antropologia Cultural No. 7.

DOBZHANSKY, T. 1955. *Evolution, Genetics and Man*, New York.

DOUGLAS M. 1967. 'If the Dogon...', *Cahiers d'Études Africaines*, 7, 28, pp. 659–672.

ERRINGTON, F. & D. GEWERTZ 1987. *Cultural Alternatives and a Feminist Anthropology. An Analysis of Culturally Constructed Gender Interests in Papua New Guinea*, Cambridge: C.U.P.

EVANS-PRITCHARD, E.E. 1940. *The Nuer. A Description of the Modes of Livelihood and Political Institutions of a Nilotic people*, New York and Oxford: O.U.P.

EVANS-PRITCHARD, E.E. 1950. 'Social anthropology: past and present' (The Marrett Lecture, 1950), in EVANS-PRITCHARD [1950] 1969, pp. 13-28.

EVANS-PRITCHARD, E.E. 1961. 'Anthropology and history', in EVANS-PRITCHARD [1962] 1969, pp. 46–65.

EVANS-PRITCHARD, E.E. [1962] 1969. *Essays in Social Anthropology*, Londn: Faber.

FABIAN, J. 1983. *Time and the Other. How Anthropology makes its Object*, New York: Columbia U.P.

FAVRET-SAADA, J. 1977. *Les Mots, la mort, les sorts. La Sorcellerie dans le Bocage*, Paris: Gallimard. (English translation, by C. Cullen: *Deadly Words, Witchcraft in the Bocage*, Cambridge: C.U.P./ Paris: Éditions de la Maison des Sciences de l'Homme.)

FEIJÓ, R., H. MARTINS & J. PINA-CABRAL (eds) 1983. *Death in*

Portugal, (Studies in Portuguese Anthropology and Modern History), Oxford: J.A.S.O.

FENTON, A. 1990. 'Phases of ethnology in Britain. With special reference to Scotland', *Ethnologia Europaea*, XX, 2, pp. 177–188.

FERNANDES-DIAS, J.A.B. 1991. 'Report from Lisbon: the current Portuguese anthropological scene', *E.A.S.A. Newsletter*, 5, pp.11-12.

FERRAROTTI, F. 1981. 'On the autonomy of the biographical method', in BERTAUX (ed), pp. 19–27.

FERREIRA DE ALMEIDA, J., A.F. DA COSTA & F.L. MACHADO 1988. 'Famílias, estudantes e Universidade – paneis de observação sociográfica', *Sociologia: Problemas e Práticas*, 4, pp. 11–44.

FINCH, J. 1989. *Family Obligations and Social Change*, Cambridge: Polity Press.

FIRMINO DA COSTA, A. & M.D. GUERREIRO 1984. *O Trágico e o Contraste: O Fado no Bairro de Alfama*, Lisbon: Don Quixote.

FIRMINO DA COSTA, A. & M.D. GUERREIRO 1986. 'The Country and the City: the Bairro of Alfama in Lisboa', *Sociologia Ruralis*, XXVI, 1, pp. 84–97. (Special Issue: Portuguese Perspectives/Perspectivas Portuguesas.)

FIRTH, R. [1936] 1983. *We, The Tikopia. A Sociological Study of Kinship in Primitive Polynesia*, Stanford, Calif.: Stanford U.P.

FIRTH, R. 1956. *Two Studies of Kinship in East London*, London: Athlone. (Extract reprinted in GRABURN (ed), 1971, pp. 385–389.)

FIRTH, R. (ed) [1957] 1970. *Man and Culture. An Evaluation of the work of Bronislaw Malinowski*, London: Routledge & Kegan Paul.

FIRTH, R. 1961. 'Family and kin ties in Britain and their social implications. Introduction', *The British Journal of Sociology*, XII, pp. 305–309.

FIRTH, R.[1963] 1983. 'Introduction to the Abridged Edition', FIRTH [1936] 1983.

FIRTH, R. 1975. 'An appraisal of modern social anthropology', *Annual Review of Anthropology*, 4, pp. 1–25.

FIRTH, R., J. HUBERT & A. FORGE. 1969. *Families and Their Relatives*, London: Routledge & Kegan Paul.

FORTES, M. 1945. *The Dynamics of Clanship among the Tallensi*, London: O.U.P.

FORTES, M. 1953. 'The structure of unilineal descent groups', *American Anthropologist*, 55, pp. 25–39.

FORTES. M. [1957] 1970. 'Malinowski and the study of kinship', in FIRTH (ed), pp. 157–188.

FORTES, M. 1958. 'Introduction', in GOODY (ed), pp. 1–14.

FORTES, M. 1969. *Kinship and the Social Order. The Legacy of Lewis*

Henry Morgan, Chicago: Aldine Publishing Company.

FORTES, M. 1978. 'An anthropologist's apprenticeship', *Annual Review of Anthropology*, 7, pp. 1–30.

FORTES, M. & E.E. EVANS-PRITCHARD (eds) 1940. *African Political Systems*, London: O.U.P.

FORTUNE, R. [1932] 1963. *Sorcerers of Dobu*, New York: Dutton.

FOX, R. 1967. *Kinship and Marriage. An Anthropological Perspective*, Harmondsworth: Penguin.

FOX, R. 1978. *The Tory Islanders. A People of the Celtic Fringe*, Cambridge: C.U.P.

FOX, R. 1982. 'Principles and pragmatics on Tory Island', in COHEN (ed), pp. 50–71.

FOX, R. 1986. *Parentesco e Casamento. Uma Perspectiva Antropológica*, Lisbon: Vega. Translation by J. Rodrigo of FOX 1967.

FRANKENBERG, R. 1966. *Communities in Britain. Social Life in Town and Country*, Harmondsworth: Penguin.

FREEMAN, J.D. [1961] 1968. 'On the concept of the kindred', reprinted in BOHANNAN & MIDDLETON (eds), pp. 255–272.

GAZE, J. 1988. *Figures in a Landscape. A History of the National Trust*, London: Barrie & Jenkins in association with The National Trust.

GEERTZ, C. 1988. *Works and Lives: The Anthropologist as Author*, Cambridge: Polity Press.

GELLNER, E. 1986. 'Original Sin: the legacy of Bronislaw Malinowski and the future of anthropology', *The Times Higher Education Supplement* (10-10-86), p.13.

GELLNER, E. n.d. Inaugural lecture. EASA first conference, Coimbra, 31.8-3.9.90.

GERHOLM, T. & U. HANNERZ 1983. 'Introduction: The Shaping of National Anthropologies', (Special Issue) *Ethnos*, 47, 1–2, pp. 5–35.

GEWERTZ, D. 1983. *Sepik River Societies. A Historical Ethnography of the Chambri and their Neighbors*, New Haven, Conn.: Yale U.P.

GIDDENS, A. [1979] 1982. *Central Problems in Social Theory. Action, Structure and Contradiction in Social Analysis*, London: The Macmillan Press.

GIDDENS, A. 1989. *Sociology*, Cambridge: Polity Press.

GOODY, J.R. (ed) 1958. *The Developmental Cycle in Domestic Groups*, Cambridge: C.U.P.

GOODY, J.R. 1983. *The Development of the Family and Marriage in Europe*, Cambridge: C.U.P.

GORER, G. 1955. *Exploring English Character*, London: The Cresset Press.

GOUGH, K. 1959. 'The Nayars and the definition of marriage', *Journal of the Royal Anthropological Institute*, 89, pp. 23-34.

GRABURN, N. (ed) 1971. *Readings in Kinship and Social Structure*, New York: Harper & Row.

GRIAULE, M. 1957. *Méthode de l'Ethnographie*, Paris: P.U.F.

GRIMSHAW, A. 1990. 'A runaway world? Anthropology as public debate', *Cambridge Anthropology*, 13, 3, pp. 75-79.

HACKENBERG, R. 1973. 'Genealogical method in social anthropology: the foundations of structural demography', in HONIGMANN (ed), pp. 289-325.

HAJNAL, J. 1965. 'European marriage patterns in perspective', in D.V. GLASS & D.E.C. EVERSLEY (eds), *Population in History*, London: Edward Arnold.

HANLEY, E. 1989. 'Undergraduate anthropology projects at Edinburgh', *B.A.S.A.P.P. Newsletter*, 3, Summer, p. 4.

HÉRITIER, F. 1976. 'L'enquête généalogique et le traitement des donées' in CRESSWELL & GODELIER (eds), pp. 223-265.

HÉRITIER, F. 1981. *L'exercise de la Parenté*, Paris: Gallimard.

HOLLIS, M. 1985. 'Of masks and men', in CARRITHERS *et al.* (eds), pp. 217-233.

HONIGMANN, J.J. (ed) 1973. *Handbook of Social and Cultural Anthropology*, Chicago: Rand McNally & Co.

HOWE, J. 1981. 'Fox hunting as ritual', *American Ethnologist*, 8, pp. 278-300.

HUIZINGA, J. 1935. *Nederland's Geestesmerk*, Leiden: A.W. Sijthoff's Uitgeversmaatschappij N.V.

INGOLD, T. (ed) 1988. *What Is an Animal?* London: Unwin Hyman.

INGOLD, T. 1989. 'Fieldwork in undergraduate anthropology: an opposing view', *B.A.S.A.P.P. Newsletter*, 3, Summer, pp. 2-3.

INGOLD, T. 1990. 'An anthropologist looks at biology', *Man*, n.s., 25, 2 (June), pp. 208-229.

INGOLD, T. 1991. 'Fieldwork projects in undergraduate anthropology', *Anthropology Today*, 7, (2), April, pp. 22-23.

JACKSON, A. 1987. *Anthropology at Home*, A.S.A. Monographs 25. London: Tavistock.

JAMARD, J.-L. 1985. 'Stability and change in French anthropology', *Dialectical Anthropology*, IX, (1-4), pp. 171-207.

JOHNSON, D. 1986. 'A House is not a Home' (Review), *New York Review*, December, 4 pp. 3-6.

JOLAS, T., Y. VERDIER & F. ZONABEND 1970. 'Parler famille', *L'Homme*, X, 3, pp. 5-26.

KABERRY, P. 1939. *Aboriginal Woman, Sacred and Profane*, London:

George Routledge & Sons.

KABERRY, P. 1957. 'Malinowski's contribution to field-work methods and the writing of ethnography', in FIRTH (ed), pp. 71–91.

KOMRIJ, G. 1990. *Over de Bergen*, Amsterdam: Uitgeverij De Arbeiderspers.

KROEBER, A.L. 1909. 'Classificatory systems of relationship', *Journal of the Royal Anthropological Institute*, 39, pp. 77-84.

KRÖLL, H. 1984. *O eufemismo e o disfemismo no português moderno*, Lisbon: Biblioteca Breve. Instituto de Cultura e Língua Portuguesa.

KRUS, L. 1985. 'A morte das fadas: a lenda genealógica da dama pé de cabra', *Ler História*, No. 6, pp. 3–34.

KUPER, A. (ed) 1977. *The Social Anthropology of Radcliffe-Brown*, London: Routledge & Kegan Paul.

KUPER, A. 1982. 'Lineage theory: a critical retrospect', *Annual Review of Anthropology*, 11, pp. 71–95.

KUPER A. 1983. *Anthropology and Anthropologists. The Modern British School*, (Completely Revised Edition), London: Routledge & Kegan Paul.

KUPER, A. 1988. *The Invention of Primitive Society. Transformations of an Illusion*, London: Routledge.

KUPER, A. 1991. 'Anthropologists and the History of Anthropology', *Critique of Anthropology*, 11, (2), pp. 125–142.

LA FONTAINE, J.S. 1985. 'Person and individual: some anthropological reflections', in CARRITHERS *et al.* (eds), pp. 123–140.

LA FONTAINE, J.S. 1990. 'Power, authority and symbols in domestic life', *International Journal of Moral and Social Studies*, 5, 3, pp. 187–205.

LANCASTER, L. 1958. 'Kinship in Anglo-Saxon society – I', *British Journal of Sociology*, IX, pp. 230–250.

LANCASTER, L. 1958. 'Kinship in Anglo-Saxon society – II', *British Journal of Sociology*, IX, pp. 359–377.

LANCASTER, L. 1961. 'Some conceptual problems in the study of family and kin ties in the British Isles', *The British Journal of Sociology*, XII, pp. 317–333.

LANCASTRE E TAVORA, L. DE, 1989. *Dicionário das Famílias Portuguesas*, Lisbon: Quetzal Editores.

LANE, M. [1946] 1985. *The Tale of Beatrix Potter, a Biography*, Harmondsworth: Penguin Books.

LANGHAM, I. 1981. *The Building of British Social Anthropology, W.H.R. Rivers and his Cambridge Disciples in the Development of Kinship Studies, 1898–1931*, Dordrecht and Boston: D. Reidel Publishing Company.

LASLETT, P. & R. WALL (eds) 1972. *Household and Family in Past Time. Comparative studies in the size and structure of the domestic group over the last three centuries in England, France, Serbia, Japan and colonial North America, with further materials from Western Europe*, Cambridge: C.U.P.

LEACH, E.R. 1955. 'Polyandry, inheritance and the definition of marriage', *Man*, 55, pp. 182-186.

LEACH E.R. 1961. *Pul Eliya, A Village in Ceylon:A Study of Land Tenure and Kinship*, Cambridge: C.U.P.

LEACH, E.R. [1964] 1972. 'Animal categories and verbal abuse', in MARANDA (ed), pp. 39–67.

LEACH, E.R. 1984. 'Glimpses of the unmentionable in the history of British social anthropology', *Annual Review of Anthropology*, 13, pp. 1–23.

LEACH, E.R. 1989–90. 'Masquerade: the presentation of self in holiday life', *Cambridge Anthropology*, 13, 3, pp. 47–69.

LE BRAS, H. & E. TODD 1981. *L'invention de la France. Atlas anthropologique et politique*, Paris: Librairie Générale Française.

LEITE DE VASCONCELLOS, J. 1928. *Antroponomia Portuguesa*, (Lix.a).

LEITE DE VASCONCELLOS, J. 1958. *Etnografia Portuguesa*, Lisbon.

LÉVI-STRAUSS, C. 1979. *La Voie des Masques*, revised, enlarged and extended edition of *Trois Excursions*, Paris: Plon.

LIE, A. 1990. 'Undergraduate anthropology projects', *Anthropology Today*, 66, (6), pp. 22–23.

LITTLEJOHN, J. 1963. *Westrigg, The Sociology of a Cheviot Parish*, London: Routledge & Kegan Paul

LÖFGREN, O. 1985. 'Our friends in Nature: class and animal symbolism', *Ethnos*, 8, pp. 184–213.

LOWE, P. & M. BODIGUEL, M. & P. LOWE (eds) 1990. *Rural Studies in Britain and France*, London: Belhaven Press. (Translated by H. Buller from BODIGUEL & LOWE.)

LOWIE, R.H. 1915. 'Exogamy and the classificatory systems of relationship', *American Anthropologist*, 17, pp. 223-239.

LURIE, A. 1990. *Don't Tell the Grown-ups. Subversive children's literature*, London: Bloomsbury.

MACFARLANE, A. 1970. *Witchcraft in Tudor and Stuart England*, London: Routledge & Kegan Paul.

MACFARLANE, A. 1977. *The Origins of English Individualism*, Oxford: Basil Blackwell.

MAINE, Sir H.S. 1883. *Ancient Law* (9th edn), London: John Murray.

MAIR, L. [1965] 1972. *An Introduction to Social Anthropology*, Oxford: Clarendon Press.

MALINOWSKI, B. [1922] 1983. *Argonauts of the Western Pacific, An Account of Native Enterprise and Adventure in the Archipelagoes of Melanesian New Guinea*, London: Routledge & Kegan Paul.

MALINOWSKI, B. 1929. *The Sexual Life of Savages in North-western Melanesia. An Ethnographic Account of Courtship, Marriage and Family Life among the Natives of the Trobriand Islands, British New Guinea*, London: Routledge & Kegan Paul.

MALINOWSKI, B. 1930. 'Kinship', Man, XXX, 17. Reprinted in GRABURN (ed) 1971, pp. 95–105.

MARANDA, P. (ed) 1972. *Mythology*, Harmondsworth: Penguin.

MASON, P. 1990. *Deconstructing America, Representations of the Other*, London: Routledge.

MATTA, R. DA 1983. *Edmund Leach. Antropologia*, São Paulo: Editora Atica.

MATTOS, A. DE 1943. *Manual de Genealogia Portuguesa*, Oporto: Editores Fernando Machado Ca. Lda.

MAUSS, M. 1924. *Sociologie et Anthropologie*, Paris: Quadrige (P.U.F.).

MAUSS, M. 1947. *Manuel d'ethnographie*, Paris: Payot.

MICHAËLIS DE VASCONCELLOS, C. 1922. *A Saudade Portuguesa*, Oporto etc.: Renascença Portuguesa.

MURDOCK, G. 1949. *Social Structure*, New York: Macmillan.

NETTING, R. M., R. WILK & E. ARNOULD (eds) 1984. *Households. Comparative and Historical Studies of the Domestic Group*, Berkeley: University of California Press.

NEWMAN, G. 1987. *The Rise of English Nationalism. A Cultural History 1740–1830*, London: Weidenfeld & Nicolson.

OKELY, J. 1983. *The Traveller-Gypsies*, Cambridge: C.U.P.

O'NEILL, B.J. 1984. *Proprietários, Lavradores e Jornaleiras. Desigualdade Social numa Aldeia Transmontana, 1870–1978*, Lisbon: Publicações Dom Quixote.

O'NEILL, B.J. 1987. 'Pul Eliya in the Portuguese mountains. A comparative essay on kinship practices and family ideology', *Sociologia Ruralis*, XXVII, 4, 278–303.

O'NEILL, B.J. 1988. 'Entre a sociologia rural e a antropologia: repensando a 'communidade' camponesa'', *Análise Social*, XXIV (103–104), 4–5: pp. 1331–1355. (Review article of José Madureira Pinto, *Estruturas Sociais e Práticas Simbólico-Ideológicas nos Campos: Elementos de Teoria e de Pesquisa Empírica*, Oporto: Edições Afrontamento, 'Biblioteca das Ciências do Homen', 5, 1985.)

O'NEILL, B.J. & J. PAIS DE BRITO (eds) 1991. *Lugares de Aqui: actas do seminário 'Terrenos Portugueses'*, Lisbon: Publicações Dom Quixote.

ORTNER, S.B. 1984. 'Theory in anthropology since the sixties', *Comparative Studies in Society and History*, 26 (1), pp. 126–166.

OVERING, J. 1989. 'Translation as a creative process: the power of the name', in L. HOLY (ed), *Comparative Anthropology*, Oxford: Basil Blackwell.

PALUCH, A. 1981. 'The Polish background to Malinowski's work', *Man* (n.s.), 16, pp. 276–285.

PERISTIANY, J. (ed) 1966. *Honour and Shame: the Values of Mediterranean Society*, Paris: Mouton/Maison des Sciences de l'Homme.

PINA-CABRAL, J. DE, 1986. *Sons of Adam, Daughters of Eve. The Peasant Worldview of the Alto Minho*, Oxford: O.U.P.

PINA-CABRAL, J. DE, 1989. 'The Mediterranean as a category of regional comparison: a critical view', *Current Anthropology*, 30, 3, (June), pp. 399–405.

PINA-CABRAL, J. DE, 1990. 'L'héritage de Maine: Repenser les catégories déscriptives dans l'étude de la famille en Europe', *Ethnologie Française*, XIX, 4, pp. 329–340.

PINA-CABRAL, J. DE, n.d. 'The bourgeois family of Oporto: tomb management and sibling vicinalities' (unpublished paper).

PITT-RIVERS, J. 1971. *People of the Sierra* (2nd edn), Chicago: University of Chicago Press.

POTTER, B. 1989. *The Complete Tales of Beatrix Potter*, Harmondsworth: Penguin Group, Frederick Warne.

PRADHAN, R. 1990. 'Much ado about food and drink...', *Etnofoor*, 3, 2, pp. 48–68.

PULMAN, B. 1989–90. 'Anthropologues et missionaires avant la rupture. Une conférence de W.H.R. Rivers' (translated form the English and presented by Bertrand Pulman), *Gradhiva*, 7, pp. 73–86.

RADCLIFFE-BROWN, A.R. [1922] 1964. *The Andaman Islanders*, New York: The Free Press of Glencoe.

RADCLIFFE-BROWN, A.R. 1923. 'The methods of ethnology and social anthropology', in GRABURN (ed), 1971, pp. 85-87.

RADCLIFFE-BROWN, A.R. 1924. 'The mother's brother in South Africa', *South African Journal of Science*, 21, pp. 542–555.

RADCLIFFE-BROWN, A.R. 1935. 'Patrilineal and matrilineal succession', *Iowa Law Review*, 20 (2), pp. 286–303.

RADCLIFFE-BROWN, A.R. 1940. 'On social structure', in *Structure and Function in Primitive Societies*, London: Cohen and West.

RADCLIFFE-BROWN, A.R. 1950. 'Introduction', in RADCLIFFE-BROWN & FORDE (eds), pp. 3-85.

RADCLIFFE-BROWN, A.R. & D. FORDE (eds), 1950. *African Systems of Kinship and Marriage*, London: O.U.P.

RAHN, S. 1984. 'Tailpiece: the Tale of Two Bad Mice', *Children's Literature*, 12, pp. 78–91.

RAPPORT, N. 1989. 'Anthropology and autobiography: an account of the 1989 A.S.A. Conference at York', *Anthropology Today*, 5, 4, August, pp. 25–26.

REIS, M. & G. NAVE 1986. 'Emigrating peasants and returning emigrants. Emigration with return in a Portuguese village', *Sociologia Ruralis*, XXVI, l, pp. 20–35. (Special Issue: Portuguese Perspectives/Perspectivas Portuguesas.)

RENTES de CARVALHO, J., *Waar de Andere God woont*, Amsterdam: Synopsis.

RENTES de CARVALHO, J., 1989. *Portugal. Een gids voor vrienden*, Amsterdam: Uitgeverij De Arbeiderspers (Translation: Harrie Lemmens).

RIBEIRO, O. 1945. *Portugal, o Mediterrâneo e o Atlântico*, Coimbra: Coimbra Editora.

RICHARDS, A.I. 1935. 'The village census in the study of culture contact', *Africa*, pp. 20–33.

RICHARDS, A.I. 1939. *Land, Labour and Diet in Northern Rhodesia. An Economic Study of the Bemba Tribe*, Oxford: O.U.P. for the International African Institute.

RICHARDS, A.I. 1981. 'Foreword', in STRATHERN, pp. xi–xxvi.

RIVERS, W.H.R. [1910] 1968. 'The genealogical method of anthropological inquiry', in *Kinship and Social Organization*, L.S.E. Monographs in Social Anthropology No. 34 (with commentaries by Raymond Firth and David M. Schneider). London: The Athlone Press. New York: Humanities Press Inc., pp. 97–109.

RIVERS, W.H.R. 1914a. *The History of Melanesian Society, I, II*, Cambridge: C.U.P.

RIVERS, W.H.R. 1914b. 'Notes on the Heron pedigree collected by the Rev. George Hall', reprinted in SLOBODIN, 1978, pp. 218–32.

RIVERS, W.H.R. [1914] 1968. 'Classificatory terminology and cross-cousin marriage', in *Kinship and Social Organisation*, pp. 39–54.

ROWLAND, D. 1984. 'Sistemas familiares e padrões demográficos em Portugal: questões para uma investigação comparada', *Ler História*, 3, pp. 13-32.

RUSSELL, N. 1986. *Like Engend'ring Like. Heredity and animal breeding in early modern England*, Cambridge: C.U.P.

SARAIVA, A.J. 1981. *A Cultura em Portugal. Teoria e História. Livro I: Introdução Geral à Cultura Portuguesa*, Amadora: Livraria Bertrand.

SCHAPERA, I. 1977. 'Kinship terminology in Jane Austen's novels', *R.A.I. Occasional Paper* No. 33.

SCHNEIDER, D.M. 1968. *American Kinship, A Cultural Account*, Chicago: University of Chicago Press.

SCHNEIDER, D.M. 1984. *A Critique of the Study of Kinship*, Ann Arbor: University of Michigan Press.

SEGALEN, M. 1985. *Quinze Générations de Bas-Bretons. Parenté et société dans le pays bigouden Sud 1720–1980*, Paris: P.U.F.

SEGALEN, M. (ed) 1989. *L'autre et le semblable. Regards sur l'ethnologie des sociétés contemporaines*, Paris: Presses du C.N.R.S.

SEGALEN, M. 1990. 'From rurality to locality: 50 years of the ethnology of France', in LOWE & BODIGUEL (eds), pp. 183–192.

SEGALEN, M. 1991. 'La famille: un regard ethnologique', in F. DE SINGLY (ed), *La Famille. L'état des savoirs*, Paris: Editions la Découverte, pp. 376–384.

SEGALEN, M. with C. MICHELAT 1991. 'L'amour de la généalogie', in M. SEGALEN (ed). *Jeux de Familles*, Paris: Presses du C.N.R.S. pp. 193–208.

SEGALEN, M. G. LENCLUD & G. AUGUSTINS 1990. 'Rural ethnology in France', in LOWE & BODIGUEL (eds), pp. 183–202.

SEGALEN, M. & F. ZONABEND 1986. 'Familles en France', in A. BURGUIRE, C. KLAPISCH-ZUBER, M. SEGALEN & F. ZONABEND (eds), *Histoire de la famille*, 2 vols, Paris: Armand Colin, pp. 497–527.

SEGALEN, M. & F. ZONABEND 1987. 'Social anthropology and the ethnology of France', in JACKSON (ed), pp. 109–119.

SHARMA, U. 1989. 'Fieldwork in undergraduate anthropology: its merits', *B.A.S.A.P.P. Newsletter*, 3, Summer, pp. 3–4.

SHORE, C. 1990. 'Teaching undergraduate anthropology: projects and placements', *Anthropology Today*, 6, 5, pp. 21–22.

SIIKALA, J. (ed) 1990. 'Culture and history in the Pacific', *Translations of the Finnish Anthropological Society*, 27,special issue.

SILVA DIAS, M. 1989. 'Pobreza choca clima encanta', *Expresso Revista*, 12.08.89, pp. 12–13.

SLOBODIN R. 1978. *W.H.R. Rivers*, New York: Columbia U.P.

SMITH, R.T. 1988. 'Review' of S. Wolfram *In-laws and Outlaws*, *Man* (n.s.), pp. 581–582.

SONTAG, S. [1973] 1977. *On Photography*, Harmondsworth: Penguin.

SOUTHWOLD, M. 1971. 'Meanings of kinship', in R. NEEDHAM (ed), *Rethinking Kinship and Marriage*, London: Tavistock, pp. 35–56.

STOCKING, G.W. 1983. 'The ethnographer's magic. Fieldwork in British anthropology from Tylor to Malinowski', in G.W. Stocking (ed) *Observers Observed. Essays on Ethnographic Fieldwork, History of Anthropology I*. Madison: University of Wisconsin Press, pp. 45–57.

STOCKING, G. 1985. 'Radcliffe-Brown and British social anthropology', in G. STOCKING (ed), *Functionalism Historicized. Essays on British Social Anthropology*, H.O.A. Vol. 2. Madison: University of Wisconsin Press, pp. 131–191.

STRATHERN, M. 1979. 'The self in self-decoration', *Oceania*, 49, pp. 241–257.

STRATHERN M. 1981. *Kinship at the Core. An anthropology of Elmdon, a village in north-west Essex in the nineteen-sixties*, Cambridge: C.U.P.

STRATHERN, M. 1982a. 'The place of kinship: kin, class and village status in Elmdon, Essex', in COHEN (ed), pp. 72–100.

STRATHERN, M. 1982b. 'The village as an idea: constructs of villageness in Elmdon, Essex', in COHEN (ed), pp. 247-277.

STRATHERN, M. 1984. 'The social meaning of localism' in BRADLEY & LOWE (eds), pp. 181–197.

STRATHERN, M. 1987. 'Out of context: the persuasive fictions of anthropology', *Current Anthropology*, 28, 3, June, pp. 251–281.

STRATHERN, M. 1988. *The Gender of the Gift. Problems with Women and Problems with Society in Melanesia*, Berkeley: University of California Press.

STRATHERN, M. 1989–90. 'Stopping the world: Elmdon and the Reith Lectures', *Cambridge Anthropology*, 13, 3, pp. 70–74.

STRATHERN, M. 1990. 'Artefacts of history. Events and the interpretation of history', in SIIKALA (ed), pp. 25–44.

STRATHERN, M. 1992a. 'Parts and wholes: refiguring relationships in a postplural world', in A. KUPER (ed), *Conceptualising Society*, London: Routledge.

STRATHERN, M. 1992b. *Reproducing the Future. Anthropology, Kinship and the New Reproductive Technologies*, Manchester: Manchester U.P.

SUNDAY TIMES INSIGHT TEAM 1975. *Insight on Portugal. The Year of the Captains*, London: André Deutsch.

SUTTON, D. 1991. 'Is there anybody out there? Anthropology and the question of audience', *Critique of Anthropology*, 11, 1, pp. 91–104.

TAYLOR, J. 1983. *That Naughty Rabbit - Beatrix Potter and Peter Rabbit*, London: Frederick Warne.

THOMAS, K. 1983. *Man and the Natural World. Changing Attitudes in England 1500–1800*, London: Allen Lane.

TYLER, S.A. 1986. 'Post-modern ethnography: from document of the occult to occult document', in CLIFFORD & MARCUS (eds), pp. 122–140

URRY, J. 1972. 'Notes and Queries on Anthropology and the development of field methods in British Anthropology, 1870–1920' (Hocart Essay Prize 1972), *Proceedings of the Royal Anthropological Institute for 1972*, pp. 45–57.

VALE DE ALMEIDA, M. 1991a. 'EASA 1: A view "from below"', *Anthropology Today*, 7, 1, pp. 19–20.

VALE DE ALMEIDA, M. 1991b. 'Leitura de um livro de leitura: a sociedade contada às crianças e lembrada ao povo', in O'NEILL & PAIS DE BRITO (eds), pp. 247–61.

VAN GENNEP, A. 1909. *Les Rites de passage*, Paris: E. Nourry.

VAN GENNEP, A. [1943] 1946. *Manuel de folklore français contemporain, Book I, Vols. 1 & 2*. Paris: A. Picard.

VERDON, M. 1981. 'Kinship, marriage and the family: an operational approach', *American Journal of Sociology*, 86 (4), pp. 796–817.

VERNIER, B. 1984. 'Putting kin and kinship to good use: the circulation of goods, labour and names on Karpathos (Greece)', in H. MEDICK & D. SABEAN (eds), *Interest and Emotion. Essays on the Study of Family and Kinship*, Cambridge: C.U.P. pp. 28–76.

WAGNER, A. 1975. *Pedigree and Progress. Essays in the genealogical interpretation of history*, London: Phillimore.

WALLACE, A.R. 1869. *The Malay Archipelago. The Land of the Orang-utan, and the Bird of Paradise. A Narrative of Travel, with Studies of Man and Nature*, London: Macmillan & Co.

WEBER, M. 1947. *The Theory of Social and Economic Organization*, trans. A.R. Henderson & Talcott Parsons, New York: Free Press.

WHATMORE, S. 1991. *Farming Women. Gender, Work and Family Enterprise*, Basingstoke and London: Macmillan.

WILLEMS, E. 1962. 'On Portuguese family structure', *International Journal of Comparative Sociology*, III, 1, pp. 65–79.

WILLIAMS, W.M. 1963. *A West Country Village, Ashworthy*, London: Routledge & Kegan Paul.

WILLIS, R.C. [1965] 1971. *An Essential Course in Modern Portuguese*, London: Harrap.

WOLFRAM, S. 1987. *In-Laws and Outlaws: Kinship and Marriage in England, 1800–1980*, New York: St. Martin's Press.

YOUNG, M. & P. WILLMOTT [1957] 1967. *Family and Kinship in East London*, Harmondsworth: Penguin.

ZONABEND, F. 1976. 'L'enquête de parenté dans la société paysanne française', in CRESSWELL & GODELIER (eds), pp. 266–276.

ZONABEND, F. 1980. 'Le nom de personne', *L'Homme*, XX, 4, pp. 7–23.

ZONABEND, F. (1980) 1984. *The Enduring Memory. Time and history in a French village*, Manchester: Manchester U.P. (English translation by A. Forster of *La Memoire Longue*, Paris: P.U.F.

ZONABEND, F. 1986. 'De la famille. Regard ethnologique sur la parenté et la famille', in A. BURGUIRE, C. KLAPISCH-ZUBER, M. SEGALEN & F. ZONABEND (eds), *Histoire de la famille*, 2 vols, Paris: Armand Colin, pp. 15–75.

APPENDIX

I.S.C.T.E. Degree course in Social Anthropology (1991)

1st Year
– Introduction to Anthropology
– General Sociology
– Introduction to Economics
– Mathematics for the Social Sciences
– Sociological Theories
2nd Year
– Social and Economic History
– Methodology for the Social Sciences
– Statistics for the Social Sciences
– Social Anthropology I
– History of Anthropology
3rd Year
– Social Anthropology II
– Portuguese Ethnography
– The Anthropology of Complex Societies
– Semiology and Linguistics
– Optional subjects
4th Year
– Political Anthropology
– Economic Anthropology
– Symbolic Anthropology
– Methods and Techniques for Anthropological Research
– Optional subjects
Options
– Urban anthropology

– Ethnography of Latin America I & II
– Sources of Ethnological Thought I & II
– Ethnographic Museology I & II
- Urban Sociology
Source: A.P.A. Dossier 'Ensino' (Annex I, part 1a).

INDEX

249

Index

Index